Foreword

This completely modern and up-to-date Lithuanian-English/English-Lithuanian Dictionary provides a quick reference to a needed word in Lithuanian and English. It is a useful tool for travelers, business people and students. It has over 8,000 entries in both languages in a concise easy-to-use format. Every entry contains a pronunciation guide to vowels and consonants and basic grammar characteristics.

Strict alphabetical order has been maintained throughout the dictionary. The main entry word appears in boldface type, usually roman, flush left to the margin of the column.

Parts of speech (nouns, adjectives, verbs, etc.) are indicated by the abbreviations and printed in italics. Each translatable word is supplied with a transcription. Keeping in mind the difference between the Lithuanian and English phonetic systems (sounds) the compiler suggested her own system of transcription.

The American pronunciation is given in the English section. A primary stress mark (') follows the syllable or syllables that normally have greater stress. The dictionary includes some new words of contemporary practical usage in both Lithuanian and English.

Guide to Pronunciation

Lithuanian Symbol	English equivalent	
a	a	in must
ą	aa	in arm
b	b	in bell
c	ts	in let's
č	ch	in chair
d	d	in damp
e	e	in end
ę	ē	in act
ė	ė	in earth
f	f	in fight
g	g	in give
h	h	in hand
i	i	in ill
į	ee	in seat
y	ee	in bee
j	y	in yellow
k	k	in kind
l	l	in low
m	m	in milk
n	n	in name
o	o	in on
p	p	in paper
r	r	in roof
s	s	in sight
š	sh	in sheep
t	t	in table
u	u	in bush
ų	oo	in smooth
ū	oo	in loop
v	v	in very
z	z	in please
ž	zh	in giraffe

HIPPOCRENE CONCISE

DICTIONARY

LITHUANIAN-ENGLISH/ ENGLISH-LITHUANIAN

HIPPOCRENE FOREIGN LANGUAGE DICTIONARIES

Byelorussian-English/English-Byelorussian
Concise Dictionary
6,500 entries • 290 pages • 0-87052-114-4 • $9.95pb • (395)

Estonian-English/English-Estonian Concise Dictionary
10,000 entries • 180 pages • 0-87052-081-4 • $11.95pb • (379)

Finnish-English/English-Finnish Concise Dictionary
12,000 entries • 410 pages • 0-87052-813-0 • $11.95pb • (142)

Icelandic-English/English-Icelandic Concise Dictionary
10,000 entries • 385 pages • 0-87052-801-7 • $9.95pb • (147)

Latvian-English/English-Latvian Practical Dictionary
16,000 entries • 491 pages • 0-7818-0059-5 • $16.95pb • (194)

Norwegian-English/English-Norwegian Concise Dictionary
10,000 entries • 599 pages • 0-7818-0199-0 • $14.95pb • (202)

Russian-English/English-Russian Concise Dictionary
10,000 entries • 536 pages • 0-7818-0132-X • $11.95pb • (262)

Prices subject to change without prior notice. To order
Hippocrene Books, contact your local bookstore, call (718)
454-2366, visit www.hippocrenebooks.com, or write to:
Hippocrene Books, 171 Madison Avenue, New York, NY
10016. Please enclose check or money order adding $5.00
shipping (UPS) for the first book and $.50 for each
additional title.

HIPPOCRENE CONCISE DICTIONARY

LITHUANIAN-ENGLISH/
ENGLISH-LITHUANIAN

Victoria Martsinkyavitshute

HIPPOCRENE BOOKS
New York

Hippocrene Books paperback edition, 1993.
Fourth printing, 2002.

Copyright©1993 by Victoria Martsinkyavitshute

For information, address:
HIPPOCRENE BOOKS, INC.
171 Madison Avenue
New York, NY 10016

ISBN 0-7818-0151-6

Printed in the United States of America

Guide to Pronunciation

a	in	act	au	in	out
ei	in	aid	ū	in	book
aa	in	art			
ie	in	air	p	in	pot
			kw	in	quard
b	in	back	r	in	read
ch	in	chief	s	in	see
d	in	do	t	in	ten
			th	in	that
e	in	ebb			
ee	in	seat	u	in	up
ea	in	mere	ė	in	burn
f	in	fit	v	in	voice
g	in	give	w	in	west
h	in	hit	ks	in	mix
			y	in	yellow
i	in	ill	z	in	zeal
ī	in	ice	zh	in	vision
j	in	just			
k	in	kept			
l	in	low			
m	in	my			
n	in	now			
o	in	box			
ou	in	over			
ō	in	ought			
oi	in	oil			
oo	in	fool			

Abbreviations used in this Dictionary

adj	adjective
adv	adverb
cnj	conjunction
int	interjection
mod	modal verb
n	noun
num	numeral
prt	particle
prp	preposition
prn	pronoun
v	verb

LITHUANIAN-ENGLISH
DICTIONARY

A

abejingas [abeyin'gas] *adj* indifferent (to)

abejingumas [abeyin'gumas] *n* indifference

abejonė [abeyo'nė] *n* doubt

abejotinas [abeyo'tinas]*adj* doubtful, questionable

abipus [abi'pus] *adv* on both sides

abonementas [abonemen'tas] *n* subscription (to, for), season ticket

abrikosas [abriko'sas] *n* apricot

absoliutus [absoliutus'] *adj* absolute

abu, abi [abu', abi'] *adj* both

ačiū [a'chioo] *n* thanks, thank you

adata [a'data] *n* needle

administratorius [administra'torius] *n* manager, administrator

adresas [a'dresas] *n* address

adresuoti [adresuo'ti] *v* address, direct

advokatas [advoka'tas] *n* barrister, lawyer

afiša [afi'sha] *n* bill, poster

agentūra [agentoo'ra]*n* agency, secret service

agrastas [agras'tas] *n* gooseberry

agresija [agre'siya] *n* aggression

aguona [aguo'na] *n* poppy, poppyseed

agurkas [agur'kas] *n* cucumber

aidas [ai'das] *n* echo

aikštė [aiksh'tė] *n* area, square, glade
aikštelė [aikshte'lė] *n* ground, playground, landing
aistra [aistra'] *n* passion (for)
aiškinti [aish'kinti]*v* explain
aiškinimas [aish'kinimas] *n* explanation
aiškus [aish'kus] *adj* clear, distinct
aitrus [aitrus'] *adj* tart, rank
akcentas [aktsen'tas] *n* accent
akcija [ak'tsiya] *n* econ. share
akcinė bendrovė [ak'tsinėbendro'vė] *n* join-stock company
akėti [akė'ti] *v* harrow
akimirka [aki'mirka] *n* instant, moment
akiniai [akiniai'] *n* spectacles, (eye-)glasses
akiplėša [aki'plėsha] *n* impudent fellow (woman)
akiplėšiškumas [akiplėshishku'mas] *n* impudence, cheek
akiratis [aki'ratis] *n* horizon
akis [akis'] *n* eye, loop
akistata [akis'tata] *n* confrontation
akivaizdus [akivaizdus'] *adj* obvious, evident
aklas [ak'las] *adj* blind
aklavietė [akla'vietė] *n* blind alley
akmeninis [akmeni'nis] *adj* stony

akmuo [akmuo'] *n* stone
akmens anglis [akmens'anglis'] *n* coal
akomponuoti [akomponuo'ti] *v* accompany
aktas [ak'tas] *n* act, deed, statement
aktyvus [akteevus'] *adj* active
aktorė [ak'torė] *n* actress
aktorius [ak'torius] *n* actor
aktualus [aktualus'] *adj* of present interest, topical, urgent
akumuliatorius [akumulia'torius] *n* battery, accumulator
akušerė [aku'šerė] *n* midwife
akvarelė [akvare'lė] *n* water-color
alavas [a'lavas] *n* tin
albumas [albu'mas] *n* album, sketchbook
alegorija [alego'riya] *n* allegory
alėja [alė'ya] *n* avenue, path, alley
alga [alga'] *n* wages, pay, salary
aliarmas [aliar'mas] *n* alarm, alert
aliejus [alie'yus] *n* oil
aludė [alu'dė] *n* beer-house, pub
aliuminis [aliumi'nis] *n* aluminum
alyva [alee'va] *n* oil, olive
alyvos [alee'vos] *n* lilac
alkanas [al'kanas] *adj* hungry
alkis [al'kis] *n* hunger

alkoholis [alkoho'lis] *n* alcohol
alksnis [alks'nis] *n* alder
alkūnė [alkoo'nė] *n* elbow
alpinistas [alpinis'tas] *n* mountaineer
alpti [alp'ti] *v* faint (away)
alsuoti [alsuo'ti] *v* breathe (heavily)
alus [alus'] *n* beer
amatas [a'matas] *n* trade, handicraft
ambasada [ambasa'da] *n* embassy
ambasadorius [ambasa'dorius] *n* ambassador
ambulatorija [ambulato'riya] *n* out-patient clinic, dispensary
amerikietis [amerikie'tis] *n* American
amfiteatras [amfiteat'ras] *n* circle, amphitheatre
amžinas [am'zhinas] *adj* eternal, everlasting, perpetual
amžinybė [amzhinee'bė] *n* eternity
amžininkas [am'zhininkas] *n* contemporary
amžius [am'zhius] *n* century, age, life, time
anądien [anaa'dien] *adv* not long ago, the other day
anaiptol [anaiptol'] *adv* by no means
anąkart [anaa'kart] *adv* that time, then
analizė [ana'lizė] *n* analysis
analogiškas [analo'gishkas] *adj* analogic

anapus [ana'pus] *adv* on that side, beyond
anas, ana [anas', ana'] *prn* that, that one
ančiukas [anchiu'kas] *n* duckling
anekdotas [anekdo'tas] *n* anecdote, funny story
anga [anga'] *n* opening, orifice
angelas [an'gelas] *n* angel
angina [angina'] *n* tonsillitis
anglai [an'glai] *n* the English
anglas [an'glas] *n* Englishman
angliakasys [angliakasees'] *n* (coal-)miner
anglis [anglis'] *n* coal, carbon
anyta [anee'ta] *n* mother-in-law
anketa [anke'ta] *n* form, questionnaire
anksčiau [ankschiau'] *adv* earlier, formerly
ankstl [anksti'] *adv* early
ankštas [anksh'tas] *adj* narrow, tight
anot [anot'] *adv* according to
ant [ant'] *prp* on, upon
antai [antai'] *adv* there, over there
antakis [an'takis] *n* eyebrow
antena [ante'na] *n* aerial, antenna
antgamtinis [antgam'tinis] *adj* supernatural
antikinis [antiki'nis] *adj* antique
antikvariatas [antikvaria'tas] *n* curiosity shop, second-hand bookshop

antinas [an'tinas] *n* drake
antipatija [antipa'tiya] *n* antipathy
antis [an'tis] *n* duck
antkapis [ant'kapis] *n* tomb
antklodė [ant'klodė] *n* blanket
antpirštis [ant'pirshtis] *n* thimble
antplūdis [ant'ploodis] *n* influx, rush
antpuolis [ant'puolis] *n* attack, assault
antra [ant'ra] *num* secondly, on the other hand
antradienis [antra'dienis] *n* Tuesday
antraeilis [antraei'lis] *adj* secondary
antrarūšis [antraroo'shis] *adj* second-rate
antraštė [ant'rashtė] *n* title, heading
antras [an'tras] *num* second
antratiek [ant'ratiek] *adv* double, twice as many
antskrydis [ant'skreedis] *n* air raid
antspaudas [ant'spaudas] *n* seal, stamp
anūkas [anoo'kas] *n* grandson
anūkė [anoo'kė] *n* granddaughter
anuliuoti [anuliuo'ti] *v* annul, cancel
anuomet [anuomet'] *adv* at that time
apačia [apachia'] *n* bottom
apačioje [apachioya'] *adv* below, downstairs
apakimas [apaki'mas] *n* loss of sight

apakinti [apa'kinti] *v* blind, dazzle
apalpti [apalp'ti] *v* faint (away), swoon
aparatas [apara'tas] *n* apparatus
apatija [apa'tiya] *n* apathy
apatinis [apati'nis] *adj* lower
apatinės kelnės [apati'nės kel'nės] *n*
drawers, pants
apatinukas [apatinu'kas] *n* pettycoat
apaugti [apaug'ti] *v* bc overgrown, overgrow
apčiuopiamas [apchiuo'piamas] *adj*
tangible, palpable, sensible
apčiuopti [apchiuop'ti] *v* feel, touch
apdaila [apdaila'] *n* finishing, trimming
apdairus [apdairus'] *adj* circumspect
apdengti [apdeng'ti] *v* cover
apdėti mokesčiais [apdė'ti mo'keschiais] *v* tax
apdergti [apderg'ti] *v* dirty, soil, defile,
profane
apdovanoti [apdovano'ti] *v* reward, decorate
apdrausti [apdraus'ti] *v* insure
apdriskęs [apdris'kēs] *adj* ragged
apdriskėlis [apdris'kėlis] *n* ragamuffin,
ragged person, tatterdemalion
apdulkėti [apdulkė'ti] *v* become dusty,
become covered with dust

apdumti [apdum'ti] *v* give a smoking, rush/run round, deceive

apdžiūti [apdzhioo'ti] *v* get dry on the surface

apeigos [a'peigos] *n* rites, ceremonies

apelsinas [apelsi'nas] *n* orange, orange-tree

apėmimas [apėmi'mas] *n* embracing, envelopment

apetitas [apeti'tas] *n* appetite, desire

apgailestauti [apgailestau'ti] *v* regret, be sorry

apgailėti [apgailė'ti] *v* mourn, weep, bewail the loss, regret

apgalėti [apgalė'ti] *v* overpower, defeat, win

apgalvotas [apgalvo'tas] *adj* well-considered, deliberate

apgamas [ap'gamas] *n* birthmark, mole

apgaubti [apgaub'ti] *v* cover, envelope, wrap up, cloak, shroud

apgaulė [apgau'lė] *n* deception, optical illusion

apgauti [apgau'ti] *v* deceive, cheat, swindle

apgavikas [apgavi'kas] *n* deceiver, swindler, knave

apgydyti [apgee'deeti] *v* cure a little

apginkluoti [apginkluo'ti] *v* arm (with)

apginti [apgin'ti] *v* defend, protect

apgyvendinti [apgeeven'dinti] *v* settle

apgižti [apgizh'ti] *v* turn (somewhat) sour

apglamžyti [apglam'zheeti] *v* make (somewhat) crumpled, rumpled

apglėbti [apglėb'ti] *v* embrace, fold in one's arms

apglumti [apglum'ti] *v* become stupid, be struck with surprise

apgraužti [apgrauzh'ti] *v* gnaw

apgręžti [apgrēzh'ti] *v* turn round

apibarti [apibar'ti] *v* give a scolding, scold a little

apybraiža [apee'braizha] *n* outline, sketch, essay

apibrėžimas [apibrėzhi'mas] *n* definition, determination

apykaklė [apee'kaklė] *n* collar

apykanta [apee'kanta] *n* tolerance

apylinkė [apee'linkė] *n* environs, country-side district

apipelėti [apipelė'ti] *v* grow musty, mouldy

apiplėšimas [apiplėshi'mas] *n* robbery, burglary, plunderage

apiplikyti [apiplikee'ti] *v* pour boiling water, scald

apiplyšęs [apiplee'shēs] *adj* ragged, shabby

apyrankė [apee'rankė] *n* bracelet, bangle, armlet

apysaka [apee'saka] *n* narrative, tale, story

apyskaita [apee'skaita] *n* account

apytikriai [apee'tikriai]*adv* approximately, roughly, about

apytikslis [apee'tikslis] *adj* pretty, fairly exact, accurate, precise, approximate

apyvarta [apee'varta] *n* money turnover, commodity circulation

apjuokti [apyuok'ti] *v* ridicule, make fun of, deride

apkalbėti [apkalbė'ti] *v* slander, calumniate, smear

apkaltinti [apkal'tinti]*v* accuse, charge

apkamšyti [apkamshee'ti] *v* stuff, fill in the holes

apkarsti [apkars'ti] *v* become bitter, turn rancid

apkrėsti [apkrės'ti] *v* infect

apkulti [apkul'ti] *v* trash, beat

apkumščiuoti [apkumschiuo'ti] *v* give a boxing

apkūnus [apkoonus'] *adj* stout, fat, corpulent

apkuopti [apkuop'ti] *v* clean, scour, tidy up

apkursti [apkurs'ti] *v* become deaf
aplaidus [aplaidus'] *adj* careless, negligent
apleisti [apleis'ti] *v* neglect, abandon, give up
aplenkti [aplenk'ti] *v* outrun, overtake, leave behind
aplink [aplink'] *adv* round, about
aplinka [aplinka'] *n* surroundings
aplinkybės [aplinkee'bės] *n* circumstance, situation
apmąstyti [apmastee'ti] *v* consider, think over, meditate
apmaudas [ap'maudas] *n* vexation, annoyance
apmauti [apmau'ti] *v* get on, put on, pull on
apmirimas [apmiri'mas] *n* faint, numbness
apmokėjimas [apmokė'yimas] *n* payment, pay
apmuilinti [apmui'linti]*v* soap all over, fool smb.
apmuitinti [apmui'tinti]*v* impose tax, tax
apmulkinti [apmul'kinti]*v* make a fool of smb.
apnakvinti [apnakvin'ti] *v* put smb. up for the night
apnešioti [apneshio'ti] *v* make treadbare, make shabby

apnuodyti [apnuo'deeti] *v* poison

aprašymas [apra'sheemas] *n* description

apsakymas [apsa'keemas] *n* story, novella, tale

apsalti [apsal'ti] *v* grow sweet, melt

apsčiai [apschiai'] *adv* many, much, plenty of, lot of

apsiaustas [apsiaus'tas] *n* cloak, mackintosh, raincoat, coat

apsigynimas [apsigeeni'mas] *n* defense

apsiginklavimas [apsiginkla'vimas] *n* armament

apsigręžti [apsigrēzh'ti] *v* turn round, swing round

apsikrėsti [apsikrės'ti] *v* catch a disease, get an infection

apsilaižyti [apsilaizhee'ti] *v* lick one's lips

apsilankyti [apsilankee'ti] *v* visit, call on, pay a call to

apsileisti [apsileis'ti] *v* become slovenly, careless, untidy

apsilenkti [apsilenk'ti] *v* miss each other

apsimesti [apsimes'ti] *v* pretend, feign, dissemble, simulate, sham

apsiniaukęs [apsiniau'kēs] *adj* gloomy, sullen

apsiprasti [apsipras′ti] *v* get used to, accustom oneself to

apsiraminti [apsiramin′ti] *v* calm, quiet, settle down

apsirengti [apsireng′ti] *v* dress oneself, put on

apsirikti [apsirik′ti] *v* make a mistake, be mistaken

apsiskusti [apsiskus′ti] *v* shave, have one's beard shaven

apsispręsti [apsisprēs′ti] *v* decide, self-determine

apsišaukėlis [apsishau′kėlis] *n* impostor, pretender

apskelbti [apskelb′ti] *v* declare, announce, make public

apstulbti [apstulb′ti] *v* become dumbfounded, be taken aback, dazzled

apsukrus [apsukrus′] *adj* dodgy, resourceful, shifty, clever

apsvaigti [apsvaig′ti] *v* get drunk, tipsy

aptarnauti [aptarnau′ti] *v* attend to, serve

aptaškyti [aptashkee′ti] *v* sprinkle, splash

apuokas [apuo′kas] *n* eagle owl

ar [ar′] *cnj* whether, if

arba [arba′] *cnj* or, either ... or

arbata [arbata'] *n* tea
arbūzas [arboo'zas] *n* watermelon
ardyti [ardee'ti] *v* unravel, unrip, pull down
areštas [a'reshtas] *n* arrest
argi [argi'] *prt* really? is it possible?
arimas [ari'mas] *n* ploughing, tillage
arkivyskupas [arkivees'kupas] *n* archbishop
arklys [arklees'] *n* horse
arti [ar'ti] *adv* near, close, nearby
asilas [a'silas] *n* donkey, ass
asmuo [asmuo'] *n* person
aš [ash'] *prn* I
ašara [a'shara] *n* tear
ašmenys [ash'menys] *n* edge, blade
aštrus [ashtrus'] *adj* sharp, acute, keen, pungent
aštuoni [ashtuoni'] *num* eight
aštuoniasdešimt [ashtuoniasde'shimt] *num* eighty
aštuoniolika [ashtuonio'lika] *num* eighteen
atbulai [atbulai'] *adv* reversedly, back to front
atbusti [atbus'ti] *v* wake up, awake
ateiti [atei'ti] *v* come
ateitis [ateitis'] *n* the future
atgal [atgal'] *adv* back, backwards

atida [atida'] *n* attention, care

atiduoti [atiduo'ti] *v* give back, return, handover, deliver

atitaisyti [atitaisee'ti] *v* correct

atitraukti [atitrauk'ti] *v* distract, divert, turn off

atkaklus [atkaklus'] *adj* persistent

atkalbinėti [atkalbinė'ti] *v* dissuade

atleisti [atleis'ti] *v* slacken, loosen, dismiss, discharge, forgive, pardon

atliekamas [atlie'kamas] *adj* unnecessary, spare, free

atlyginimas [atlee'ginimas] *n* pay, salary, wages

atlikti [atlik'ti] *v* carry out, fulfill, perform

atlyžti [atleezh'ti] *v* calm, quiet, settle down

atmintis [atmintis'] *n* memory

atnešti [atnesh'ti] *v* bring, fetch

atodūsis [ato'doosis] *n* deep breath, sigh

atostogos [atos'togos] *n* vacation, holiday

atprasti [atpras'ti] *v* fall out of a habit

atrakinti [atrakin'ti] *v* unlock

atrodyti [atro'deeti] *v* look like, look

atsakingas [atsakin'gas] *adj* responsible, crucial

atsakyti [atsakee'ti] *v* answer, reply, return

atsargiai [atsargiai'] *adv* carefully, cautiously, warily, gingerly

atsidaryti [atsidaree'ti] *v* open

atsidavęs [atsida'vēs] *adj* devoted, staunch

atsidurti [atsidur'ti] *v* find oneself, get, come

atsigauti [atsigau'ti] *v* come to one's senses, collect oneself, recover

atsikąsti [atsikaas'ti] *v* bite off

atsikelti [atsikel'ti] *v* get up, stand up

atsiklaupti [atsiklaup'ti] *v* kneel down

atsikratyti [atsikratee'ti] *v* get rid of, throw off, shake off

atsimerkti [atsimerk'ti] *v* open one's eyes

atsipalaiduoti [atsipalaiduo'ti] *v* loosen, relax

atsiprašyti [atsiprashee'ti] *v* apologize, excuse, beg smb's pardon

atsirasti [atsiras'ti] *v* be found, turn up, appear

atsiraugėti [atsirau'gėti] *v* belch, berp

atsisakyti [atsisakeeti] *v* refuse, decline, repudiate

atsisėsti [atsisės'ti] *v* sit down, take a seat

atsiskirti [atsiskir'ti] *v* separate, isolate, part with, keep aloof

atsispirti [atsispir'ti] *v* resist, withstand

atsitiktinis [atsitikti'nis] *adj* accidental, casual, fortuitous

atsitrenkti [atsitrenk'ti] *v* hit, strike

atskiras [ats'kiras] *adj* separate,individual, special

atspausdinti [atspaus'dinti] *v* print, offprint, type

atspėti [atspė'ti] *v* guess, solve

atstovas [atsto'vas] *n* representative, spokesman for

atstovybė [atstovee'bė] *n* embassy, representatives

atsukti [atsuk'ti] *v* turn on, turn back

atšalti [atshal'ti] *v* get colder, grow cool

atšilti [atshil'ti] *v* grow warmer, thaw, melt

atvaizdas [at'vaizdas] *n* picture, image, portrayal, reflection

atvesti [atves'ti] *v* bring, lead, make smb. come

atvykti [atveek'ti] *v* arrive, come, appear

atviras [at'viras] *adj* open, frank, public

atviraširdis [atvirashir'dis] *adj* open-hearted

atvirukas [atviru'kas] *n* postcard

audeklas [au'deklas] *v* cloth, material, textile

audinė [audi'nė] *n* mink

audra [audra'] *n* storm, tempest
augalas [au'galas] *n* plant
augalija [augali'ya] *n* vegetation, verdure, flora
augti [aug'ti] *v* grow, increase
auka [auka'] *n* sacrifice, victim, donation
auklė [auk'lė] *n* nurse, nannie
auklėti [auk'lėti] *v* educate, train
auksas [auk'sas] *n* gold
aukščiau [aukshchiau'] *adv* above, over
aukščiausias [aukshchiau'sias] *adj* the highest, supreme, superior
aukštas [auksh'tas] *adj* high, tall, lofty
ausis [ausis'] *n* ear
auskaras [aus'karas] *n* earring
aušra [aushra'] *n* dawn, daybreak
auti [au'ti] *v* put on or take off one's shoes
autobusas [autobu'sas] *n* bus, motor bus
automašina [automashina'] *n* car, truck
autorius [au'torius] *n* author
avalynė [avalee'nė] *n* footwear, footgear
avarija [ava'rija] *n* crash, accident, mishap
avėti [avė'ti] *v* wear (shoes, boots)
aviena [avie'na] *n* mutton, lamb
avietė [avie'tė] *n* raspberry

avigalvis [avi'galvis] *n* gawk, blockhead, dolt, oaf

avikailis [avi'kailis] *n* sheepskin

avilys [avilees'] *n* beehive

avinas [a'vinas] *n* ram, wether

avinėlis [avinė'lis] *n* lamb

avis [avis'] *n* sheep, ewe

aviža [avizha'] *n* oat

azartas [azar'tas] *n* excitement, hazard

ąžuolas [aa'zhuolas] *n* oak tree

B

badas [ba'das] *n* hunger, starvation, famine, dearth

badyti [badee'ti] *v* prick, poke, stick, jab

bagažas [baga'zhas] *n* luggage, baggage

baidarė [baida'rė] *n* kayak, canoe

baidyklė [baidee'klė] *n* scarecrow, bugbear

baigimas [baigi'mas] *n* graduation, finish

baigti [baig'ti] *v* end, finish, stop

bailys [bailees'] *n* coward

baimė [bai'mė] *n* fear, fright, apprehension

baiminti [bai'minti] *v* frighten, scare, intimidate

baisenybė [baisenee'bė] *n* monster, scarecrow

bakalėja [bakalė'ya] *n* grocery
bakas [ba'kas] *n* cistern, tank
baklažanas [baklazha'nas] *n* aubergine, eggplant
bala [bala'] *n* marsh, bag, slough
baladojimas [balado'yimas] *n* knocking, noise
balaganas [balaga'nas] *n* booth, showbooth
balandėlė [balandė'lė] *n* my dear
balandis [balan'dis] *n* pigeon, dove, April
baldai [bal'dai] *n* furniture
baldakimas [baldaki'mas] *n* canopy
baldžius [bal'dzhius] *n* furniture maker
baletas [bale'tas] *n* ballet
balionas [balio'nas] *n* balloon
balius [ba'lius] *n* ball, dance, fancy-dress ball
balkonas [balko'nas] *n* balcony
balkšvas [balksh'vas] *adj* whitish, somewhat white
balnakilpė [balna'kilpė] *n* stirrup
balnas [bal'nas] *n* saddle
balotiravimas [balotira'vimas] *n* vote, ballot, poll
balsas [bal'sas] *n* voice, part, vote
balsastygės [balsa'steegės] *n* vocal chords

balsavimas [baksa'vimas] *n* voting, ballot

balsė [bal'sė] *n* vowel letter

balsiai [bal'siai] *adv* loudly, aloud

baltai [bal'tai] *n* the Balts

baltakiuoti [baltakiuo'ti] *v* look sideways, askew

baltakraujystė [baltakrauyees'tė] *n* leukemia

baltaodis [baltao'dis] *adj* white (about skin)

baltaplaukis [baltaplau'kis] *adj* white-haired

baltarankė [baltaran'kė] *adj* lady of leisure

baltas [bal'tas] *adj* white, clean

baltymas [bal'teemas] *n* egg-white

baltiniai [baltiniai'] *n* linen, underwear, bed-clothes

bamba [bam'ba] *n* navel, belly-button

bamblys [bamblees'] *n* toddler, tot

banalus [banalus'] *adj* commonplace, trite, hackneyed, banal

bananas [bana'nas] *n* banana

bandelė [bande'lė] *n* roll

banderolė [bandero'lė] *n* printed matter, postal wrapper

banditas [bandi'tas] *n* bandit, brigand, thug, cut-throat

bandyti [bandee'ti] *v* experiment, try, put to the test

bankas [ban'kas] *n* bank
bankrotas [bankro'tas] *n* bankrupt
baras [ba'ras] *n* bar, tavern, saloon
baravykas [baravee'kas] *n* boletus
barnis [bar'nis] *n* quarrel
barstyti [barstee'ti] *v* pour, strew
barsukas [barsu'kas] *n* badger
barti [bar'ti] *v* scold, chide, inveigh
barzda [barzda'] *n* beard
basakojis [basako'yis] *adj* barefooted
basas [ba'sas] *adj* bare
baseinas [basei'nas] *n* basin, reservoir
baslys [baslees'] *n* stake, picket
bastytis [bastee'tis] *v* wander, roam, rove
basutės [basu'tės] *n* sandals
batas [ba'tas] *n* shoe, boot
batlaižys [batlaizhees'] *n* toady, bootlicker
batonas [bato'nas] *n* long loaf
batraištis [bat'raishtis] *n* shoelace,
shoe-string
batsiuvys [batsiuvees'] *n* shoemaker,
bootmaker
baubas [bau'bas] *n* bugaboo, bugbear
baubti [baub'ti] *v* moo, roar
bauda [bauda'] *n* fine, penalty
baudimas [baudi'mas] *v* punishment, fining

bausmė [bausmė'] *n* punishment

bausti [baus'ti] *v* punish, chastise, inflict penalty

baužas [bau'zhas] *adj* hornless

bažnyčia [bazhnee'chia] *n* church

be [be'] *prp* without

beatodairiškas [beato'darishkas] *adj* decisive, resolute, firm, all-out

bebaimis [bebai'mis] *adj* fearless, intrepid

bebras [beb'ras] *n* beaver

bėda [bėda'] *n* misfortune, trouble

bedantis [bedan'tis] *adj* toothless

bedievis [bedie'vis] *adj* atheist

bėdoti [bėdo'ti] *v* complain, lament

bedugnė [bedug'nė] *n* precipice, abyss, gulf, chasm

bėdulis [bėdu'lis] *n* unfortunate creature, poor devil

begalė [bc'galė] *n* a huge number of, a lot, a great deal

begalvis [bega'lvis] *adj* headless, brainless

begarsis [begar'sis] *adj* soundless, voiceless

begėdis [begė'dis] *adj* shameless creature

begemotas [begemo'tas] *n* hippopotamus

bėgikas [bėgi'kas] *n* runner

bėgimas [bėgi′mas] *n* run, running, race, sprint

beginklis [begink′lis] *adj* unarmed, defenseless

bėgis [bė′gis] *n* rail, track

bėglys [bėglees′] *n* fugitive, runaway, refugee, prison-breaker

beglobis [beglo′bis] *adj* stray, homeless, waif

bėgti [bėg′ti] *v* run

bei [bei′] *cnj* and

beje [beye′] *prt* by the way

bejėgis [beyė′gis] *adj* helpless, weak person

bekelnis [bekel′nis] *adj* without trousers, poor man, beggar

bekonas [beko′nas] *n* hog

bekraštis [bekrash′tis] *adj* infinite, boundless

bekraujis [bekrau′yis] *adj* bloodless, pale, anemic

bekūnis [bekoo′nis] *adj* immaterial, incorporeal, bodiless

bekvapis [bekva′pis] *adj* scentless

belaikis [belai′kis] *adj* untimely, premature, early

belaisvis [belais′vis] *n* slave, captive, prisoner

belangė [belan'gė] *n* dungeon, prison

bematant [bema'tant] *adv* immediately, at once, presently

bemaž [bemazh'] *adv* almost, nearly

bemiegis [bemie'gis] *adj* sleepless

bemokslis [bemoks'lis] *adj* uneducated, unlearned

benamis [bena'mis] *adj* homeless, stray

bendraamžis [bendraam'zhis] *n* coeval, contemporary

bendrabutis [bendra'butis] *n* hostel, dormitory

bendradarbiauti [bendradarbiau'ti] *v* collaborate, cooperate, contribute

bendrai [bendrai'] *adv* together, jointly

bendras [ben'dras] *adj* general, commmon

bendratis [bendratis'] *n* infinitive

bendrauti [bendrauti'] *v* associate, keep company, rub shoulders with

bendrija [bendriya'] *n* community, association

bendrininkas [bendrinin'kas] *n* participator, accomplice

bendrovė [bendro'vė] *n* company

benzinas [benzi'nas] *n* petrol, gasoline, gas

beprasmis [bepras'mis] *adj* meaningless, senseless

beprotybė [beprotee'bė] *n* folly, madness, insanity

berankis [beran'kis] *adj* armless, one-armed, awkward, clumsy

beregint [bere'gint] *adv* immediately, at once

bergždžiai [bergzhdzhiai'] *adv* in vain, vainly

beribis [beri'bis] *adj* boundless, infinite, limitless

bernas [ber'nas] *n* fellow, lad, chap, hired man

berti [ber'ti] *v* strew, scatter

beržas [ber'zhas] *n* birch

besaikis [besai'kis] *adj* immoderate

besąlygiškas [besaa'leegishkas] *adj* unconditional, unreserved

besarmatis [besarma'tis] *adj* shameless, barefaced

beskausmis [beskaus'mis] *adj* painless

beskonis [besko'nis] *adj* tasteless, insipid

besmegenis [besmege'nis] *adj* brainless

besotis [beso'tis] *adj* insatiable, greedy, grasping

bespalvis [bespal'vis] *adj* colorless, flat

besvoris [besvo'ris] *adj* weightless

bešalis [besha'lis] *adj* impartial, unbiased
bet [bet'] *cnj* but
betarpiškai [betar'pishkai] *adv* directly
betėvis [betė'vis] *adj* fatherless, orphan
betikslis [betiks'lis] *adj* aimless, idle,
pointless
betonas [beto'nas] *n* concrete
betgi [bet'gi] *cnj* but, still, neveheless
bevaisis [bevai'sis] *adj* barren, sterile
bevalis [beva'lis] *adj* weak-willed
beveik [beveik'] *adv* almost, nearly
bevertis [bever'tis] *adj* worthless, of no value
beviltiškas [bevil'tishkas] *adj* hopeless
beždžionė [bezhdzhio'nė] *n* monkey, ape
bežiūrint [bezhioo'rint] *adv* presently, soon,
at once, immediately
biblioteka [biblioteka'] *n* library
bičiulis [bichiu'lis] *n* friend
bidonas [bido'nas] *n* can
bijoti [biyo'ti] *v* be afraid, dread
bijūnas [biyoo'nas] *n* peony
byla [beela'] *n* case, file, dossier
bildukas [bildu'kas] *n* brownie
biliardas [biliar'das] *n* billiards, pool
bilietas [bi'lietas] *n* ticket
byloti [beelo'ti] *v* say, tell

birus [birus'] *adj* dry, friable
birža [bir'zha] *n* exchange
birželis [birzhe'lis] *n* June
bitė [bi'tė] *n* bee
bizūnas [bizoo'nas] *n* whip, lash
bjaurybė [byauree'bė] *n* abominable,
villain, ugly
blakė [bla'kė] *n* bug
blakstiena [blakstie'na] *n* eyelash
blaškytis [blashkee'tis] *v* rush about, toss,
knock about
blaustis [blaus'tis] *v* grow cloudy, grow dim,
dull
blauzda [blauzda'] *n* shin, shank, calf
blefas [ble'fas] *n* bluff
blėsti [blės'ti] *v* go out, die out, burn down
blevyzga [blevee'zga] *n* ribaldry, foul
language
bliauti [bliau'ti] *v* bleat, boa, howl, blubber
blykčioti [bleek'chioti] *v* sparkle, twinkle
blykšti [bleeksh'ti] *v* grow pale
blynas [blee'nas] *n* pancake
bliūkšti [bliooksh'ti] *v* become flat, sink
blizgesys [blizgesees] *n* luster, brilliancy
blogai [blogai'] *adv* bad, badly
blogas [blo'gas] *adj* bad, ill, evil

bloknotas [blokno′tas] *n* notebook
blokšti [bloksh′ti] *v* throw, cast, fling, hurl, toss
blondinas [blondi′nas] *n* fair-haired man, blonde
blukti [bluk′ti] *v* fade, lose color
blusa [blusa′] *n* flea
boba [bo′ba] *n* woman, wife
bocmanas [bots′manas] *n* boatswain
bokalas [boka′las] *n* mug, glass, goblet
boksas [bok′sas] *n* boxing
bokštas [boksh′tas] *n* tower, derrick
bordo [bordo′] *adj* claret
bortas [bor′tas] *n* side
boružė [boru′zhė] *n* ladybird
botagas [bota′gas] *n* whip, lash
botai [bo′tai] *n* high overshoes, high galoshes
braidyti [braidee′ti] *v* wade, ford
braižas [brai′zhas] *n* handwriting
braižyti [braizhee′ti] *v* scratch, draw
brakonierius [brakonie′rius] *n* poacher
branduolinis [branduoli′nis] *adj* nuclear
brandus [brandus′] *adj* ripe, mature
brangakmenis [brang′akmenis] *n* gem, jewel

brangenybė [brangenee'bė] *n* jewel,
treasure, dearness
branginti [brangin'ti] *v* value, highly
appreciate
brangti [brang'ti] *v* rise in price, grow dearer
brasta [brasta'] *n* ford
braškesys [brashkesees'] *n* crack, crackling
braškė [brash'kė] *n* strawberry
braukyti [braukee'ti] *v* cross, underline,
wipe, dry
brautis [brau'tis] *v* squeeze one's way
through
brazdėjimas [brazdė'yimas] *n* tap, slight
knock, rustle
brėkšti [brėksh'ti] *v* dawn, break
bręsti [brēs'ti] *v* ripen, mature
brėžinys [brėzhinees'] *n* draft, sketch
brėžti [brėzh'ti] *v* draw
briauna [briauna'] *n* edge, verge
briedis [brie'dis] *n* elk
brigada [brigada'] *n* brigade, team
briliantas [brilian'tas] *n* diamond, brilliant
brinkti [brink'ti] *v* swell, bloat
bristi [bris'ti] *v* ford, wade
britas [bri'tas] *n* British man
brolis [bro'lis] *n* brother

bruknė [bruk'nė] *n* cranberry, red bilberry, cowberry

brukti [bruk'ti] *v* poke into, thrust, shove

bruožas [bruo'zhas] *n* stroke, trait, feature

brūzgai [brooz'gai] *n* brushwood, thicket, undergrowth

brūžuoti [broozhuo'ti] *v* rub, file, roll, mangle

bučiavimas [buchia'vimas] *n* kissing

bučinys [buchinees'] *n* kiss

būda [booda'] *n* box, cabin

būdas [boo'das] *n* disposition, temper, character

budėjimas [budė'yimas] *n* duty, watch, keeping awake

būdelė [boode'lė] *n* stall, stand, box, cabin

budelis [bu'delis] *n* executioner, hangman, butcher

būdingas [boodin'gas] *adj* characteristic

budinti [bu'dinti] *v* wake, awake

budrumas [budru'mas] *n* vigilance, watchfulness

būdvardis [bood'vardis] *n* adjective

bufetas [bu'fetas] *n* sideboard, refreshment room, buffet

būgštauti [boogsh'tauti] *v* be afraid, fear, apprehend

buhalterija [buhalte'riya] *n* bookkeeping, counting house

buivolas [bui'volas] *n* buffalo

bukagalvis [bukagal'vis] *adj* numskull, blockhead

bukas [bu'kas] *adj* blunt, obtuse

būklė [book'lė] *n* state, condition

buksyras [buksee'ras] *n* tug-boat, tow-boat

bulius [bu'lius] *n* bull

buljonas [bulyo'nas] *n* bouillon, broth

bulvė [bul'vė] *n* potato

buožė [buo'zhė] *n* knob, butt, steelyard, kulak

buožgalvis [buozh'galvis] *n* tadpole

burbėti [burbė'ti] *v* mutter, mumble, grumble

burbulas [bur'bulas] *n* bubble

burbuolė [burbuo'lė] *n* corn-cob

burė [bu'rė] *n* sail

būrelis [boore'lis] *n* circle, society, club

buriavimas [buria'vimas] *n* yachting

būrys [boorees'] *n* detachment, detached force

burkavimas [burka'vimas] *n* coo, purr

burna [burna'] *n* mouth
burokas [buro'kas] *n* beet, beet-root
burti [bur'ti] *v* charm, enchant, bewitch, unite
burtininkas [bur'tininkas]*n* sorcerer, magician, wizard
būsena [boo'sena] *n* state, condition
būsimas [boo'simas] *adj* future
būstas [boos'tas] *n* lodging, dwelling, apartment, room
būstinė [boos'tinė] *n* abode, residence

C

cechas [tse'khas] *n* shop, departament
centras [tsen'tras] *n* center
cerata [tsera'ta] *n* oilcloth, oilskin
cerkvė [tserk'vė] *n* church
chalatas [khala'tas] *n* dressing gown, bathrobe
chamas [kha'mas] *n* cad, boor
charakteris [kharak'teris] *n* disposition, temper, character
chirurgas [khirur'gas] *n* surgeon
chuliganas [khuliga'nas] *n* hooligan, ruffian
ciferblatas [tsiferbla'tas] *n* clockdial, clockface

cypauti [tsee'pauti] *v* screech, squeak
cypė [tsee'pė] *n* lock-up
cipenti [tsipen'ti] *v* walk with short steps
cit! [tsit'] *int* hush! be silent! shut up!
citrina [tsitrina'] *n* lemon, citron, lime
cukrainė [tsukrai'nė] *n* confectionary,
pastry-cook's
cukrus [tsuk'rus] *n* sugar

Č

čaižyti [chai'zheeti] *v* lask, switch, whip, bet
česnakas [chesna'kas] *n* garlic
čežėjimas [chezhė'yimas] *n* rustle, rustling
čia [chia'] *adv* here
čiaudėti [chiau'dėti] sneeze
čiauškėjimas [chiaushkė'jimas] *n* chatter,
chirping
čigonas [chigo'nas] *n* gipsy
čiobrelis [chiobre'lis] *n* thyme
čiulbėti [chiulbė'ti] *v* chirp, twitter, warble,
sing
čiulpti [chiulp'ti] *v* suck
čiuopti [chiuop'ti] *v* grasp, seize, feel, touch
čiuožti [chiuozh'ti] *v* skate
čiurlenti [chiurlen'ti] *v* purl, babble, murmur
čiužinys [chiuzhi'nees] *n* mattress

D

dabar [dabar'] *adv* now, at present

dabinti [dabin'ti] *v* adorn, beautify

daboklė [dabok'lė] *n* guard-room, guard-house

dagilis [dagi'lis] *n* goldfinch

dagys [dagees'] *n* thistle

daigas [dai'gas] *n* sprout, shoot

daiktas [daik'tas] *n* thing, object

daiktavardis [daikta'vardis] *n* noun, substantive

dailė [dailė'] *n* art, fine arts

daina [daina'] *n* song

dainuoti [dainuo'ti] *v* sing

dairytis [dairee'tis] *v* turn back to look at smb., look round

daktaras [dak'taras] *n* doctor

dalia [dalia'] *n* fate, lot

dalykas [dalee'kas] *n* thing, object

dalis [dalis'] *n* part, share, portion

dalyti [dalee'ti] *n* divide, distribute

dalyvauti [daleevau'ti] *v* take part in, participate, be present

dama [dama'] *n* lady

danga [danga'] *n* cover

danginti [dangin'ti] *v* carry smth. somewhere else, go to a new place

dangoraižis [dango'raizhis] *n* skyscraper

dangtis [dang'tis] *n* lid, cover

dangus [dangus'] *n* sky, heaven

dantenos [dan'tenos] *n* gums

dantis [dantis'] *n* tooth

dar [dar'] *prn* still, yet, some more

darbadienis [darba'dienis] *n* work-day

darbas [dar'bas] *n* work, labor, toil, working, job, occupation

darbymetis [darbee'metis] *n* busy season

darbingas [darbin'gas] *adj* able-bodied, able to work

darbininkas [darbinin'kas] *n* worker, workman

darbštumas [darbshtu'mas] *n* industry, diligence

dargana [dargana'] *n* bad weather, rainy weather

dargi [dar'gi] *prep* even

daryti [daree'ti] *v* do, make, produce

darkyti [darkee'ti] *v* spoil, mar, distort, pervert

darna [darna'] *n* harmony, concord

daržas [dar'zhas] *n* garden

daržovė [daržo'vė] *n* vegetable
dašis [da'shis] *n* savory
data [data'] *n* date
dauba [dauba'] *n* ravine
daug [daug'] *prn* much, plenty of, a lot of
daugelis [dau'gelis] *prn* many
daugėti [daugė'ti] *v* increase, rise,
accumulate
daugiaamžis [daugiaam'zhis] *adj* centuries
old
daugiakovė [daugia'kovė] *n* round events
daugialaipsnis [daugialaips'nis] *adj*
multi-stage, multi-step
daugyba [daugee'ba] *n* multiplication
dauginti [dau'ginti] *v* multiply, manifold,
duplicate
daugiskaita [daugis'kaita] *n* plural
daužyti [dauzhee'ti] *v* break, crush, smash,
bit
davatka [davatka'] *n* bigot, hypocrite
dažai [dazhai'] *n* paint
dažymas [da'zheemas] *n* painting, dyeing,
making up
dažnai [dazhnai'] *adv* often, frequently
dėbčioti [dėb'chioti] *v* look with an
unfavorable eye

debesis [debesis'] *n* cloud
dėdė [dė'dė] *n* uncle
dėdienė [dėdie'nė] *n* aunt
defektas [defek'tas] *n* defect, blemish
degalai [degalai'] *n* fuel, oil
degėsiai [degė'siai] *n* site of a fire
degimas [degi'mas] *n* burning, combustion
deglas [deg'las] *n* torch, *adj* motley
degti [deg'ti] *v* burn, bake, kiln, light
degtinė [degti'nė] *n* whisky, brandy
degtukas [degtu'kas] *n* match
deguonis [deguo'nis] *n* oxygen
degutas [degu'tas] *n* tar
deimantas [dei'mantas] *n* diamond
deja [deja'] *int* unfortunately, alas
dejonė [dejo'nė] *n* moaning, groan,
lamentation
dėka [dėka'] *prp* thanks to, owing to
dėkingas [dėkin'gas] *adj* grateful, thankful
dėklas [dėk'las] *n* holster, case
dėl [dėl'] *prp* because of, due to
delčia [delchia'] *n* wane
dėlė [dėlė'] *n* leech
dėlioti [dėlio'ti] *v* put, place, set, lay out
delnas [del'nas] *n* palm
delsti [dels'ti] *v* linger, loiter, delay, tarry

dėlto [dėlto'] *prp* still, all the same

dėmė [dėmė'] *n* spot, patch, blot, stain

dėmesys [dėmesees'] *n* attention, notice

dengti [deng'ti] *v* cover, roof, thatch, tile

denis [de'nis] *n* deck

deponentas [deponen'tas] *n* depositor

deramai [deramai'] *adv* properly, thoroughly

derėti [derė'ti] *v* bargain with, be fit

dergti [derg'ti] *v* foul, make dirty, defile

derinti [de'rinti]*v* conform, coordinate with, tune

derlingas [derlin'gas] *adj* fertile, fecund

derlius [der'lius] *n* harvest, yield, crop

derva [derva'] *n* resin, pitch, tar, rosin

dėsningas [dėsnin'gas] *adj* natural, regular

dėsnis [dės'nis] *n* law

dėstymas [dės'teemas] *n* teaching, instruction

dešimt [de'shimt] *num* ten

dešimtakart [deshimtakart'] *num* ten times

dešimtis [deshimtis'] *num* tenfold

dešimtmetis [deshimt'metis] *n* decade, ten years

dešinė [deshinė'] *n* right side, off side

dešra [deshra'] *n* sausage

detalė [deta'lė] *n* detail

dėti [dė'ti] *v* lay, put, place
dėtis [dė'tis] *v* pretend, feign
dėvėti [dėvė'ti] *v* wear
devyni [deveeni'] *num* nine
devyniasdešimt [deveeniasde'shimt] *num* ninety
devyniolika [deveenio'lika] *num* nineteen
devynmetis [deveen'metis] *n* nine-year-old
devizas [devi'zas] *n* motto
dėžė [dėžė'] *n* box, chest
didelis [di'delis] *adj* big, large, tall
didenybė [didenee'bė] *n* majesty
didėti [didė'ti] *adj* increase, grow, rise
didis [di'dis] *adj* great
dydis [dee'dis] *n* size
didmenomis [didmenomis'] *adv* wholesale
didmiestis [did'miestis] *n* city
diduma [diduma'] *n* majority
didvyris [didvee'ris] *n* hero
didžiadvasis [didzhiadva'sis] *n* magnanimous, generous
didžiai [didzhiai'] *adv* greatly, very highly
didžiulis [didzhiu'lis] *adj* enormous, vast, huge
diegti [dieg'ti] *v* plant, spread, implant, ingraft

diemedis [die'medis] *n* wormwood, absinthe

diena [diena'] *n* day

dienynas [dienee'nas] *n* diary

dieta [die'ta] *n* diet

dievaitė [dievai'tė] *n* goddess

dievas [die'vas] *n* god

dieveris [die'veris] *n* brother-in-law

dygsnis [deegs'nis] *n* stitch

dykaduonis [deekaduo'nis] *n* drone, parasite, sponger

dykai [deekai'] *adv* free of charge, gratis

dykinėti [deekinė'ti] *v* idle, loaf

dykuma [deekuma'] *n* desert, wilderness

dilbis [dil'bis] *n* forearm

dilgėlė [dilgėlė'] *n* nettle

dilgus [dilgus'] *adj* stingy, smarting

dingstis [dingstis'] *n* pretext, occasion

dingti [ding'ti] *v* disappear, vanish

dirbti [dirb'ti] *v* work, do, perform

dirbtuvė [dirbtu'vė] *n* workshop, studio

dirginti [dir'ginti] *v* irritate

dirigentas [dirigen'tas] *n* conductor, leader, band-master

dirsčioti [dirs'chioti] *v* shoot glances at, fling one's eyes

dirti [dir'ti] *v* flay, bark

dirva [dirva'] *n* soil, ground, field

dìržas [dir'zhas] *n* belt, girdle

dobilas [do'bilas] *n* clover

dobti [dob'ti] *v* beat, hit, kill

domėtis [domė'tis] *v* be interested in, care for

dora [dora'] *n* morals, honesty

doroti [doro'ti] *v* put in order, reap, work up, treat

dosnus [dosnus'] *adj* generous, liberal

dovana [dovana'] *n* gift, present

drabstyti [drabstee'ti] *v* sprinkle with, splash over

drabužinė [drabuzhi'nė] *n* cloakroom

drabužis [drabu'zhis] *n* clothes, garments

draikytis [draikee'tis] *v* spread, float, drift

drakonas [drako'nas] *n* dragon

dramblys [dramblees'] *n* elephant

drąsa [draasa'] *n* courage, boldness, audacity

draskyti [draskee'ti] *v* tear, rend

draugas [drau'gas] *n* friend, crony, chum

drausmė [drausmė'] *n* discipline

drausti [draus'ti] *v* forbid, prohibit, ban

draustinis [drausti'nis] *n* preserve, reservation, forest reserve

drebantis [dre'bantis] *adj* shivering, trembling, shaking

drebėti [drebě'ti] *v* quiver, tremble, shake

drėbti [drėb'ti] *v* throw, hurl, chuck

drebučiai [drebu'chiai] *n* galantine, meat-jelly, jelly

drebulė [drebulė'] *n* asp

drebulys [drebulees'] *n* tremor, shiver, quiver

drėgmė [drėgmė'] *n* dampness, moisture, humidity

drėgnas [drėg'nas] *adj* damp, humid, moist, wet

drėksti [drėks'ti] *v* tear, scratch, scribble

drevė [drevė'] *n* hollow

dribsniai [dribs'niai] *n* flakes

drybsoti [dreebso'ti] *v* lie awkwardly, lie lazily

dribti [drib'ti] *v* fall, drop, tumble

driežas [drie'zhas] *n* lizard

drimba [drim'ba] *n* lout, bumpkin

drioksėti [drioksė'ti] *v* thunder

driskius [dris'kius] *n* ragamuffin, vagabond

drįsti [drees'ti] *v* venture, risk, dare, make bold

dryžas [dree'zhas] *adj* striped

drobė [dro'bė] *n* linen, canvas

drobulė [drobu'lė] *n* sheet, bed sheet, linen cloth

drovus [drovus'] *adj* shy, diffident, bashful

drožti [drozh'ti] *v* plane, shave, cut out, carve, fret

dručkis [druch'kis] *n* fat, plump

drugys [drugees'] *n* fever, butterfly, moth

drumsti [drums'ti] *v* stir up, disturb

drumzlės [drumz'lės] *n* lees, dregs

drungnas [drung'nas] *adj* warmish, tepid, fresh, cool, chilly

druska [druska'] *n* salt

drūtas [droo'tas] *adj* thick, rich deep, strong, firm

du [du'] *num* two

dubenėlis [dubenė'lis] *n* small dish

dubuo [dubuo'] *n* tureen, dish, bowl

dūda [dooda'] *n* brass instrument, bag pipes

dūduoti [dooduo'ti] *v* pipe, fife

dudutis [dudu'tis] *n* hoopoe

dugnas [dug'nas] *n* bottom, ground

dujos [du'yos] *n* gas

dukart [du'kart] *num* twice, double

dūkinti [dookin'ti] *v* enrage, infuriate, madden

dukra [dukra'] *n* daughter
duktė [duktė'] *n* daughter
dūkti [dook'ti] *v* romp, frolic, gambol
dūlėti [doolė'ti] *v* rot, decay, moulder
dulkės [dul'kės] *n* dust, pollen
dulksnoti [dulksno'ti] *v* drizzle
dūluoti [dooluo'ti] *v* lurk, loom
dūmai [doo'mai] *n* smoke
dumblas [dumb'las] *n* silt
dūmyti [doo'meeti] *v* smoke, fumigate
dumti [dum'ti] *v* rush, speed, tear along
dundulis [dundu'lis] *n* thunder
duobė [duobė'] *n* pit, pot-hole
duoklė [duok'lė] *n* tribute, contribution
duomenys [duo'menees] *n* data,facts,
information
duona [duo'na] *n* bread
duoneliauti [duoneliau'ti] *v* beg, live by
begging
duoti [duo'ti] *v* give, let
durininkas [du'rininkas]*n* hall-porter,
doorman
durys [du'rees] *n* door
dūris [doo'ris] *n* prick, stitch
durklas [durk'las] *n* spit, dagger, poniard
durpės [dur'pės] *n* peat

durti [dur'ti] *v* thrust, stab, ache, hurt
dūsauti [doo'sauti] *v* sigh
dusyk [du'seek] *num* twice, twice as much
dusinti [du'sinti] *v* choke, suffocate, smother
duslus [duslus'] *adj* hollow, toneless, voiceless
dusulingas [dusulin'gas] *adj* short-winded, asthmatic
dušas [du'shas] *n* shower, douche
dužti [duzh'ti] *v* break
dvaras [dva'ras] *n* estate, landed property, manor
dvasia [dvasia'] *n* spirit, soul, ghost
dvasinis [dva'sinis] *adj* spiritual, emotional
dvejaip [dveyaip'] *num* in two ways
dvejetas [dve'jetas] *num* two
dvejinti [dve'yinti] *v* double, redouble
dvejonė [dveyo'nė] *n* hesitation, wavering, vacilation
dvelkti [dvelk'ti] *v* blow, smell
dvėsena [dvė'sena] *n* carrion
dvėsti [dvės'ti] *v* die, croak
dvibalsis [dvibal'sis] *n* diphthong
dvidešimt [dvi'deshimt] *num* twenty
dviese [dvie'se] *num* two together
dvigubai [dvi'gubai] *num* double

dvikova [dvi′kova] *n* duel
dvylika [dvee′lika] *num* twelve
dvilypis [dvilee′pis] *adj* twofold,
double-faced
dvynys [dveenees′] *n* twin
dviratis [dvi′ratis] *n* bicycle, bike
dvišakas [dvi′shakas] *adj* forked, bifurcated
dviveidis [dvivei′dis] *adj* double-dealer
dvokas [dvo′kas] *n* stink, stench, bad smell
džiaugsmas [dzhiaugs′mas] *n* joy, gladness
džiauti [dzhiau′ti] *v* hang up to dry
džiovinti [dzhiovin′ti] *v* dry, dry-cure, jerk
džiūgauti [dzhiȯo′gauti]*v* rejoice, triumph
džiūti [dzhioo′ti] *v* dry, get dry, fade, droop
džiūvėsis [dzhioovė′sis] *n* piece of dried
bread

E, Ė

ėdalas [ė′dalas] *n* wash, mash, swill
ėdamas [ė′damas] *adj* eatable, edible
ėdrumas [ėdru′mas] *n* greediness for food,
gluttony
ėdžios [ė′dzhios] *n* feeding-trough, crib,
manger
ėgi [ė′gi] *int* well, you see
eglė [eg′lė] *n* fir tree

ėglis [ėg'lis] *n* juniper

egoistas [egois'tas] *n* egoist

egzempliorius [egzemplio'rius] *n* copy, specimen

ei [ei'] *int* halloo! ahoy!

eibė [ei'bė] *n* damage, loss, detriment

eiga [eiga'] *n* motion, run, course

eigulys [eigulees'] *n* forest-guard, woodman

eiklus [eiklus'] *adj* swift-footed, nimble-footed

eikš [eiksh'] *v* come here, come up

eikvoti [eikvo'ti] *v* dissipate, waste

eilė [eilė'] *n* row, line, file, rank, turn

eilėraštis [eilė'rashtis] *n* poem, rhyme, verse

eilinis [eili'nis] *adj* next, ordinary, common

einamasis [einama'sis] *adj* current, present-day

eisena [ei'sena] *n* walk, gait, step

eismas [eis'mas] *n* traffic

eiti [ei'ti] *v* go, walk

eitynės [eitee'nės] *n* demonstration, procession

ekipažas [ekipa'zhas] *n* carriage, crew

ekonomika [ekono'mika] *n* economics

ekranas [ekra'nas] *n* screen

eksponatas [ekspona'tas] *n* exhibit

ekspromtas [eksprom'tas] *adj* impromptu, extemporaneous

elastingas [elastin'gas] *adj* elastic

elektra [elektra'] *n* electricity

elgesys [elgesees'] *n* conduct, behaviour

elgeta [el'geta] *n* beggar, mendicant

elgetynas [elgetee'nas] *n* almshouse

elnė [el'nė] *n* doe

elnias [el'nias] *n* deer

ėmimas [ėmi'mas] *n* raising, levy, collection

emocija [emo'tsiya] *n* emotion

entuziastas [entuzias'tas] *n* enthusiast

epušė [e'pushė] *n* asp

erdvė [erdvė'] *n* space

erelis [ere'lis] *n* eagle

ėriukas [ėriu'kas] *n* lamb

erkė [er'kė] *n* tick

eršketas [ershke'tas] *n* sturgeon

erškėčiuotas [ershkėchiuo'tas] *adj* thorny, prickly

erškėtis [ershkė'tis] *n* blackthorn, sloe

ertmė [ertmė'] *n* cavity

erzeliuoti [erzeliuo'ti] *v* make noise, hubbub, din, row

erzinti [er'zinti] *v* irritate

eržilas [er'zhilas] *n* stallion, colt

esamas [e'samas] *adj* available, existing, being

esybė [esee'bė] *n* being, creature

eskadra [eskad'ra] *n* squadron

eskizas [eski'zas] *n* sketch, study, cartoon, outline

esmė [esmė'] *n* essence, main point

estafetė [estafe'tė] *n* baton

ėsti [ės'ti] *v* eat, devour, gorge, guzzle

estrada [estra'da] *n* stage, platform, variety art

ešerys [esherees'] *n* perch

etatai [eta'tai] *n* staff, personnel

etažerė [etazhe'rė] *n* book stand

etiketė [etike'tė] *n* label

europietis [europie'tis] *n* European

ežeras [e'zheras] *n* lake

ežia [ezhia'] *n* boundary, bound, bed

ežys [ezhees'] *n* hedgehog

F

fabrikas [fab'rikas] *n* factory, mill, plant

fabula [fa'bula] *n* plot, story

fajansas [fayan'sas] *n* pottery

fakelas [fa'kelas] *n* torch

faktas [fak'tas] *n* fact

faktūra [faktoo'ra] *n* invoice, bill, texture

familiariai [familia'riai] *adj* unceremoniously, without ceremony

fanera [fane'ra] *n* veneer, plywood

fantazuoti [fantazuo'ti] *v* dream, fib

faršas [far'shas] *n* stuffing, ground meat, force-meat

fasonas [faso'nas] *n* fashion, style, cut

fasuoti [fasuo'ti] *v* pack up

fėja [fė'ya] *n* fairy

ferma [fer'ma] *n* farm

fermeris [fer'meris] *n* farmer

filialas [filia'las] *n* branch, subsidiary

filmas [fil'mas] *n* film, movie

flakonas [flako'nas] *n* bottle

fonas [fo'nas] *n* background

forma [for'ma] *n* shape, form

fortepionas [fortepio'nas] *n* piano

fotelis [fo'telis] *n* armchair

fotoaparatas [fotoapara'tas] *n* camera

frakas [fra'kas] *n* dress-coat, tuxedo

freza [fre'za] *n* cutter, mill, milling

futliaras [futlia'ras] *n* case

G

gabalas [ga'balas] *n* piece, bit, lump, bar, slice

gabaritas [gabari'tas] *n* size

gabenti [gaben'ti] *v* transport, remove

gabumas [gabu'mas] *n* ability, aptitude, gift

gadinti [gadin'ti] *v* spoil, corrupt, demoralize

gaida [gaida'] *n* note, melody, tune

gaidys [gaidees'] *n* cock, rooster

gailestis [gai'lestis] *n* pity, regret, remorse

gailéti [gailé'ti] *v* feel sorry, grudge, regret, repent

gailiaširdis [gailiashir'dis] *adj* tender-hearted, compassionate

gainiotis [gai'niotis] *v* chase, pursue

gairé [gai'ré] *n* stake, landmark

gaisras [gais'ras] *n* fire, conflagration

gaišinti [gaishin'ti] *v* waste, delay, detain

gaišti [gaish'ti] *v* loiter, linger, tarry, die

gaiva [gaiva'] *n* liveliness, vivacity, freshness

gaivinti [gaivin'ti] *v* freshen, enliven, vivify

gaižus [gaizhus'] *adj* rank, rancid, peevish, grumpy

gajus [gayus'] *adj* of great vitality

gal [gal'] *prt* maybe, perhaps

galabyti [gala'beeti] *v* kill, slay

galanterija [galante'riya] *n* haberdashery

galantiškas [galan'tishkas] *adj* gallant

galas [ga'las] *n* end, butt, finish

galąsti [galaast'ti] *v* sharpen, grind

galėti [galė'ti] *v* be able

galia [galia'] *n* power, might

galiausiai [galiau'siai] *adv* in the end, after all

galima [ga'lima] *mod* one can, one may

galimas [ga'limas] *adj* possible

galynėtis [galeenė'tis] *v* wrestle, grapple

galinis [gali'nis] *adj* final, last, end

galiojimas [galio'yimas] *n* validity, run

galioti [galio'ti] *v* be valid, be in operation

galiukas [galiu'kas] *n* tip

galiūnas [galioo'nas] *n* mighty man, giant

galop [galop'] *adv* towards the end, finally

galūnė [galoo'nė] *n* tip, point, limb, extremity

galutinai [galutinai'] *adv* finally, once and for all

galva [galva'] *n* head, mind, chief

galvažudybė [galvazhudee'bė] *n* murder

galvijai [galvi'yai] *n* cattle, livestock, neat

galvočius [galvo'chius] *n* wise man, sage, intelligent

gama [gama'] *n* scale

gamyba [gamee'ba] *n* production, manufacture

gamykla [gameekla'] *n* works, factory, mill, plant

gaminys [gaminees'] *n* manufactured article, finished product

gamta [gamta'] *n* nature

gana [gana'] *adv* rather, fairly, enough

gandas [gan'das] *n* rumor, hearsay

gandras [gand'ras] *n* stork

ganyti [ganee'ti] *v* graze, pasture

garantija [garan'tiya] *n* guarantee, security

garas [ga'ras] *n* steam, vapor

garbana [gar'bana] *n* curl, lock, ringlet

garbė [garbė'] *n* honor

garbingas [garbin'gas] *adj* honorable, respectable

garbinti [gar'binti] *v* honor, respect, glorify, worship

gardėsis [gardė'sis] *n* dainty, delicate

gardžiai [gardzhiai'] *adv* tastefully, fragrantly

gargždas [gargzh'das] *n* gravel

garinti [ga'rinti]*v* evaporate

garlaivis [gar'laivis]*n* steamer, steamboat, steamship

garmėti [garmė'ti] *v* flock, throng, sink, plunge

garsas [gar'sas] *n* sound, rumor, glory

garstyčia [garstee'chia] *n* mustard

garsus [garsus'] *adj* sonorous, loud, famous, well-known

garvežys [garvezhees'] *n* railway engine, locomotive

gąsdinti [gaas'dinti]*v* frighten, scare, threaten

gastrolės [gastro'lės] *n* tour

gastronomas [gastrono'mas] *n* grocery

gašlus [gashlus'] *adj* voluptuous, sensual

gatavas [ga'tavas] *adj* finished, ready-made

gatvė [gat'vė] *n* street

gaudesys [gaudesees'] *n* drone, din, hum, buzz

gaudyti [gau'deeti] *v* catch

gauja [gauya'] *n* band, gang, pack

gauruotas [gauruo'tas] *adj* shaggy, dishevelled

gausa [gausa'] *n* abundance, plenty

gauti [gau'ti] *v* receive, get, obtain

gavènia [gavė'nia] *n* lent, fast
gėda [gė'da] *n* shame
gedėti [gedė'ti] *v* grieve, mourn
gedimas [gedi'mas] *n* deterioration,
spoiling, rotting, damage
gegutė [gegu'tė] *n* cuckoo
gegužė [geguzhė'] *n* May
geibti [geib'ti] *v* wither, grow sickly, pine
geidulys [geidulees'] *n* lust, passion
geismas [geis'mas] *n* longing, hunger, wish,
desire
gėlas [gė'las] *adj* fresh, sweet
gelbėti [gel'bėti] *v* save, rescue
gėlė [gėlė'] *n* flower
geležinis [gelezhi'nis] *adj* iron
geležinkelis [gelezhin'kelis] *n* railway,
railroad
geležtė [gelezh'tė] *n* blade
gėlynas [gėlee'nas] *n* flower garden
gelmė [gelmė'] *n* depth
geltligė [gelt'ligė] *n* jaundice
geltonas [gelto'nas] *adj* yellow
gelumbė [gelumbė'] *n* cloth
geluonis [geluo'nis] *n* sting
gemalas [ge'malas] *n* embryo, germ
genėti [genė'ti] *v* lop, prune, trim

genys [genees'] *n* woodpecker
gentis [gentis'] *n* tribe
geradarybė [geradaree'bė] *n* benefaction, good deal, boon
gerai [gerai'] *adv* well
geras [ge'ras] *adj* good, kind
gerbti [gerb'ti] *v* honor, respect, esteem
gerėti [gerė'ti] *v* become better, recover
gėrėtis [gėrė'tis] *v* admire, be delighted
gėrybė [gėree'bė] *n* wealth
gėrimas [gė'rimas] *n* drink, beverage
gerinti [ge'rinti]*v* improve, make better
gėris [gė'ris] *n* goodness, kindness
gerklė [gerklė'] *n* throat, windpipe
gerokai [gero'kai] *adv* rather
gerti [ger'ti] *v* drink, sip, gulp
gervė [ger'vė] *n* crane, sweep, winch
gervuogė [ger'vuogė] *n* blackberry, bramble
gesinti [gesin'ti] *v* put out, switch off, extinguish
gesti [ges'ti] *v* spoil, decay, rot, die out, become dim
gydyti [gee'deeti] *v* treat medically, cure
gydytojas [gee'deetoyas] *n* doctor
giedoti [giedo'ti] *v* chant, pipe, warble, crow
giedra [giedra'] *n* fine weather

giedrintis [gied'rintis]*v* brighten up, clear up

giesmė [giesmė'] *n* canto, song

gilė [gi'lė] *n* acorn

giliamintis [giliamin'tis] *adj* profound

gilyn [gileen'] *adv* deep down

gylis [gee'lis] *n* depth, deepness

gilus [gilus'] *adj* deep, profound

gimdykla [gimdykla'] *n* maternity home

giminaitis [giminai'tis] *n* relative, kinsman

giminė [giminė'] *n* family, kin, relatives, gender

gimtadienis [gimta'dienis] *n* birthday

gimtas [gim'tas] *adj* native

gimti [gim'ti] *v* be born

ginčas [gin'chas] *n* argument, controversy, debate

gynimas [geeni'mas] *n* defense, protection

ginklas [gink'las] *n* arm, weapon

gintaras [gin'taras] *n* amber

ginti [gin'ti] *v* defend, protect

gira [gira'] *n* sour drink, kvass

girdėti [girdė'ti] *v* hear

girdyti [gir'deeti] *v* give smb. a drink, make drunk

girgždėjimas [girgzhdė'yimas] *n* squeak, creak, crunch

giria [giria'] *n* forest, wood
girna [gir'na] *n* millstone, grindstone
girtas [gir'tas] *adj* drunk, tipsy, intoxicated
girti [gir'ti] *v* praise, commend
gysla [gees'la] *n* vein, artery, fiber, rib
gitara [gitara'] *n* guitar
gyti [gee'ti] *v* get better, recover, heal, skin over
gyvas [gee'vas] *adj* live, living, alive
gyvatė [geeva'tė] *n* snake, serpent, viper
gyvatvorė [geeva'tvorė] *n* hedgerow, green hedge
gyvavimas [geeva'vimas] *n* existence, living, being
gyventi [geeven'ti] *v* live, exist, reside, dwell
gyvybė [geevee'bė] *n* life
gyvis [gee'vis] *n* living being
gyvsidabris [geev'sidabris] *n* mercury, quicksilver
gyvulys [geevulees'] *n* animal, cattle, beast
gyvūnija [geevooni'ya] *n* fauna
gižti [gizh'ti] *v* turn sour
glamonėti [glamonė'ti] *v* caress, fondle, pet
glamžyti [glam'zheeti] *v* rumple, crumple
glaudės [glau'dės] *n* shorts, trunks, slips
glaudus [glaudus'] *adj* serried, solid, close

glaustas [glaus'tas] *adj* concise, close
glausti [glaus'ti] *v* close, clasp, press
glėbys [glėbees'] *n* embrace, armful
glebus [glebus'] *adj* flabby, flaccid, sluggish
gleivės [glei'vės] *n* mucus, mucilage, slime
glemžti [glemzh'ti] *v* grab, seize, capture
gležnas [glezh'nas] *adj* delicate, flabby, sickly
gliaudyti [gliau'deeti] *v* crack, pod, hull
glitus [glitus'] *adj* viscous, sticky, slimy
globoti [globo'ti] *v* be guardian, be warden, take care
glostyti [glos'teeti] *v* stroke, smooth, flatter
glotnas [glot'nas] *adj* smooth, sleek
glūdėti [gloodė'ti] *v* be, lie, be concealed, be hidden
glūduma [glooduma'] *n* depth
gluosnis [gluos'nis] *n* willow
glusti [glus'ti] *v* snuggle to, cuddle up
gnaibyti [gnai'beeti] *v* pinch, nip
gniaužyti [gniau'zheeti] *v* squeze, rumple, crumple
gniutulas [gniu'tulas] *n* piece, lump, bundle
gniūžtė [gnioozh'tė] *n* lump, clod, wisp, tuft
gobšus [gobshus'] *adj* greedy, avid, covetous

gobtuvas [gobtu'vas] *n* cover, shed, lampshade

godus [godus'] *adj* covetous, greedy, avid

gomurys [gomurees'] *n* palate

grabalioti [grabalio'ti] *v* grope, feel about

gracija [gra'tsiya] *n* grace, refinement, elegance

grafa [grafa'] *n* column

grafika [gra'fika] *n* drawing, graphics arts

grafikas [gra'fikas] *n* time-table, schedule

grandinė [grandi'nė] *n* chain

grandionizinis [grandio'zinis] *adj* mighty, grand, grandiose

grandis [grandis'] *n* ring, link, team

graudinti [graudin'ti] *v* touch, move, grieve

graudumas [graudu'mas] *v* woefulness, grief, sorrow

graužikas [grauzhi'kas] *n* rodent, gnawer

graužti [grauzh'ti] *v* gnaw, nibble

graužtukas [grauzhtu'kas] *n* core

grąža [graazha'] *n* change

gražiai [grazhiai'] *adv* beautifully, nicely, well

gražybė [grazhee'bė] *n* beauty, charm, prettiness

gražinti [gra'zhinti] *v* adorn, beautify, decorate, ornament

grąžinti [graazhin'ti] *v* return, give back, repay

gražiuoju [grazhiuo'ju] *adv* in a friendly way, on good terms

gražus [grazhus'] *adj* beautiful, nice, lovely, pretty

grėblys [grėblees'] *n* rake

grėbti [grėb'ti] *v* rake

greičiausiai [greichiau'siai] *adv* most probably, very likely

greitai [grei'tai] *adv* quickly, fast, rapidly, soon

greitis [grei'tis] *n* speed, rate

grėsmė [grėsmė'] *n* threat, menace

greta [greta'] *adv* side by side, near, by, beside

gretimas [gre'timas] *adj* adjacent, neighboring, next

gretinimas [gre'tinimas] *n* comparison, confrontation

gręžti [grēzh'ti] *v* bore, drill, perforate, wring

griaučiai [griau'chiai] *n* skeleton, frame

griaudėti [griau'dėti] *v* thunder, roar

griauti [griau′ti] *v* destroy, demolish, raze

grybas [gree′bas] *n* fungus, mushroom

griebti [grieb′ti] *v* snack, seize, catch, grap

grietinė [grieti′nė] *n* sour cream

grietinėlė [grietinė′lė] *n* cream

griežtai [griezhtai′] *adv* strictly, severely

grikšėti [grikshė′ti] *v* crunch, crackle

grimas [gri′mas] *n* make-up, grease-paint

grimzti [grimz′ti] *v* sink, plunge, submerge, dive

grynai [greenai′] *adv* purely, merely, barely

grynakraujis [greenakrau′yis] *adj* pure-blooded

grynas [gree′nas] *adj* pure, bare

grindinys [grindinees′] *n* roadway, carriage-way

grindys [grin′dees] *n* floor

griova [griova′] *n* ravine, cave, cavern

griovys [griovees′] *n* ditch

gripas [gri′pas] *n* influenza, flu

gristi [grees′ti] *v* floor, pave, ground, base

griūti [grioo′ti] *v* fall down, tumble down, crash down

griuvėsiai [griuvė′siai] *n* ruins

grįžti [greezh′ti] *v* return, come back, recur

grobti [grob′ti] *v* plunder

grobuonis [grobuo'nis] *n* predatory animal, beast of prey

gromuliuoti [gro'muliuoti]*v* chew the cud, ruminate

groti [gro'ti] *v* play

grotos [gro'tos] *n* railing, trellis

grožėtis [grozhė'tis] *v* admire, be delighted

grublėtas [grublė'tas] *adj* coarse, rough, smooth

grubus [grubus'] *adj* rough, rude, uneven

grūdas [groo'das] *n* grain, corn

grūdėtas [groodė'tas] *adj* grainy

grūdinti [groo'dinti]*v* temper, harden, steel

grumstas [grums'tas] *n* clod

grumtis [grum'tis] *v* fight, struggle, battle

gruntas [grun'tas] *n* soil, ground, bottom

gruodis [gruo'dis] *n* December

grupė [gru'pė] *n* group, cluster

grūsti [groos'ti] *v* crush, pound, push, cram

gubernatorius [guberna'torius] *n* governor

gudragalvis [gudragal'vis] *adj* clear head, clever person

gudrus [gudrus'] *adj* clever, sly, cunning, artful

gūdus [goodus'] *adj* dreary, gloomy, somber

gulbė [gul'bė] *n* swan, pen

guldyti [guldee'ti] *v* lay down

gulėti [gulė'ti] *v* lie, keep one's bed

gumbas [gum'bas] *n* bump, growth

gundyti [gun'deeti] *v* entice, allure, tempt, seduce

guoba [guo'ba] *n* elm, ulmus

guolis [guo'lis] *n* bed, couch, lair, den

guosti [guos'ti] *v* comfort, console

guotas [guo'tas] *n* group, clump, flock, colony

gurgždėti [gurgzhdė'ti] *v* squeak, creak

gurklys [gurklees'] *n* crop, craw, double chin

gurkšnis [gurksh'nis] *n* drink, mouthful, sip, gulp

gūsis [goo'sis] *n* gust, rush

guvus [guvus'] *adj* quick, prompt, swift, agile

gūžta [goozh'ta] *n* nest

gūžtelėti [goozh'telėti] *v* shrug, give a shrug

gvazdikas [gvazdi'kas] *n* pink, clove-pink, sweet-william

gvėra [gvė'ra] *n* gawk, booby, fool

gvieštis [gviesh'tis] *v* covet, hanker

gvildenti [gvilden'ti] *v* crack, examine, discuss

H

herbas [her'bas] *n* coat of arms, armorial bearings

hercogas [her'tsogas] *n* duke

hidroelektrinė [hidroelektri'nė] *n* hydroelectric power station

honoraras [honora'ras] *n* author's emoluments, royalties

horizontas [horizon'tas] *n* horizon

I, Į, Y

į [ee'] *cnj* in, into, to

įamžinti [eeam'zhinti]*v* perpetuate, immortalize

įaudrinti [eeau'drinti]*v* excite, agitate, make stormy

įbauginti [eebaugin'ti] *v* intimidate, frighten, scare

įbėgti [eebėg'ti] *v* come running, flow into

įbrėžti [eebrėzh'ti] *v* scratch

įbristi [eebris'ti] *v* wade in, ford in

įbrolis [ee'brolis] *n* step-brother

įbrukti [eebruk'ti] *v* shove in, foist, palm off

yda [eeda'] *n* vice, defect

idant [i'dant] *cnj* in order that

įdaras [ee'daras] *n* filling, stuffing

įdegęs [eede'gēs] *adj* tanned, sunburnt, brown

įdėmiai [eedėmiai'] *adv* attentively, carefully, intently

įdėti [eedė'ti] *v* put in, insert in

įdiegti [eedieg'ti] *v* plant

įdomus [eedomus'] *adj* interesting, prepossessing

įdribti [eedrib'ti] *v* tumble in

įduba [ee'duba] *n* hollow, cavity

įdukra [ee'dukra] *n* foster-daughter, adopted daughter

įdūkti [eedook'ti] *v* rage, become furious, go mad

įduoti [eeduo'ti] *v* hand in, deliver to

įdurti [eedur'ti] *v* prick, thrust into

įdužti [eeduzh'ti] *v* crack slightly, split slightly

įeiti [iei'ti] *v* enter, go in, come in

įėjimas [iėyi'mas] *n* entrance, entry

ieškoti [ieshko'ti] *v* look for, search, seek

iešmas [iesh'mas] *n* spit, railway point

ietis [ie'tis] *n* spear, lance, pike

ieva [ie'va] *n* bird-cherry

įforminti [eefor'minti] *v* register officially

įgalinti [eega'linti]*v* enable, give a chance

įgarsinti [eegar'sinti] *v* make a sound recording

įgelti [eegel'ti] *v* sting, bite

įgimtas [eegim'tas] *adj* innate, inborn, native

įgyti [eegee'ti] *v* get, acquire, gain

įgyvendinti [eegeeven'dinti]*v* realize, put into, practice, fulfill, carry out

įgnybti [eegneeb'ti] *v* pinch, nip, tweak

ignoruoti [ignoruo'ti] *v* ignore, disregard

įgristi [eegris'ti] *v* pester smb., bother smb., bore smb.

įgrūsti [eegroos'ti] *v* push in, shove in, hustle in

įgudęs [eegu'dēs] *adj* skilful, experienced

įgūdis [ee'goodis] *n* habit, practice, skill

įgula [ee'gula] *n* garrison, crew

įjungti [eeyung'ti] *v* engage, start, switch on

įkainis [ee'kainis] *n* valuation

įkainoti [eekaino'ti] *v* fix the price, estimate, evaluate

įkaisti [eekais'ti] *v* become heated, get hot

įkaitas [ee'kaitas] *n* pledge, pawn, hostage

įkalbėti [eekalbė'ti] *v* persuade, induce

įkalinti [eeka'linti]*v* imprison, jail, incarcerate

įkalti [eekal′ti] *v* drive in, hammer in

įkarštyje [ee′karshteeye] *adv* in full swing

įkaušęs [eekau′shēs] *adj* intoxicated, drunk, tipsy

įkeisti [eekeis′ti] *v* pawn, mortgage

iki [iki′] *prp* as far as, to, till, until

iki- [iki′] pre-

ikimokyklinis [ikimokeek′linis] *adj* pre-school

įkypai [eekeepai′] *adv* obliquely, aslant

įkyrėti [eekeerė′ti] *v* pester, bother, bore

įkyruolis [eekeeruo′lis] *n* bore, nuisance

ikišiolinis [ikishio′linis] *adj* previous, former, up to now

įkišti [eekish′ti] *v* put in, shove in

įklampinti [eeklampin′ti] *v* stick in, involve, entangle

įklimpti [eeklimp′ti] *v* stick in, sink in

įkliūti [eeklioo′ti] *v* be caught, get into, be entrapped

įkopti [eeckop′ti] *v* climb up, clamber

ikrai [ik′rai] *n* roe, spawn, caviar

įkraustyti [eekraus′teeti] *v* bring in, lodge in, move in

įkrėsti [eekrės′ti] *v* pour in, put in, thrash, give a thrashing

įkristi [eekris′ti] *v* fall into, sink into

įkūnyti [eekoo'neeti] *v* incarnate, embody
įkurdinti [eekur'dinti] *v* settle
įkurti [eekur'ti] *v* found, form, set up
įkvėpimas [eekvėpi'mas] *n* inspiration, inhalation
yla [eela'] *n* awl
įlanka [ee'lanka] *n* bay, gulf
įleisti [eeleis'ti] *v* let in, admit, inject
įlėkti [eelėk'ti] *v* fly in
įlenkimas [eelenki'mas] *n* curve, bend
ilgaamžis [ilgaam'zhis] *adj* lasting, long-lived
ilgainiui [ilgai'niui] *adv* in time, in due course
ilgametis [ilgame'tis] *adj* of many years
ilgas [il'gas] *adj* long, prolonged
ilgesys [ilgesees'] *n* longing for, grief for
ilgis [il'gis] *n* length
ilgumas [ilgu'mas] *n* length, duration
įlipti [eelip'ti] *v* climb up, get on
ilsėtis [ilsė'tis] *v* rest, have a rest
ilsti [ils'ti] *v* get tired, get out of breath
iltis [il'tis] *n* fang, tusk
įmaišyti [eemaishee'ti] *v* mix in, involve
įmanomas [eema'nomas] *adj* possible, clear

įmantrus [eemantrus'] *adj* fanciful, pretentious

imbieras [imbie'ras] *n* ginger

įmerkti [eemerk'ti] *v* make wet, soak, dip into

įmesti [eemes'ti] *v* throw into, drop into

įmigti [eemig'ti] *v* fall deeply asleep

įminti [ccmin'ti] *v* guess, solve

įmisti [eemis'ti] *v* fatten, become fat

imlus [imlus'] *adj* receptive, consuming

įmokėti [eemokė'ti] *v* pay in

įmonė [ee'monė] *n* undertaking, enterprise

įmotė [ee'motė] *n* foster-mother

imperija [impe'riya] *n* empire

impilas [im'pilas] *n* tick

imti [im'ti] *v* take, harvest, gather in

imtinai [imtinai'] *adv* inclusive

imtynės [imtœ'nœs] *n* wrestling

imurdyti [imurdee'ti] *v* push into, dip into

įmūryti [eemoo'reeti] *v* brick in

įnašas [ee'nashas] *n* contribution

indas [in'das] *n* dish, plate

įnerti [eener'ti] *v* pass through, thread, dive into

įnikti [eenik'ti] *v* apply oneself to, be absorbed in

įniršis [ee'nirshis] *n* fury, rage

inkaras [in'karas] *n* anchor

inkilas [in'kilas] *n* nesting-box

inkstas [inks'tas] *n* kidney

inkšti [inksh'ti] *v* whine, squeal, screech, yelp

įnoris [ee'noris] *n* whim, caprice, fancy

intakas [in'takas] *n* tributary, affluent

intarpas [in'tarpas] *n* insertion, infix

interesantas [interesan'tas] *n* visitor, caller

internatas [interna'tas] *n* boarding school

investicija [investi'tsiya] *n* investment

ypač [ee'pach] *adv* especially, particularly

įpainioti [eepai'nioti] *v* entange, involve, implicate

įpareigoti [eepareigo'ti] *v* obligate, bind

ypatybė [eepatee'bė] *n* specific feature, peculiarity

įpėdinis [ee'pėdinis] *n* heir, legatee

įpilti [eepil'ti] *v* pour in

įpiršti [eepirsh'ti] *v* match, foist

įpjova [ee'pyova] *n* cut, incision, saw-cut

įplaukos [ee'plaukos] *n* income, receipts

įplyšti [eepleesh'ti] *v* become torn slightly

įprasminti [eepras'minti] *v* give a sense to

įprastas [ee'prastas] *adj* usual, ordinary

įpratimas [eeprati′mas] *n* habit

įpratinti [eepra′tinti]*v* train

ir [ir′] *cnj* and

įranga [ee′ranga] *n* equipment, requisites

įrankis [ee′rankis] *n* instrument, tool,
implement

įrašas [ee′rashas] *n* record, entry, inscription

įregistravimas [eeregistra′vimas] *n* visa,
registration

įrėminti [eerė′minti]*v* set in a frame

įremti [eerem′ti] *v* rest against, set against

įrengimai [eerengi′mai] *n* equipment, outfit,
machinery

įrėplioti [eerėplio′ti] *v* crawl on all fours,
crawl

irgi [ir′gi] *cnj* also, as well, too

įriedėti [eeriedė′ti] *v* roll in

irklas [irk′las] *n* oar, scull

irkluotojas [irkluo′tojas] *n* rower, oarsman,
puller

įrodymas [eero′deemas] *n* proof, evidence,
argument

įrodymas [eero′deeti] *v* prove,
demonstration

ironija [iro′nija] *n* irony

įropoti [eeropo′ti] *v* crawl in

irti [ir'ti] *v* disintegrate, fall to pieces

irtis [ir'tis] *v* row, pull

irzlus [irzlus'] *adj* irritable, short of temper, petulant

irzti [irz'ti] *v* get irritated, get annoyed, chafe

įsakas [ee'sakas] *n* decree, edict

įsakyti [eesakee'ti] *v* order, command, tell, direct

įsakmiai [eesakmiai'] *adv* insistently, in a commanding way

įsegti [eeseg'ti] *v* fasten, attach, stick in

įsėlinti [eesė'linti]*v* steal in, creep in, slip in

įsėsti [eesės'ti] *v* get in, take board

įsibėgėti [eesibėgė'ti] *v* make one's run, full speed

įsibrauti [eesibrau'ti] *v* invade, encroach, break in

įsidėmėti [eesidėmė'ti] *v* pay attention, take notice, take into account

įsigalioti [eesigalio'ti] *v* come into force

įsigeisti [eesigeis'ti] *v* want, get a strong desire

įsigerti [eesiger'ti] *v* soak in, be absorbed

įsigilinti [eesigi'linti]*v* go deep, delve deeply

įsigyti [eesigee'ti] *v* acquire, gain, buy

įsigrūsti [eesigroos'ti] *v* squeeze into, shoulder one's way into

įsijausti [eesijaus'ti] *v* feel one's part

įsikabinti [eesikabin'ti] *v* seize, grasp

įsikarščiuoti [eesikarshchiuo'ti] *v* flush, become excited, grow heated

įsikišti [eesikish'ti] *v* interfere, intervene, meddle with

įsiklausyti [eesiklausee'ti] *v* listen attentively, lend one's ear to

įsikniaubti [eesikniaub'ti] *v* bury oneself in

įsiknisti [eesiknis'ti] *v* dig oneself into

įsikūnijimas [eesikoo'niyimas] *n* incarnation, embodiment, personification

įsikurti [eesikur'ti] *v* settle, make one's home

įsilaužėlis [eesilau'zhėlis] *n* burglar, housebreaker

įsileisti [eesileis'ti] *v* start, set out, let in, admit

įsiliepsnoti [eesiliepsno'ti] *v* flare up, blaze up, burst into flame

įsilieti [eesilie'ti] *v* flow into, join the ranks

įsimaišyti [eesimaishee'ti] *v* interfere, meddle, step in

įsimylėti [eesimeelė'ti] v fall in love, lose one's heart

įsiminti [eesimin'ti] v memorize

įsipareigojimas [eesipareigo'yimas] n obligation, engagement

įsipareigoti [eesipareigo'ti] v pledge oneself, commit oneself

įsipiršti [eesipirsh'ti] v woo oneself, foist oneself

įsiristi [eesirish'ti] v roll in, run in, stumble in

įsisąmoninti [eesisaa'moninti] v realize

įsisiautėti [eesisiau'tėti] v rage, bluster, run high

įsisiūbuoti [eesisioobuo'ti] v swing, rock oneself to and fro, sway

įsisiūlyti [eesisioo'leeti] v thrust oneself upon

įsiskverbti [eesiskverb'ti] v penetrate into, get through

įsismaginti [eesismaa'ginti] v cheer up, grow merry

įsispirti [eesispir'ti] v rest one's feet against

įsisvajoti [eesisvayo'ti] v give oneself up to dreams, be day dreaming

įsitaisyti [eesitaisee'ti] v provide oneself with, settle

įsiteikti [eesiteik'ti] *v* worm oneself into smb's favor

įsitempimas [eesitempi'mas] *n* strain, effort, exertion

įsitikinęs [eesiti'kirēs] *adv* assured, sure, confident

įsitvirtinti [eesitvir'tinti]*v* consolidate, fortify

įsivaizduoti [eesivaizduo'ti] *v* imagine, fancy

įsižeisti [eesizheis'ti] *v* take offense

įskaitant [eeskai'tant] *adv* including, included

įskaitomas [eeskai'tomas] *adj* legible

įskųsti [eeskoos'ti] *v* denounce, inform against, report on

įsmukti [eesmuk'ti] *v* fall into, rush into, slip in

įsodinti [eesodin'ti] *v* plant, embark, take smb. aboard

įspėti [eespė'ti] *v* warn, guess, solve

įspirti [eespir'ti] *v* kick

įsprausti [eespraus'ti] *v* insert, put in, force in

įspūdingas [eespoodin'gas] *adj* imposing, impressive

įspūdis [ee'spoodis] *n* impression, effect

įstaiga [ee'staiga] *n* institution, establishment

įstanga [ee'stanga] *n* effort

įstatai [ee'statai] *n* regulations, statutes

įstatymai [eesta'teemai] *n* law, statute

įsteigti [eesteig'ti] *v* found, establish

įstengti [eesteng'ti] *v* be able

įstoti [eesto'ti] *v* enter, join

įstrigti [eestrig'ti] *v* stick

įsūnyti [eesoo'neeti] *v* adopt

išaiškėti [ishaishkė'ti] *v* turn out

išaiškinimas [ishaish'kinimas] *n* elucidation, clearing up

įšalas [ee'shalas] *n* frozen ground

išalkti [ishalk'ti] *v* grow hungry

išankstinis [ishanksti'nis] *adj* preliminary, advance

išardyti [ishardee'ti] *v* rip up

išauklėti [ishauk'lėti] *v* educate, bring up, train

išaukštinti [ishauksh'tinti] *v* praise, extol, exalt

išbaidyti [ishbaidee'ti] *v* scare away

išbalęs [ishba'ēs] *adj* pale

išbandyti [ishbandee'ti] *v* try, test, put to the test

išbarstyti [ishbarstee'ti] *v* spill, scatter, strew

išbėgti [ishbėg'ti] *v* run out

išbėrimas [ishbėri'mas] *n* rash, eruption, spilling

išblaivėti [ishblaivė'ti] *v* get sober, clear up

išblaškyti [ishblashkee'ti] *v* scatter, dispel, dissipate

išblėsti [ishblės'ti] *v* go out, die out, be out

išblizginti [ishbliz'ginti] *v* polish

išbraukti [ishbrauk'ti] *v* cross out

išbrinkęs [ishbrin'kēs] *adj* swollen

išbučiuoti [ishbuchiuo'ti] *v* cover with kisses

išburti [ishbur'ti] *v* prophesy, foretell

išbūti [ishboo'ti] *v* stay, remain

iščiulpti [ishchiulp'ti] *v* suck out, suck dry

išdabinti [ishdabin'ti] *v* decorate, adorn, embellish

išdaiga [ishdai'ga] *n* trick, prank, escapade

išdalyti [ishdalee'ti] *v* distribute, dispense

išdava [ish'dava] *n* result

išdavikas [ishdavi'kas] *n* traitor

išdeginti [ishde'ginti] *v* burn out, scorch, etch

išderinti [ishde'rinti] *v* disorder, disturb

išdėstyti [ishdės'teeti] *v* lay out, spread out, set forth

išdidumas [ishdidu'mas] *n* pride, arrogance, haughtiness

išdygti [ishdeeg'ti] *v* spring, sprout, shoot up

išdykauti [ishdeekau'ti] *v* play pranks, be naughty, romp

išdilti [ishdil'ti] *v* disappear, vanish, fade

išdrįsti [ishdrees'ti] *v* dare, make bold

išdrožti [ishdrozh'ti] *v* cut out, engrave, carve

išduoti [ishduo'ti] *v* hand, give, betray

išdurti [ishdur'ti] *v* prick out

išeiga [ish'eiga] *n* outlet, mouth, yield, output

išeikvojimas [isheikvo'yimas] *n* peculation, defalcation, embezzlement

išeiti [ishei'ti] *v* go out, leave

išeitis [isheitis'] *n* way out

išerzinti [isher'zinti] *v* tease

išformuoti [ishformuo'ti] *v* disband, disembody

išgabenti [ishgaben'ti] *v* take out, export, carry out

išgaląsti [ishgalaas'ti] *v* edge, sharpen

išgarsėti [ishgarsė'ti] *v* become famous

išgąsdinti [ishgaas'dinti] *v* frighten, scare

išgelbėti [ishgel'bėti] *v* save, rescue, liberate

išgerti [ishger'ti] *v* drink

išgirsti [ishgirs'ti] *v* hear

išgirti [ishgir'ti] *v* lavish praise, shower praise

išgyvendinti [ishgeeven'dinti] *v* evict, overcome, get rid of

išgręžti [ishgrēzh'ti] *v* drill

išgriebti [ishgrieb'ti] *v* get out, fish out

išgvildenti [ishgvilden'ti] *v* analyze, examine, husk, shell

išieškoti [ishieshko'ti] *v* exact, recover, search everywhere

išilgai [ishilgai'] *adv* along

išilgas [ish'ilgas] *adj* lengthwide, fore-and-aft

išimti [ishim'ti] *v* take out, pull out, extract, withdraw

įširsti [eeshirs'ti] *v* become angry

išjungti [ishyung'ti] *v* turn off, switch off, shut off

išjuokti [ishyuok'ti] *v* ridicule

iškaba [ish'kaba] *n* sign, signboard

iškalti [ishkal'ti] *v* forge, hew, cram, con

iškarpa [ish'karpa] *n* cutting, clipping, press-cutting

iškart [ishkart'] *adv* at once, right away, straight off

iškasti [ishkas'ti] *v* dig out, mine, extract

iškąsti [ishkaas'ti] *v* bite out

iškaulyti [ishkau'leeti] *v* beg and get

iškeikti [ishkeik'ti] *v* scold, rail at, curse, damn

iškeisti [ishkeis'ti] *v* exchange

iškeliauti [ishkeliau'ti] *v* set off, start, leave, go to

iškentėti [ishkentė'ti] *v* undergo, bear, suffer, endure

iškepti [ishkep'ti] *v* bake, fry, roast, broil, grill

iškyla [ish'keela] *n* picnic, trip

iškilmės [ish'kilmės] *n* festival, celebrations, festivities

iškilti [ishkil'ti] *v* rise, advance, be promoted, emerge

iškirptė [ish'kirptė] *n* decollete

iškloti [ishklo'ti] *v* cover, flag, line

išknisti [ishknis'ti] *v* dig up, make a litter of, nose out

iškošti [ishkosh'ti] *v* filter

iškovoti [ishkovo'ti] *v* conquer, win, gain, achieve

iškraipyti [ishkraipee'ti] *v* misrepresent, distort, mutilate

iškratyti [ishkratee'ti] *v* strew, shake out, search

iškraustyti [ishkraus'teeti] *v* unload, evict

iškrypimas [ishkreepi'mas] *n* bend, crook, distortion, perversion

iškristi [ishkris'ti] *v* fall out

iškvėpinti [ishkvėpin'ti] *v* scent, perfume

iškviesti [ishkvies'ti] *v* call out of, send for

išlaidos [ish'laidos] *n* expenditure, expense, outlay

išlaisvinti [ishlais'vinti] *v* liberate, emancipate, set free, release

išleisti [ishleis'ti] *v* let out

išlepėlis [ishle'pėlis] *n* pet, mollycoddle

išlepęs [ishle'pēs] *adj* spoilt

išlikti [ishlik'ti] *v* survive, remain alive

išlipti [ishlip'ti] *v* climb out, get out, alight, land

išlošti [ishlosh'ti] *v* win, gain

išmaitinti [ishmaitin'ti] *v* keep, maintain, provide

išmalda [ish'malda] *n* alms, charity

išmanyti [ishmanee'ti] *v* understand, know, grasp

išmarginti [ishmar'ginti] *v* speckle, spot, dot, mottle

išmatos [ish'matos] *n* feces, excrement, dung

išmatuoti [ishmatuo'ti] *v* measure

išmaudyti [ishmau'deeti] *v* bathe, bath, give smb. a bath

išmėginti [ishmėgin'ti] *v* try, test, put to the test

išmesti [ishmes'ti] *v* throw out, drop, dismiss

išmintis [ishmintis'] *n* wisdom

išmirkyti [ishmirkee'ti] soak, steep

išmokėti [ishmokė'ti] *v* pay out

išmokyti [ishmo'keeti] *v* teach

išmokti [ishmok'ti] *v* learn, master

išmonė [ish'monė] *n* quick thinking, trick, joke

išnaikinti [ishnaikin'ti] *v* destroy, annihilate

išnaudoti [ishnaudo'ti] *v* exhaust

išnaudotojas [ishnaudo'tojas] *n* exploiter

išnešti [ishnesh'ti] *v* carry out, take out, remove

išniekinti [ishnie'kinti] *v* disgrace, outrage, profane, desecrate

išnykti [ishneek'ti] *v* disappear, vanish, die out

išnokti [ishnok'ti] *v* ripen, mature

išorė [ish'orė] *n* exterior, appearance, look

išparduoti [ishparduo'ti] *v* sell, sell out

išpažinti [ishpazhin'ti] *v* confess

išpildyti [ishpil'deeti] *v* fulfil

išpirka [ish'pirka] *n* ransom, recovery price

išpirkti [ishpirk'ti] *v* redeem, buy up, repurchase, expiate

išplatinti [ishpla'tinti]*v* spread

išplėsti [ishplės'ti] *v* enlarge, widen, broaden

išprievartauti [ishprievartau'ti] *v* ravish, force, constrain

išprotėti [ishprotė'ti] *v* go mad, go crazy

išpuikėlis [ishpui'kėlis] *n* arrogant, haughty, lofty person

išpuoselėti [ishpuo'selėti] *v* cherish, foster, tend carefully

išpurvinti [ishpur'vinti]*v* soil, dirty, besmear

išradėjas [ishradė'jas] *n* inventor

išradingas [ishradin'gas] *adj* inventive, resourceful

išraiška [ish'raishka] *n* expression

išrankus [ishrankus'] *adj* fastidious, squeamish

išrašas [ish'rashas] *n* extract, excerpt

išreikšti [ishreiksh'ti] *v* express

išrinkti [ishrink'ti] *v* choose, select, pick out, sort out

išsamus [ishsamus'] *adj* exhaustive, comprehensive

išsaugoti [ishsau'goti] *v* safe, keep, preserve, retain, maintain

išsiblaškęs [ishsiblash'kēs] *adj* absentminded, tossed about

išsidėstymas [ishsidės'teemas] *n* situation, arrangement, location

išsigąsti [ishsigaas'ti] *v* be frightened with

išsigimėlis [ishsigi'mėlis] *n* degenerate

išsiilgti [ishsiilg'ti] *v* miss

išsyk [ishseek'] *adv* at once, right away

išsikelti [ishsikel'ti] *v* move, migrate

išsikišti [ishsikish'ti] *v* lean out, protrude, jut out

išsilavinimas [ishsila'vinimas] *n* development, intelligence

išsiliejimas [ishsilieyi'mas] *n* effusion, outpouring

išsimokslinęs [ishsimoks'linēs] *adj* educated

išsinešdink! [ishsinesh'dink] *v* be off! get away!

išsipildyti [ishsipil'deeti] *v* be fulfilled, come true

išsipirkti [ishsipirk'ti] *v* ransom
išsirinkti [ishsirink'ti] *v* choose
išsiskirti [ishsiskir'ti] *v* divorce, separate, differ, stand out
išsisklaidyti [ishsisklaidee'ti] *v* disperse, dissipate, clear away
išsiskleisti [ishsiskleis'ti] *v* open
išsisukinėti [ishsisukinė'ti] *v* dodge, avoid, shun, evade, elude
išsitepti [ishsitep'ti] *v* make oneself dirty, besmear oneself
išsiveržimas [ishsiverzhi'mas] *n* eruption
išsivystęs [ishsivees'tēs] *adj* developed
išsižadėti [ishsizhadė'ti] *v* renounce, disavow
išsižiojėlis [ishsizhio'yėlis] *n* gawk
išsižioti [ishsizhio'ti] *v* open one's mouth
išskalauti [ishskalau'ti] *v* rinse
išskyrus [ishskee'rus] *adv* except, excepting, barring
išspręsti [ishsprēs'ti] *v* solve
išsprūsti [ishsproos'ti] *v* slip away
iššūkis [ish'shookis] *n* challenge
ištaigingas [ishtaigin'gas] *adj* comfortable
ištaka [ish'taka] *n* source
ištarti [ishtar'ti] *v* pronounce, utter, articulate

ištaškyti [ishtashkee'ti] *v* spill, splash, spray
išteisinti [ishtei'sinti] *v* acquit
ištekėti [ishtekė'ti] *v* flow out, marry smb.
išteklius [ish'teklius] *n* stock, supply, reserve
ištempti [ishtemp'ti] *v* stretch, pull out
išterlioti [ishterlio'ti] *v* daub, soil, dirty
ištesėti pažadą [ishtesė'ti pa'zhadaa] *v n*
keep one's promise
ištežti [ishtezh'ti] *v* soften, grow pulpy
išties [ishties'] *adv* really, indeed
ištiesti [ishties'ti] *v* straighten, extend,
stretch out
ištikimas [ish'tikimas] *adj* faithful, loyal,
true to
ištikti [ishtik'ti] *v* strike, overtake, be fall
ištinti [ishtin'ti] *v* swell up, bloat out
ištirpti [ishtirp'ti] *v* smelt, melt, fuse, thaw
ištisai [ishtisai'] *adv* completely, entirely
ištįsti [ishtees'ti] *v* stretch, lengthen out
ištremti [ishtrem'ti] *v* exile, banish,
transport, deport
ištrūkti [ishtrook'ti] *v* break away, escape
ištuoka [ish'tuoka] *n* divorce
ištvermė [ishtvermė'] *n* tenacity, staying
power, endurance
ištverti [ishtver'ti] *v* bear, stand, endure

išugdyti [ishugdee'ti] *v* bring up, train, prepare, cultivate

išvada [ish'vada] *n* deduction, conclusion, inference

išvaduoti [ishvaduo'ti] *v* liberate, emancipate, set free

išvaizda [ish'vaizda] *n* appearance, looks

išvargęs [ishvar'gēs] *adj* exhausted, tired, worn out

išvaryti [ishvaree'ti] *v* drive out

išvažiuoti [ishvazhiuo'ti] *v* leave

išvėdinti [ishvėdin'ti] *v* air, ventilate

išvemti [ishvem'ti] *v* vomit, throw up

išversti [ishvers'ti] *v* overturn, translate, pull down

išvežti [ishvezh'ti] *v* take out, remove, drive away

išvien [ishvien'] *adv* together, in common, jointly

išvietė [ish'vietė] *n* lavatory, restroom

išvyka [ish'veeka] *n* excursion, trip, outing, journey

išvykti [ishveek'ti] *v* depart from, leave for, quit

išvilioti [ishvilioti] *v* coax, wheedle out of, fool

išvilkti [ishvilk'ti] *v* drag out, pull out

išvis [ishvis'] *adv* on the whole, in all, altogether

išvystyti [ishvees'teeti] *v* develop

išvyti [ishvee'ti] *v* drive out, drive away

įtaiga [ee'taiga] *n* suggestion, hypnosis

įtaka [ee'taka] *n* influence

įtampa [ee'tampa] *n* voltage, strain, stress

įtarimas [eetari'mas] *n* suspicion

įtarti [eetar'ti] *v* suspect

įteisinti [eetei'sinti] *v* legalize, legitimate

įtempimas [eetempi'mas] *n* tension, intensity, strain, stretch

įterpti [eeterp'ti] *v* put in, insert, introduce

įtėvis [ee'tėvis] *n* foster-father

įtikinti [eeti'kinti] *v* convince, persuade, make believe

įtikti [eetik'ti] *v* please

itin [itin'] *adv* especially, very, particularly

įtrinti [eetrin'ti] *v* rub in

įtūžti [eetoozh'ti] *v* get furious, become enraged

įtvirtinti [eetvir'tinti] *v* strengthen, consolidate

įvadas [ee'vadas] *n* introduction, preface

įvaikinti [ee'vaikinti] *v* adopt a child

įvairus [eevairus'] *adj* various, diverse, different

įvaizdis [ee'vaizdis] *n* image, trope

įvartis [ee'vartis] *n* goal

įvažiavimas [eevazhia'vimas] *n* entrance, entry for cars

įveikti [eeveik'ti] *v* overcome, get over

įvelti [eevel'ti] *v* mix up, involve, entangle

įvertinti [eever'tinti] *v* estimate, evaluate

įvykdyti [eeveek'deeti] *v* carry out, execute, fulfill

įvykti [eeveek'ti] *v* happen, occur

įvirsti [eevirs'ti] *v* tumble down, burst into

įžanga [ee'zhanga] *n* introduction, prelude

iždas [izh'das] *n* exchequer, treasury

įžeisti [eezheis'ti] *v* insult, outrage

įžnybti [eezhneeb'ti] *v* pinch, nip, tweak

įžulus [eezhulus'] *adj* impudent, insolent, saucy

įžvalgus [eezhvalgus'] *adj* sagacious, astute

įžvelgti [eezhvelg'ti] *v* perceive, discover

J

jau [yau'] *adv* already, no longer

jaudinti [yau'dinti] *v* agitate, trouble, excite, worry, alarm

jaukas [yau'kas] *n* lure, enticement, bait
jaukinti [yaukin'ti] *v* domesticate
jaukus [yaukus'] *adj* comfortable, cosy
jaunamartė [yauna'martė] *n* bride
jaunas [yau'nas] *adj* young, youthful
jaunavedys [yaunavedees'] *n* groom
jaunystė [yaunees'tė] *n* youth
jausti [yaus'ti] *v* feel, sense, have a sensation
jautiena [yautie'na] *n* beef
jautis [yau'tis] *n* ox, bullock
jautrus [yautrus'] *adj* sensitive, keen, sentimental
javai [yavai'] *n* corn, grain
jazminas [yazmi'nas] *n* jasmine
jėga [yėga'] *n* strength, force, power
jei, jeigu [yei', yei'gu] *cnj* if
ji [yi'] *prn* she
jie, jos [yie', yos'] *prn* they
jis [yis'] *prn* he
jodinėti [yodinė'ti] *v* ride, go on horseback
jog [yog] *cnj* that
joks [yoks'] *adj* no, none
jonvabalis [yon'vabalis] *n* glowworm
joti [yo'ti] *v* ride on horse back
judėti [yudė'ti] *v* move, stir, budge

jungti [yung'ti] *v* join, connect, combine with

jungtukas [yungtu'kas] *n* conjunction

jungtuvės [yungtu'vės] *n* marriage, wedding

juodas [yuo'das] *adj* black

juokas [yuo'kas] *n* laughter, laugh, trifle

juokauti [yuokau'ti] *v* joke, jest

juosta [yuos'ta] *n* waist-band, tape, film

juosti [yuos'ti] *v* gird, begird

jūra [yoo'ra] *n* sea

jurginas [yurgi'nas] *n* dahlia

jūrininkas [yoo'rininkas]*n* sailor, seaman, navigator

jūs [yoos'] *prn* you

jūsų [yoo'soo] *prn* of you

jutimas [yuti'mas] *n* sensation

K

kabėti [kabė'ti] *v* hang, be suspended

kabykla [kabeek'la] *n* pegboard, rack, stand

kabinti [kabin'ti] *v* hang, suspend, hook, hitch

kablelis [kable'lis] *n* hook, comma

kačiukas [kachiu'kas] *n* kitten

kad [kad'] *cnj* that

kada [kada'] *cnj* when, while, as

kadagys [kadagees'] *n* juniper
kadaise [kadai'se] *adv* once upon a time
kadangi [kadan'gi] *cnj* as, since, because
kai [kai'] *cnj* when, while
kailiniai [kailiniai'] *n* fur coat
kailis [kai'lis] *n* skin, hide, fell, fur
kaimas [kai'mas] *n* village, countryside
kaimynas [kaimee'nas] *n* neighbor
kaina [kai'na] *n* price, cost, worth
kaip [kaip'] conj how, what
kairė [kairė'] *n* left hand
kaitinti [kai'tinti] *v* incandesce, heat red hot
kaitra [kaitra'] *n* heat, intense heat
kajutė [kaju'tė] *n* room, cabin
kaklaraištis [kakla'raishtis] *n* tie, necktie
kaklas [kak'las] *n* neck
kakta [kakta'] *n* forehead, brow
kalakutas [kalaku'tas] *n* turkey-cock
kalavijas [kalavi'jas] *n* sword
kalba [kalba'] *n* language, tongue, speech
kalbėti [kalbė'ti] *v* speak, talk
kalė [kalė'] *n* bitch
Kalėdos [kalė'dos] *n* Christmas
kalėjimas [kalė'yimas] *n* prison, jail
kalenti [kalen'ti] *v* chatter
kalnas [kal'nas] *n* mountain, hill

kaltas [kal'tas] *adj* guilty
kalti [kal'ti] *v* forge, hammer, cram, con
kaltinti [kal'tinti] *v* accuse, charge, indict, prosecute
kalva [kalva'] *n* hill
kalvis [kal'vis] *n* blacksmith, hammersmith, farrier
kam [kam'] *adv* what for
kamanė [kama'nė] *n* bumble-bee
kame [kame'] *adv* where
kamera [ka'mera] *n* cell, chamber
kamienas [kamie'nas] *n* trunk, stem, bole
kaminas [ka'minas] *n* chimney
kampas [kam'pas] *n* corner, angle
kamštis [kamsh'tis] *n* cork, stopper
kamuolys [kamuolees'] *n* ball, clew, globe
kamuoti [kamuo'ti] *v* torment, torture, weary, tire
kanapė [kana'pė] *n* hemp
kanceliarija [kancclia'rija] *n* office
kančia [kanchia'] *n* suffering, pain, torment, torture
kankinti [kankin'ti] *v* torture, torment, martyr
kanopa [kano'pa] *n* hoof
kantrybė [kantree'bė] *n* patience

kapas [ka'pas] *n* grave
kapai [kapai'] *n* graveyard, churchyard
kapinės [ka'pinės] *n* cemetery
kapoti [kapo'ti] *v* hew, hack, chop, flog
kaprizas [kapri'zas] *n* whim, caprice
karalaitė [karalai'tė] *n* princess
karalaitis [karalai'tis] *n* prince
karalienė [karalie'nė] *n* queen
karalius [kara'lius] *n* king
karas [ka'ras] *n* war, warfare
kardas [kar'das] *n* sword, sabre
kareivis [karei'vis] *n* soldier
kariauti [kariau'ti] *v* fight, make war
karklas [kark'las] *n* asier, willow
karoliai [karo'liai] *n* beads
karpa [kar'pa] *n* wart
karpyti [karpee'ti] *v* cut, clip
karstas [kars'tas] *n* coffin
karščiavimas [karshchia'vimas] *n* fever,
feverishness
karštai [karshtai'] *adv* hotly, with heat,
warmly
karštas [karsh'tas] *adj* hot
karštis [karsh'tis] *n* heat, fever
karta [karta'] *n* generation

kartais [kar'tais] *adv* sometimes, at times, now and then

kartas [kar'tas] *n* time

kartėlis [kartė'lis] *n* bitterness, bitter taste

kartoti [karto'ti] *v* repeat, reiterate, multiply

kartu [kartu'] *adv* together, in common, jointly

kartus [kartus'] *adj* bitter

karūna [karoo'na] *n* crown

karuselė [karuse'lė] *n* merry-go-round, carousel

karvė [kar'vė] *n* cow

kas [kas'] *prn* who, what

kasa [kasa'] *n* plait, tress, braid, cach, desk

kasdien [kasdien'] *adv* daily, every day

kaskart [kaskart'] *adv* every time, each time

kąsnis [kaas'nis] *n* piece, bit

kaspinas [kas'pinas] *n* ribbon, bow, fillet

kasryt [kasreet'] *adv* every morning

kassyk [kasseek'] *adv* every time, each time

kasti [kas'ti] *v* dig, mine

kąsti [kaas'ti] *v* bite, sting, nibble

kaštonas [kashto'nas] *n* chestnut

katė [katė'] *n* cat

katedra [ka'tedra] *n* chair, department, cathedral

katilas [ka'tilas] *n* copper, boiler, cauldron

katinas [ka'tinas] *n* tomcat

katras [katras'] *prn* which of the two

kaukas [kau'kas] *n* goblin

kaukė [kau'kė] *n* mask

kaukti [kauk'ti] *v* howl, wail, hoot

kaulas [kau'las] *n* bone

kaupas [kau'pas] *n* heap, pile, excess, overmeasure

kaustyti [kaus'teeti] *v* shoe, bind with metal

kava [kava'] *n* coffee

kavinė [kavi'nė] *n* cafe, coffeehouse

kažin [kazhin'] *adv* scarcely, hardly

keblus [keblus'] *adj* difficult

kėdė [kėdė'] *n* chair

kėglis [kėg'lis] *n* skittle

keiksmažodis [keiksma'zhodis] *n* curse, oath, swearword

keikti [keik'ti] *v* scold, rail, abuse

keistas [keis'tas] *adj* strange, queer, odd

keisti [keis'ti] *v* change, substitute, relieve

kekšė [kek'shė] *n* bitch

keleivis [kelei'vis] *n* passenger, traveller, wayfarer

keli, keletas [keli', ke'letas] *prn* several, some

kelias [ke'lias] *n* road, way, path

keliauti [keliau'ti] *v* travel, voyage, wander
kelintas [kelin'tas] *prn* which
kelis [ke'lis] *n* knee
kelmas [kel'mas] *n* stump, stub
kelnės [kel'nės] *n* trousers
keltas [kel'tas] *n* ferryboat, raft
kelti [kel'ti] *v* lift, raise
keltis [kel'tis] *v* get up, ferry, go up
kenkėjas [kenkė'jas] *n* pest
kenkti [kenk'ti] *v* injure, harm, hurt
kentėti [kentė'ti] *v* suffer, endure, undergo
kepenys [ke'penees] *n* liver
kepykla [kepeek'la] *n* bakery, baker's shop
kepti [kep'ti] *v* bake, broil, fry, roast
kepurė [kepu'rė] *n* cap
kerėpla [kerėp'la] *n* clumsy person, clod
kerėti [kerė'ti] *v* conjure, practice witchcraft
keršyti [ker'sheeti] *v* avenge oneself, take
revenge
kėsintis [kėsin'tis] *v* attempt, encroach on
kėslas [kės'las] *n* evil intent, malicious plan
ketinimas [keti'nimas] *n* intention, purpose
keturi [keturi'] *num* four
keturiasdešimt [ke'turiasdėshimt] *num* forty
keturiolika [keturio'lika] *num* fourteen

ketvirtadalis [ketvirta'dalis] *num* quarter, one fourth

ketvirtadienis [ketvirta'dienis] *n* Thursday

ketvirtas [ketvir'tas] *num* fourth

kevalas [ke'valas] *n* shell, nutshell

kiaulė [kiau'lė] *n* pig, swine, hog, sow, boar

kiaulpienė [kiaul'pienė] *n* dandelion

kiaurai [kiaurai'] *adv* through

kiaušinienė [kiaushinie'nė] *n* omelette

kiaušinis [kiaushi'nis] *n* egg

kibiras [ki'biras] *n* bucket, pail

kibirkštis [kibirkshtis'] *n* spark

kiek [kiek'] *adv* how much

kiekybė [kiekee'bė] *n* quantity, amount

kiemas [kie'mas] *n* court, yard, courtyard

kieno [kieno'] *prn* whose

kietas [kie'tas] *adj* hard, solid, tough

kilimas [ki'limas] *n* carpet, rug

kilkė [kil'kė] *n* sprat

kilmė [kilmė'] *n* origin, provenance

kilnoti [kilno'ti] *v* move, shift, lift, raise, heave

kilnus [kilnus'] *adj* generous, noble, brave

kilpa [kil'pa] *n* loop, buttonhole, stitch

kilti [kil'ti] *v* rise

kimšti [kimsh'ti] *v* cram, fill, stuff

kirčiuoti [kirchiuo'ti] *v* stress, accent

kirmėlė [kirmėlė'] *n* worm

kirpėjas [kirpė'jas] *n* hairdresser, barber

kirpti [kirp'ti] *v* cut, clip, shear

kirsti [kirs'ti] *v* fell, peck, strike

kirvis [kir'vis] *n* axe

kišenė [kishe'nė] *n* pocket

kyšis [kee'shis] *n* bribe, palmoil, hushmoncy

kiškis [kish'kis] *n* hare

kišti [kish'ti] *v* poke, thrust, shove, slip

kitaip [kitaip'] *adv* differently, otherwise

kitas [ki'tas] *prn* other, another

kitoks [kitoks'] *adv* different, another

kitur [kitur'] *adv* elsewhere, somewhere else

kivirčas [kivir'chas] *n* discord, strife, conflict, quarrel

klaida [klaida'] *n* mistake, error, blunder

klaikus [klaikus'] *adj* terrible, dreadful, horrid, frightful

klajoti [klayo'ti] *v* be a nomad, roam, wander, ramble

klasta [klasta'] *n* insidiousness, perfidy

klastingas [klastin'gas] *adj* insidious, perfidious, crafty

klastoti [klasto'ti] *v* falsity, duff, fabricate, forge

klausimas [klau'simas] *n* question, matter

klausyti [klausee'ti] *v* listen, obey, follow

klausti [klaus'ti] *v* ask, inquire, question

klestėti [klestė'ti] *v* prosper, flourish, thrive

klevas [kle'vas] *n* maple

klibinti [kli'binti] *v* shake, loose, tap, patter

klijai [kliyai'] *n* glue, paste, gum

klimpti [klimp'ti] *v* stick in, sink in, get tied up in

klysti [klees'ti] *v* be mistaken, err, be wrong

kliudyti [kliudee'ti] *v* touch, prevent, hinder, hamper

klupti [klup'ti] *v* stumble over, trip on

klusnus [klusnus'] *adj* obedient, dutiful

kmynas [kmee'nas] *n* caraway

knarkti [knark'ti] *v* snore

knyga [kneega'] *n* book

knygynas [kneegee'nas] *n* bookshop, bookstore

ko [ko'] *adv* why, what for

kodėl [kodėl'] *adv* why

koja [ko'ya] *n* foot, leg

kokybė [kokee'bė] *n* quality

koks [koks'] *adv* what

koktus [koktus'] *adj* nasty, disgusting, repulsive

kol [kol'] *adv* while

konditerija [kondite'riya] *n* confectionery

konjakas [konya'kas] *n* cognac

konkursas [konkur'sas] *n* competition

konservai [konser'vai] *n* canned food

konstatuoti [konstatuo'ti] *v* state, ascertain

kopa [ko'pa] *n* dune

kopėčios [ko'pėchios] *n* ladder

koplyčia [koplee'chia] *n* chapel

kopūstas [kopoos'tas] *n* cabbage

korta [kor'ta] *n* playing card

kosėti [ko'sėti] *v* cough, have a cough

kostiumas [kostiu'mas] *n* suit, costume

košė [ko'shė] *n* porridge, gruel, jumble

košmaras [koshma'ras] *n* nightmare

kotas [ko'tas] *n* handle, grip, haft, helve, stalk

kotletas [kotle'tas] *n* cutlet, chop, rissole

kova [kova'] *n* struggle, fight

kovas [ko'vas] *n* rook, March

kraipyti [kraipee'ti] *v* shake, wag

kramtyti [kramtee'ti] *v* chew, masticate, bite

krantas [kran'tas] *n* bank, seashore

krapas [kra'pas] *n* fennel, dill

krapštyti [krapshtee'ti] *v* peck, pick, claw, scratch

kraštas [krash'tas] *n* edge, verge, brim, brink, curb

kraštutinybė [krashtutinee'bė] *n* extreme

kraujas [krau'jas] *n* blood

kraupus [kraupus'] *adj* terrible, horrible, frightful, dreadful

krauti [krau'ti] *v* pile, heap up, lade, charge

krautuvė [krau'tuvė] *n* shop, store

kregždė [kregzh'dė] *n* swallow, martin

kreida [kreida'] *n* chalk

kreipti [kreip'ti] *v* direct at, turn, concentrate

kreivas [krei'vas] *adj* crooked, curved, wry

krepšinis [krepshi'nis] *n* basketball

krėslas [krės'las] *n* armchair, easychair

kriauklė [kriauk'lė] *n* shell, cockleshell, mussel, sink

kriaušė [kriau'shė] *n* pear

krienas [krie'nas] *n* horseradish

krioklys [krioklees'] *n* waterfall, falls, cascade

kryptis [kreeptis'] *n* direction, trend, tenor

kristi [kris'ti] *v* fall, drop, slump

kryžius [kree'zhius] *n* cross

krūmas [kroo'mas] *n* bush, shrub

kruopos [kruo'pos] *n* groats, grain

kruopštus [kruopshtus'] *adj* thorough, tedious, careful

krūpčioti [kroop'chioti] *v* start, flinch, wince

krūtinė [krooti'nė] *n* breast, bosom

krūva [kroova'] *n* heap, pile, lots

kūdikis [koo'dikis] *n* baby, infant

kuklus [kuklus'] *adj* modest

kukurūzas [kukuroo'zas] *n* maize, corn

kulka [kulka'] *n* bullet, projectile

kulnas [kul'nas] *n* heel

kumpis [kum'pis] *n* ham, gammon

kumštis [kumsh'tis] *n* fist

kūnas [koo'nas] *n* body

kunigas [ku'nigas] *n* priest

kupinas [ku'pinas] *adj* full

kur [kur'] *adv* where, which way

kuras [ku'ras] *n* fuel, firing

kūryba [kooree'ba] *n* creative work, creation

kūrimas [koori'mas] *n* creation, establishment, lightning

kuris [kuris'] *prn* which

kutenti [kuten'ti] *v* tickle

kuždėti [kushdė'ti] *v* whisper

kvadratas [kvadra'tas] *n* square

kvailas [kvai′las] *adj* foolish, stupid, silly, inane

kvapas [kva′pas] *n* smell, odor, scent

kvatoti [kvato′ti] *v* laugh, shout with laughter

kvepalai [kvepalai′] *n* perfume, scent

kvėpuoti [kvėpuo′ti] *v* breathe, respire

kviesti [kvies′ti] *v* invite, ask

kvietys [kvietees′] *n* wheat

L

labądien [la′baadien] *mod* good day! good afternoon

labai [labai′] *adv* very, very much, greatly, extremely

labdara [labdara′] *n* charity, philantropy

labinti [la′binti] *v* greet, welcome, hail

lagaminas [lagami′nas] *n* trunk, suitcase

laibas [lai′bas] *adj* thin, slender, slim, delicate

laida [laida′] *n* sunset, issue, edition, telecast

laidas [lai′das] *n* guarantee, deposit, wires, installation

laidoti [lai′doti] *v* bury

laidotuvės [lai'dotuvės] *n* burial, funeral, obsequies

laiduoti [laiduo'ti] *v* warrant, guarantee, certify, vouch

laikas [lai'kas] *n* time, tense

laikinai [laikinai'] *adv* temporarily, provisionally

laikyti [laikee'ti] *v* hold, keep

laikraštis [laik'rashtis] *n* newspaper, paper

laikrodis [laik'rodis] *n* clock, watch, alarmclock

laiku [laiku'] *adv* in time, in proper time

laimė [lai'mė] *n* happiness, luck, good fortune

laimėti [laimė'ti] *v* win, gain

laimikis [laimi'kis] *n* prize, plunder, booty, catch

laiminti [lai'minti] *v* wish luck, bless

laipsnis [laips'nis] *n* degree, extent

laiptai [laip'tai] *n* stairs, staircase

laistyti [lais'teeti] *v* pour, water, hose

laisvalaikis [laisva'laikis] *n* leisure

laisvas [lais'vas] *adj* free, unrestricted, vacant

laisvė [lais'vė] *n* freedom, liberty

laiškanešys [laishkaneshees] *n* postman

laiškas [laish'kas] *n* letter
laivas [lai'vas] *n* ship, vessel, craft
laižyti [laizhee'ti] *v* lick
lakštingala [lakshtin'gala] *n* nightingale
lakūnas [lakoo'nas] *n* flier, flyer, pilot, aviator
langas [lan'gas] *n* window, casement-window
lankyti [lankee'ti] *v* call on, visit, resort
lankstytis [lankstee'tis] *v* bend, fold
lapas [la'pas] *n* leaf, sheet
lapė [la'pė] *n* fox, vixen
lapkritis [lap'kritis]*n* November
lašas [la'shas] *n* drop, bit
lašiša [lashi'sha] *n* salmon
lauk! [lauk'] *v* away! get away!
laukas [lau'kas] *n* open air, field
laukinis [lauki'nis] *adj* wild, savage, fierce
laukti [lauk'ti] *v* wait, expect, anticipate
laumė [lau'mė] *n* witch, hag
laužas [lau'zhas] *n* bonfire, campfire, scrap
laužyti [lau'zheeti] *v* break
lavinti [la'vinti]*v* develop, train, exercise, practice
lavonas [lavo'nas] *n* corpse, dead body, carcass

lazda [lazda'] *n* stick, cane
lažintis [la'zhintis] *v* wager
lėbauti [lė'bauti] *v* debauch
ledas [le'das] *n* ice
leisti [leis'ti] *v* let, allow, permit
lėkštas [lėksh'tas] *adj* flat, plane, trivial
lėktuvas [lėktu'vas] *n* aircraft, airplane,
plane
lėlė [lėlė'] *n* doll
lempa [lem'pa] *n* lamp, valve
lemtis [lemtis'] *n* fate, destiny, fortune,
doom
lengvabūdis [lengvaboo'dis] *adj*
light-minded person, flippant person
lengvas [leng'vas] *adj* light, easy
lengvata [lengva'ta] *n* privilege, advantage
lenkas [len'kas] *n* Pole
lenktynės [lenktee'nės] *n* the races,
competition, emulation
lenta [lenta'] *n* board, plank, table
lepinti [le'pinti] *v* spoil, indulge, pamper,
coddle
lėšos [lė'shos] *n* means
lėtas [lė'tas] *adj* slow, quiet, peaceful
letena [le'tena] *n* paw, pad, foot
liaudis [liau'dis] *n* people, nation

liautis [liau'tis] *v* stop, cease
lydeka [leedeka'] *n* pike, ling
lydėti [leedė'ti] *v* accompany, see off
lydyti [lee'deeti] *v* melt, smelt, fuse
liekana [lie'kana] *n* remainder, remnant, survival
lieknas [liek'nas] *adj* slender, slim
liemenė [lieme'nė] *n* waistcoat, vest
liemuo [liemuo'] *n* body, trunk, stem, bole
liepa [lie'pa] *n* lime-tree, linden, July
liepsna [liepsna'] *n* flame, flare, blaze
liepti [liep'ti] *v* order, tell, bid
liesas [lie'sas] *adj* lean, thin
lieti [lie'ti] *v* pour
lietus [lietus'] *n* rain
Lietuva [lietuva'] *n* Lithuania
liežuvis [liezhu'vis] *n* tongue
lyg [leeg'] *adv* as if, like
liga [liga'] *n* illness, disease, ailment
lygiai [lee'giai] *adv* smoothly, equally
lygiavertis [leegiaver'tis] *adj* equivalent, of equal value
lyginti [lee'ginti] *v* compare, smooth, collate
lygis [lee'gis] *n* level
ligoninė [ligo'ninė] *n* hospital
lygus [lee'gus] *adj* flat, even, equal

likimas [liki'mas] *n* staying, fate, destiny, fortune

likti [lik'ti] *v* remain, stay

linas [li'nas] *n* flax

linija [li'niya] *n* line

lininis [lini'nis] *adj* linen, flaxen

liniuotė [liniuo'tė] *n* ruler

link [link'] *adv* towards, in the direction of

linkėti [linkė'ti] *v* wish smb. smth.

linksmas [links'mas] *adj* merry, gay, lively, joyful, jolly

linkti [link'ti] *v* bend, stoop, incline

lynoti [leeno'ti] *v* drizzle

lipdyti [lipdee'ti] *v* glue, stick, paste, model, sculpture

lipti [lip'ti] *v* climb, scale, stick

lįsti [lees'ti] *v* get in, crawl into

lyti [lee'ti] *v* rain

liūdėti [lioodė'ti] *v* grieve, be sad, be melancholy

liudyti [liu'deeti] *v* witness, testify

liurbis [liur'bis] *n* lout, lubber, bumpkin, booby

liūtas [lioo'tas] *n* lion

lizdas [liz'das] *n* nest, socket

lobis [lo'bis] *n* wealth, riches, treasure

lokys [lokees'] *n* bear
lošti [losh'ti] *v* play, recurve, recline
loti [lo'ti] *v* bark, bay
lova [lo'va] *n* bedstead, bed, cot, crib
lubos [lu'bos] *n* ceiling
lukštas [luksh'tas] *n* husk, peel, sheel
luošas [luo'shas] *adj* lame
lūpa [loo'pa] *n* lip, labium
lupti [lup'ti] *v* bark, peel, skin, strip off
lūšna [loosh'na] *n* hut, hovel, shanty, shack
lūžis [loo'zhis] *n* break, breaking, fracture
lūžti [loozh'ti] *v* break, burst with smth.

M

mada [mada'] *n* fashion, vogue
maigyti [mai'geeti] *v* rumple, crumple, mash, crush
mainyti [mainee'ti] *v* exchange
maistas [mais'tas] *n* food, foodstuffs
maišas [mai'shas] *n* bag, sack
maišyti [maishee'ti] *v* stir, agitate, mix, hinder
maitinti [maitin'ti] *v* feed, nourish
maitoti [maito'ti] *v* defile, profane
makleris [mak'leris] *n* broker
malda [malda'] *n* prayer, grace

malka [mal′ka] *n* log, firewood
malonė [malo′nė] *n* favor, grace
malonėti [malonė′ti] *v* be kind, wish
malšinti [malshin′ti] *v* supress, repress, put down, calm
malti [mal′ti] *v* grind, mill
malūnas [maloo′nas] *n* mill
mama [mama′] *n* mummy, mamma
man [man′] *prn* me, to me, for me
mandagus [mandagus′] *adj* polite, courteous, civil
manyti [manee′ti] *v* think, have the intention
mankšta [mankshta′] *n* gymnastic, drill
mano [ma′no] *prn* my, mine
manta [manta′] *n* property, belongings, things
margas [mar′gas] *adj* motley, variegated, of many colors
marinuotas [marinuo′tas] *adj* pickled
marios [ma′riòs] *n* sea, lagoon, land-locked bay
marmeladas [marmela′das] *n* jam, candied fruit jelly
marškiniai [marshkiniai′] *n* shirt, chemise
maršrutas [marshru′tas] *n* route, itinerary
marti [marti′] *n* daughter-in-law, bride

masinti [ma'sinti] *v* attract, carry away

mąslus [maaslus'] *adj* prudent, clever

mąstyti [maastee'ti] *v* think, reflect,
meditate, ponder

mašina [mashina'] *n* machine, car, lorry

matyt [mateet'] *adv* evidently, obviously,
apparently

matyti [matee'ti] *v* see

matomas [ma'tomas] *adj* visible

maudytis [mau'deetis] *v* bathe, take a bath

mausti [maus'ti] *v* ache

mazgas [maz'gas] *n* knot, bend, hitch

mažai [mazhai'] *adv* little, few

mažas [ma'zhas] *adj* small, little, short

mažėti [mazhė'ti] *v* diminish, decrease

mažylis [mazhee'lis] *n* baby, little one,
youngster

mažne [mazhne'] *adv* nearly, almost

mažuma [mazhuma'] *n* minority

mediena [medie'na] *n* wood, timber

medis [me'dis] *n* tree, wood

meduolis [meduo'lis] *n* honey cake

medus [medus'] *n* honey

medvilnė [med'vilnė] *n* cotton, raw cotton,
cotton wool

medžiaga [medzhiaga'] *n* material, stuff, cloth

medžioti [medzhio'ti] *v* hunt, shoot, chase, battle

mėgautis [mė'gautis] *v* take pleasure, revel, enjoy

mėgdžioti [mėg'dzhioti] *v* imitate, mimic

mėginti [mėgin'ti] *v* attempt, try, essay

mėgti [mėg'ti] *v* like, be fond of

megzti [megs'ti] *v* knot, knit, crochet

megztinis [megsti'nis] *n* sweater, jumper

meilė [mei'lė] *n* love

meilikauti [meilikau'ti] *v* flatter, adulate

meilus [meilus'] *adj* friendly, kind, tender, sweet

meistras [meist'ras] *n* foreman, master

meitėlis [mei'tėlis] *n* hog, barrow

menkė [men'kė] *n* ide

melagis [mela'gis] *n* liar, fibster, fibber

mėlynė [mėlcc'nė] *n* bruise, black eye, bilberry

mėlynas [mė'leenas] *adj* blue

melsti [mels'ti] *v* pray, entreat, supplicate

meluoti [meluo'ti] *v* lie, tell lies

melžti [melzh'ti] *v* milk

menas [me'nas] *n* art, skill, proficiency

mėnesiena [mėnesie'na] *n* moonlight, moonlit night

menkas [men'kas] *adj* poor, small, weak, of little importance

mentė [men'tė] *n* paddle, trowel, shovel

mėnulis [mėnu'lis] *n* moon

mėnuo [mė'nuo] *n* month

merdėti [mer'dėti] *v* agonize, be in agony

mergaitė [mergai'tė] *n* girl, lass, little girl

mergina [mergina'] *n* girl, lass

merkti [merk'ti] *v* soak, steep, drizzle, close one's eyes

mes [mes'] *prn* we

mėsa [mėsa'] *n* flesh, meat

mėsamalė [mėsa'malė] *n* meat grinder, meat-chopper

mesti [mes'ti] *v* throw, hurl, chuck, shed

meška [meshka'] *n* bear

meškerioti [meshkerio'ti] *v* fish, angle

mėšlas [mėsh'las] *n* dung, manure, excrement

mėšlungis [mėshlun'gis] *n* cramp, convulsion

metai [me'tai] *n* year

metas [me'tas] *n* time

metinės [me'tinės] *n* anniversary

mėtyti [mė'teeti] *v* throw, cast

miegoti [miego'ti] *v* sleep, slumber
mielai [mielai'] *adv* with pleasure
mielas [mie'las] *adj* nice, sweet, dear
miestas [mies'tas] *n* town, city
miežis [mie'zhis] *n* barley
migdyti [migdee'ti] *v* lull to sleep
migla [migla'] *n* haze, mist, fog
miklus [miklus'] *adj* flexible, lithe, lissom
miksėti [miksė'ti] *v* stutter, stammer
mylėti [meelė'ti] *v* love
mylimas [mee'limas] *adj* beloved, dear, loved
miltai [mil'tai] *n* flour, meal
milžinas [mil'zhinas] *n* giant, colossus
mindžioti [min'dzhioti] *v* trample down
minėti [minė'ti] *v* mention, refer, celebrate
minia [minia'] *n* crowd, throng
minkštas [minksh'tas] *adj* soft
mintis [mintis'] *n* thought, reflection, idea
miręs [mi'rēs] *adj* dead
mirgėti [mirgė'ti] *v* twinkle, shimmer, glimmer, sparkle
mirksėti [mirksė'ti] *v* wink, blink
mirti [mir'ti] *v* die, pass away, depart
mirtingas [mirtin'gas] *adj* mortal
mirtis [mirtis'] *n* death

mįslė [meeslė'] *n* riddle, puzzle, enigma
mišios [mi'shios] *n* Mass
miškas [mish'kas] *n* forest, wood, woods
mišrainė [mishrai'nė] *n* salad
mitrus [mitrus'] *adj* quick, prompt, swift, agile
močiutė [mochiu'tė] *n* granny
mokestis [mo'kestis] *n* tax, rent, customs duty
mokėti [mokė'ti] *v* pay, be able, can
mokykla [mokeekla'] *n* school
mokinys [mokinees'] *n* pupil, apprentice, disciple
mokyti [mo'keeti] *v* teach, instruct
mokytojas [mo'keetoyas] *n* teacher, schoolmaster, tutor
mokslas [moks'las] *n* science, study, knowledge
molis [mo'lis] *n* clay
moliūgas [molioo'gas] *n* pumpkin
moneta [moneta'] *n* coin
morka [mor'ka] *n* carrot
mostas [mos'tas] *n* gesture
mosuoti [mosuo'ti] *v* wave, swing, wag
moteris [moteris'] *n* woman
motina [mo'tina] *n* mother

mudu, mudvi [mu'du, mu'dvi] *prn* both of us, we two

muilas [mui'las] *n* soap

muitas [mui'tas] *n* duty, customs

mulkinti [mul'kinti] *v* fool, dupe, make a fool

mūras [moo'ras] *n* stone wall, brick wall, brick building

murmėti [murmė'ti] *v* mutter, mumble, murmur

musė [mu'sė] *n* fly

mūsiškai [moo'sishkai] *adv* after our manner

mūsų [moo'soo] *prn* our, ours

mūšis [moo'shis] *n* battle

mušti [mush'ti] *v* beat, thrash, hit, strike, drum

N

nafta [nafta'] *n* oil, petroleum

nagas [na'gas] *n* nail, fingernail, claw

nagi [na'gi] *int* well, well then

nagrinėti [nagrinė'ti] *v* examine, investigate, look

naikinti [naikin'ti] *v* destroy, annihilate, devastate, ravage

naktis [naktis'] *n* night

nakvoti [nakvo'ti] *v* spend the night, sleep

namas [na'mas] *n* house, home
namie [namie'] *adv* at home
nardyti [nar'deeti] *v* dive, plunge, duck
narys [narees'] *n* member, fellow
narsa [narsa'] *n* courage, valor
narsus [narsus'] *adj* brave, courageous, valiant
naršyti [narshee'ti] *v* ransack, rummage
narvas [nar'vas] *n* cage, coop
nasrai [nasrai'] *n* jaws, mouth
našlaitis [nashlai'tis] *n* orphan
našlys [nashlees'] *n* widower
našta [nashta'] *n* burden, weight, load
našus [nashus'] *adj* productive, efficient, fruitful
nauda [nauda'] *n* use, profit, advantage, benefit
naujagimis [nauya'gimis] *n* newborn
naujametis [nauya'metis] *n* New Year
naujas [nau'yas] *adj* new, fresh, novel
naujiena [nauyie'na] *n* news, tidings, novelty
ne [ne'] *prt* not, no
neabejotinas [nɛabeyo'tinas] *adj* undoubted, unmistakable, indubitable
neaiškus [neaish'kus] *adj* indistinct, dim, obscure, vague

neapibrėžtas [neapi'brėzhtas] *adj* indefinite, indeterminate, uncertain

neapykanta [neapee'kanta] *n* hatred, hate, odium

neapsimoka [neapsimo'ka] *v* it is not worth

neatidėliotinas [neatidėlio'tinas] *adj* urgent, pressing, immediate

nebe [nebe'] *adv* no longer, no more

nebent [nebent'] *adv* unless, if only, except

nebėra [nebėra'] *v* there is no more

nebylus [nebeelus'] *adj* dumb, mute

nedaug [nedaug'] *adv* a little, little, not much

nedaugelis [nedau'gelis] *adv* few, not many

nedidelis [nedi'delis] *adj* small, not great

negaluoti [negaluo'tl] *v* feel unwell

neganda [ne'ganda] *n* disaster, calamity

negeras [nege'ras] *adj* bad, not good

negi [ne'gi] *adv* really

negilus [negilus'] *adj* shallow, not deep

negyvas [negee'vas] *adj* dead, inanimate, lifeless

negu [ne'gu] *adv* than

nei ... nei [nei' nei'] *cnj* neither ... nor, as ... as

neigti [neig'ti] *v* deny, disclaim, negate

neišmanėlis [neishma'nėlis] *n* simpleton, ignoramus

neišvaizdus [neishvaizdus] *adj* plain, uncomely, unprepossessing

nejautrus [neyautrus'] *adj* insensible, insensitive, impassive

nejučia [neyuchia'] *adv* imperceptibly, unwittingly

nejudrus [neyudrus'] *adj* slow, sluggish

nekaltas [nekal'tas] *adj* innocent, guiltless, harmless

nekantriai [nekant'riai] *adj* impatiently

nekęsti [nekēs'ti] *v* hate, detest

nekoks [nekoks'] *adj* poor, bad

nelaimė [nelai'mė] *n* misfortune, bad luck, disaster, calamity

nelauktai [nelauktai'] *adv* unexpectedly, suddenly

neleisti [neleis'ti] *v* prohibit, not allow, prevent

nematomas [nema'tomas] *adj* invisible

nėmaž [nėmazh'] *adv* not in the least, not a bit, not at all

nendrė [nend'rė] *n* reed, cane

nenuorama [nenuo'rama] *n* fidget, rolling-stone

nepaisant [nepai'sant] *adv* regardless of, in spite of

nepaisyti [nepai'seeti] *v* neglect, disregard

nepanašus [nepanashus'] *adj* unlike, dissimilar

nepaprastas [nepap'rastas] *adj* unusual, remarkable, extraordinary

nepriklausomas [nepriklau'somas] *adj* independent

nėra [nėra'] *v* there is no, is not

neramus [neramus'] *adj* anxious, uneasy, troubled

nerti [ner'ti] *v* knit, crochet, weave, dive

nes [nes'] *cnj* for, as, because

nesąmonė [nesaa'monė] *n* nonsense, rubbish, absurdity

nesėkmė [nesėkmė'] *n* failure, misfortune

neskaitant [neskai'tant] *adv* not counting, apart from

nesudėtingas [nesudėtin'gas] *adj* simple, not complicated

nėščia [nėshchia'] *adj* pregnant

nešti [nesh'ti] *v* carry, bear, bring

neštuvai [neshtu'vai] *n* stretcher, litter

nešvankus [neshvankus'] *adj* obscene, improper, indecent

nešvarus [neshvarus'] *adj* unclean, dirty, soiled

net [net'] *adv* even

neteisingai [neteisin'gai] *adv* wrong, incorrectly

netekimas [neteki'mas] *n* loss

netyčia [netee'chia] *adv* accidentally, inadvertently

netikėtas [netikė'tas] *adj* unexpected, sudden

netikras [netik'ras] *adj* untrue, false, artificial

netoli [netoli'] *adv* not far, near, close

netrukus [netru'kus] *adv* soon, shortly after

neva [neva'] *adv* as if, as though, ostensibly

nevaisingas [nevaisin'gas] *adj* barren, sterile, fruitless, unproductive

nevalyvas [nevalee'vas] *adj* slovenly, untidy, dirty

neveltui [nevel'tui] *adv* not without reason

neviltis [neviltis'] *n* despair

nežymus [nezheemus'] *adj* insignificant, unimportant

nežinia [nezhinia'] *n* ignorance, obscurity, uncertainty

niekada [niekada'] *adv* never

niekaip [nie'kaip] *adv* in no way, by no means

niekas [nie'kas] *prn* nobody, no one, nothing

niekieno [nie'kieno] *prn* nobody's, no one's

niekinti [nie'kinti] *v* despise, scorn, look down

niekšas [niek'shas] *n* scoundrel, villain, knave

niekur [nie'kur] *adv* nowhere, not anywhere

nykštys [neekshtees'] *n* thumb

nykus [neekus'] *adj* grim, dismal, dreary, weird

niršti [nirsh'ti] *v* rage, grow angry

niūrus [nioorus'] *adj* gloomy, sullen, somber, dismal

nokti [nok'ti] *v* ripen, mature

noras [no'ras] *n* wish, desire, longing, itch

norėti [norė'ti] *v* want, like, wish, desire

noriai [no'riai] *adv* willingly, readily

nors [nors'] *cnj* though, although, if, even if

nosinė [no'sinė] *n* handkerchief

nosis [no'sis] *n* nose, snout, nozzle

nubausti [nubaus'ti] *v* punish, penalize, fine

nublukti [nubluk'ti] *v* fade, lose color, pale

nubrėžti [nubrėzh'ti] *v* draw, trace

nubusti [nubus'ti] *v* wake up, awake

nučiupti [nuchiup'ti] *v* seize, catch, filch, bag, swipe

nudažyti [nudazhee'ti] *v* paint, color, dye, tincture

nudėti [nudė'ti] *v* kill, lay out

nudirti [nudir'ti] *v* flay, skin

nudribti [nudrib'ti] *v* tumble, fall down

nudvėsti [nudvės'ti] *v* die, croak

nudžiauti [nudzhiau'ti] *v* take down, pinch

nugalėti [nugalė'ti] *v* overcome, defeat, surmount, conquer

nugara [nugara'] *n* back

nuilsęs [nuil'sēs] *adj* tired, weary

nuimti [nuim'ti] *v* take off, remove, take down

nujausti [nuyaus'ti] *v* forebode, have a presentiment

nukalti [nukal'ti] *v* forge, coin

nukentėti [nukentė'ti] *v* suffer, smart

nukirpti [nukirp'ti] *v* cut off, clip off, crop, dock, shear

nuklysti [nuklees'ti] *v* stray, go astray, lose one's way

nukrypti [nukreep'ti] *v* diverge, deviate, digress

nukryžiuoti [nukreezhiuo'ti] *v* crucify

nulis [nu'lis] *num* nought, zero, nil

nulupti [nulup'ti] *v* strip, peel, shell

numalšinti [numalshin'ti] *v* suppress, put down, slake, satisfy

numatyti [numatee'ti] *v* foresee, foreknow, provide, forecast

numauti [numau'ti] *v* take off

numeris [nu'meris] *n* number

numesti [numes'ti] *v* throw down, drop

numirti [numir'ti] *v* die, pass away, depart

nuo [nuo'] *prep* from, off, down

nuobauda [nuo'bauda] *n* penalty, punishment

nuobodus [nuobodus'] *adj* dull, boring, tedious

nuodai [nuodai'] *n* poison, venom

nuodėmė [nuodėmė'] *n* offense, trespass, sin

nuodugniai [nuodugniai'] *adv* thoroughly

nuogas [nuo'gas] *adj* naked, nude

nuogąstauti [nuogaastauti] *v* fear, be apprehensive

nuogirdos [nuo'girdos] *n* rumor, hearsay

nuograuža [nuo'grauzha] *n* gnawed bit

nuojauta [nuo'yauta] *n* feeling, flair, presentiment

nuolaidus [nuolaidus'] *adj* yielding, pliant, compliant

nuolankus [nuolankus'] *adj* submissive, obedient, resigned

nuolat [nuo'lat] *adv* constantly, continually

nuolauža [nuo'lauzha] *n* fragment, fraction, splinter, debris

nuomonė [nuo'monė] *n* opinion, mind

nuomoti [nuomo'ti] *v* let, rent, lease, tenant

nuopelnas [nuo'pelnas] *n* merit, desert

nuorašas [nuo'rashas] *n* copy, transcript, duplicate

nuorūka [nuo'rooka] *n* stump, cigarette-butt

nuosaikus [nuosaikus'] *adj* moderate, temperate

nuosavas [nuo'savas] *adj* own

nuosavybė [nuosavee'bė] *n* property, ownership

nuosėdos [nuo'sėdos] *n* sediment, settlings, deposition

nuoseklus [nuoseklus'] *adj* successive, consecutive

nuoskauda [nuo'skauda] *n* wrong, mortification

nuosprendis [nuo'sprendis] *n* sentence, verdict, decree

nuostaba [nuostaba'] *n* wonder, amazement, astonishment, surprise

nuostabus [nuostabus'] *adj* wonderful, marvelous, amazing, striking

nuostolis [nuo'stolis] *n* loss, detriment, damage

nuošaliai [nuoshaliai'] *adv* aloof, apart, in solitude

nuoširdus [nuoshirdus'] *adj* sincere, heartfelt, hearty, frank

nuotaika [nuo'taika] *n* mood, humor, temper

nuotaka [nuo'taka] *n* bride

nuotykis [nuo'teekis] *n* adventure

nuotolis [nuo'tolis] *n* distance, space

nuotrauka [nuo'trauka] *n* photograph, picture

nuovada [nuo'vada] *n* police office, police station

nuovargis [nuo'vargis] *n* tiredness, weariness

nuoviras [nuo'viras] *n* broth

nuožiūra [nuo'zhioora] *n* discretion

nuožmus [nuozhmus'] *adj* fierce, ferocious, truculent

nupirkti [nupirk'ti] *v* buy, purchase

nuraminti [nuramin'ti] *v* quiet, calm, soothe, set at ease

nurausti [nuraus'ti] *v* redden, flush, blush

nuryti [nuree'ti] *v* swallow, choke down

nurodyti [nuro'deeti] *v* indicate, point, explain

nusakyti [nusakee'ti] *v* define

nusiaubti [nusiaub'ti] *v* devastate, ravage, lay waste

nusibosti [nusibos'ti] *v* bore, bother

nusigerti [nusiger'ti] *v* get drunk, get tight

nusiginkluoti [nusiginkluo'ti] *v* disarm

nusikalsti [nusikals'ti] *v* commit a crime, be guilty, trespass

nusikaltėlis [nusikal'tėlis] *n* criminal, offender, felon

nusikeikti [nusikeik'ti] *v* curse, utter a curse

nusileisti [nusileis'ti] *v* come down, descend

nusilengvinti [nusileng'vinti] *v* defecate, relieve nature

nusimanyti [nusimanee'ti] *v* understand, know, be versed in

nusiminęs [nusimi'nēs] *adj* downhearted, dispirited, depressed

nusiraminti [nusiramin'ti] *v* calm down, compose oneself

nusirengti [nusireng'ti] *v* undress, strip

nusiskusti [nusiskus'ti] *v* shave

nusispjauti [nusispyau'ti] *v* spit

nusišaipyti [nusishaipee'ti] *v* smirk, simper

nusišypsoti [nusisheepso'ti] *v* smile, give a smile

nusišlapinti [nusishla'pinti] *v* urinate, relieve oneself

nusišnekėti [nusishnekė'ti] *v* talk nonsense

nusišnypšti [nusishneepsh'ti] *v* blow one's nose

nusiteikti [nusiteik'ti] *v* be disposed

nusitęsti [nusitēs'ti] *v* linger, last, drag on

nusivilti [nusivil'ti] *v* be disappointed, be disillusioned

nusižeminti [nusizhe'minti] *v* abase oneself, eat humble pie

nusižudyti [nusizhudee'ti] *v* commit suicide

nuskęsti [nuskės'ti] *v* sink, go down, drown

nuskinti [nuskin'ti] *v* pick, pluck off

nuskurėlis [nusku'rėlis] *n* ragamuffin

nuskursti [nuskurs'ti] *v* grow poor, become a pauper

nusnūsti [nusnoos'ti] *v* take a nap, have a doze

nuspręsti [nusprēs'ti] *v* decide, determine, resolve

nustebti [nusteb'ti] *v* be astonished, be surprised

nustoti [nusto'ti] *v* lose, stop, cease

nustulbinti [nustul'binti] *v* stun, astound

nusvirti [nusvir'ti] *v* hang down, droop

nušalimas [nushali'mas] *n* cold, shill, frostbite

nušiuręs [nushiu'rēs] *adj* shabby, frayed, dilapidated

nušviesti [nushvies'ti] *v* light up, illuminate

nutarti [nutar'ti] *v* enact, decree, decide, resolve

nuteisti [nuteis'ti] *v* convict, sentence, condemn

nutikti [nutik'ti] *v* happen, occur

nutrūktgalvis [nutrooktgal'vis] *adj* madcap, romp, daredevil

nutrūkti [nutrook'ti] *v* come off, break, snap

nutukęs [nutu'kēs] *adj* obese, fat

nutuokti [nutuok'ti] *v* see the point, realize, catch on

nutūpti [nutoop'ti] *v* land, touch down, alight, perch

nutverti [nutver'ti] *v* catch, snatch, seize

nuvalyti [nuvalee'ti] *v* clean off, brush off, polish

nuvalkioti [nuval'kioti] *v* wear out, carry, drag

nuvargęs [nuvar'gēs] *adj* tired, weary

nuversti [nuvers'ti] *v* overturn, throw down

nuvesti [nuves'ti] *v* take to, lead to, lead away

nuvysti [nuvees'ti] *v* fade, wither, wilt

nuvyti [nuvee'ti] *v* drive away, wind off

nužudyti [nuzhudee'ti] *v* kill, murder, assassinate

O

o [o'] *cnj* and, but

obelis [obelis'] *n* appletree

obuolys [obuolees'] *n* apple

oda [oda'] *n* skin, hide

okeanas [okea'nas] *n* ocean

ola [ola'] *n* burrow, hole, cave, cavern

omaras [oma'ras] *n* lobster

ondatra [ondat'ra] *n* muskrat

opa [opa'] *n* ulcer, sore

opšrus [opsh'rus] *n* badger

opus [opus'] *adj* delicate, frail, sore, tender

oras [o'ras] *n* air, weather

oriai [o'riai] *adv* with dignity

orientyras [orientee'ras] *n* landmark, reference, guide

orkaitė [or'kaitė] *n* oven

orlaidė [or'laidė] *n* ventilation pane, air-hole

ošti [osh'ti] *v* murmur, rustle, sough

ožys [ozhees'] *n* he-goat

ožka [ozhka'] *n* goat, she-goat

P

paauglys [paauglees'] *n* juvenile, teenager

pabaiga [pabaiga'] *n* end, conclusion

pabaigti [pabaig'ti] *v* finish, end, complete

pabaisa [pabai'sa] *n* monster

pabėgėlis [pabė'gėlis] *n* fugitive, runaway, refugee, escape

pabėgti [pabėg'ti] *v* run away, take to flight, make off

pabrangti [pabrang'ti] *v* rise in price

pabraukti [pabrauk'ti] *v* underline, underscore, pass smth. over

pabrinkti [pabrink'ti] *v* swell, be swollen, become puffy

pabučiuoti [pabuchiuo'ti] *v* kiss, give a kiss

pabusti [pabus'ti] *v* wake up, awake

padanga [pa'danga] *n* tire

padangė [padan'gė] *n* the skies, the heavens

padaras [pa'daras] *n* being, creature

padaryti [padaree'ti] *v* make, do

padas [pa'das] *n* sole

padavėjas [padavė'yas] *n* waiter, bearer

padažas [pa'dazhas] *n* sauce, gravy, dressing

padėjėjas [padėyė'yas] *n* assistant, help, helper

padėka [padėka'] *n* thanks, gratitude

padėklas [padėk'las] *n* tray, salver, saucer

padėkoti [padėko'ti] *v* thank

padėti [padė'ti] *v* lay down, place, lay, help, assist

padėtis [padėtis'] *n* position, location

padorus [padorus'] *adj* decent, decorous, seemly, passable

padugnės [pa'dugnės] *n* riff-raff, scum, dregs of society

paduoti [paduo'ti] *v* give, serve, hand

paeiliui [paeiliui'] *adv* one after another, in turn, by turns

pagal [pa'gal] *adv* along, according to, by

pagalba [pagal'ba] *n* help, assistance, aid

pagaliau [pagaliau'] *adv* at last, finally

pagalys [pagalees'] *n* stick

pagalvė [pa'galvė] *n* pillow, cushion

pagarba [pagarba'] *n* honor, respect, esteem

pagauti [pagau'ti] *v* catch, seize, snatch

pagedęs [page'dēs] *adj* spoilt, rotten, decayed, tainted

pageidauti [pageidau'ti] *v* wish, desire

pagirios [pa'girios] *n* hangover, the morning after

pagirti [pagir'ti] *v* praise, commend

pagyrūnas [pageeroo'nas] *n* boaster, swaggerer, braggart

pagyvenęs [pageeve'nēs] *adj* elderly

paglemžti [paglemzh'ti] *v* usurp, take possession, lay hands on

pagrindas [pa'grindas] *n* foundation, base, bottom, basis

pagrobti [pagrob'ti] *v* grab, seize, kidnap, abduct

pagunda [pagunda] *n* temptation

paguoda [paguo'da] *n* comfort, consolation, solace

pagurklis [pagurk'lis] *n* double chin

paikas [pai'kas] *adj* silly, foolish, imbecile

pailgas [pail'gas] *adj* oblong

pailsęs [pail'sēs] *adj* tired, weary, fatigued

paimti [paim'ti] *v* take

painioti [pai'nioti] *v* tangle, confuse, muddle, mix up

pajamos [pa'yamos] *n* receipts, returns, income

pajėgti [payėg'ti] *v* be able, have the strength

pajudėti [payudė'ti] *v* stir, move, start, be off

pajuokti [payuok'ti] *v* ridicule, make fun of, mock, gibe at

pajūris [payoo'ris] *n* seaside, beach, seashore

pajusti [payus'ti] *v* feel, sense, have a sensation

pakaba [pakaba'] *n* tab, hanger, peg, rack, clothes hanger

pakabinti [pakabin'ti] *v* hang, suspend

pakalnutė [pakalnu'tė] *n* lily of the valley

pakankamai [pakan'kamai] *adv* sufficiently, enough, rather, fairly

pakarpa [pakarpa'] *n* scruff

pakartoti [pakarto'ti] *v* repeat, revise, go over

pakaušis [pakau'shis] *n* back of the head, occiput

pakeisti [pakeis'ti] *v* change, alter, modify, replace

pakelė [pakelė'] *n* wayside, roadside

pakelti [pakel'ti] *v* lift, raise, heave

pakenkti [pakenk'ti] *v* damage, harm, injure

pakęsti [pakēs'ti] *v* bear, endure, tolerate

pakirpti [pakirp'ti] *v* trim, cut

paklausa [paklausa'] *n* demand, run on

paklausti [paklaus'ti] *v* ask, inquire, question

paklusnus [paklusnus'] *adj* obedient, dutiful, submissive

pakopa [pako'pa] *n* step, footstep, stage

pakrantė [pakran'tė] *n* shore, coast, seabord, riverside

pakraštys [pakrashtees] *n* border, edge

pakrikti [pakrik'ti] *v* disperse, scatter, straggle

pakrypti [pakreep'ti] *v* tilt, lean, turn, bend, heel over

pakviesti [pakvies'ti] *v* invite, ask

palaidas [palai'das] *adj* loose, untied, loose-fitting

palaidinė [palaidi'nė] *n* tunic, field shirt

palaima [palai'ma] *n* bliss, felicity, blessing

palaipsniui [palaipsniui'] *adv* gradually, progressively, little by little

palangė [palan'gė] *n* windowsill

palankus [palankus'] *adj* disposed, benevolent

palapinė [palapi'nė] *n* tent, marquee, hut

palei [pa'lei] *adv* by, near

paleisti [paleis'ti] *v* let go, set free, loosen, release

palengvėjimas [palengvė'yimas] *n* relief

palengvinti [paleng'vinti]*v* facilitate, make easier

palenkti [palenk'ti] *v* bend, incline, bow

palyda [palee'da] *n* retinue, escort, train

palydėti [paleedė'ti] *v* accompany, see off

paliepimas [paliepi'mas] *n* order, command, bidding

paliesti [palies'ti] *v* touch

palyginti [palee'ginti] *v* compare, liken, collate

palikimas [paliki'mas] *n* leaving behind, abandonment, inheritance, legacy

palikti [palik'ti] *v* leave

palmė [pal'mė] *n* palmtree

paltas [pal'tas] *n* overcoat, topcoat

pamaiva [pamai'va] *n* affected creature, all airs and graces

pamatas [pa'matas] *n* base, foundation, groundwork

pamazgos [pa'mazgos] *n* slops, dishwater, rinsings

pamėgdžioti [pamėg'dzhioti] *v* imitate, mimic

pamėginti [pamėgin'ti] *v* try, attempt, endeavor

paminėti [paminė'ti] *v* mention, commemorate

paminklas [pamink'las] *n* monument, memorial, tombstone

pamiršti [pamirsh'ti] *v* forget

pamišęs [pami'shēs] *adj* mad, lunatic, crazy, insane

pamoka [pamoka'] *n* lesson, class, task

pamokyti [pamo'keeti] *v* teach, instruct, lecture, edify

pamokslas [pamoks'las] *n* sermon, homily, lecture

pamotė [pa'motė] *n* stepmother

panaikinti [panaikin'ti] *v* abolish, do away

panardinti [panardin'ti] *v* immerse, submerge, plunge, dip, douse

panašus [panashus'] *adj* resembling, alike, similar

panaudoti [panaudo'ti] *v* use, utilize, employ, apply

paneigti [paneig'ti] *v* deny, disclaim, negate, refute

panelė [pane'lė] *n* young lady, girl

panieka [panieka'] *n* contempt, scorn, disdain

papartis [papar'tis] *n* fern, brake

papasakoti [papa'sakoti] *v* relate, narrate, tell

papildyti [papil'deeti] *v* replenish, fill up, refill, add

papildomai [papil'domai] *adv* in addition

papjauti [papyau'ti] *v* kill, butcher, slaughter

paprastai [paprastai'] *adv* simply, easily, usually

paprastas [pap'rastas] *adj* usual, common, ordinary, plain

paprotys [paprotees'] *n* custom, usage

papuošalas [papuo'shalas] *n* decoration, ornament

para [para'] *n* twenty four hours, day

paragauti [paragau'ti] *v* taste, sample

paraiška [paraishka'] *n* claim, application, demand

parama [parama'] *n* support, prop, maintenance, help

parašas [pa'rashas] *n* signature

pardavėjas [pardavė'jas] *n* seller, salesman, shop assistant, vendor

pardavinėti [pardavinė'ti] *v* sell, market

pareiga [pareiga'] *n* duty, obligation

pareikšti [pareiksh'ti] *v* declare, state, announce

pareiškimas [pareishki'mas] *n* application

parengti [pareng'ti] *v* prepare, make ready, train

pargabenti [pargaben'ti] *v* bring up

parinkti [parink'ti] *v* select, choose, pick, glean

parkeris [par'keris] *n* fountain pen

paroda [paroda'] *n* exhibition

parodyti [paro'deeti] *v* show

paršas [par'shas] *n* pig

paršiena [parshie'na] *n* pork

paruošti [paruosh'ti] *v* prepare, make ready

parūpinti [paroo'pinti] *v* supply, provide

parvykti [parveek'ti] *v* return, come back

pas [pas'] *prep* by, to, with

pasaka [pa'saka] *n* fairy tale, tale, fable

pasakinėti [pasakinė'ti] *v* prompt

pasakyti [pasakee'ti] *v* say, tell, utter, speak

pasas [pa'sas] *n* passport

pasaulis [pasau'lis] *n* world

pasekmė [pasekmė'] *n* consequence, result, sequel

pasenęs [pase'nēs] *adj* aged, old, old-fashioned, out- of-date

pasėti [pasė'ti] *v* sow

pasidaryti [pasidaree'ti] *v* become, get

pasiduoti [pasiduo'ti] *v* yield, give way, surrender to

pasiekti [pasiek'ti] *v* reach, touch, attain, achieve

pasiguosti [pasiguos'ti] *v* console oneself

pasiilgti [pasiilg'ti] *v* yearn, pine, long, miss

pasikliauti [pasikliau'ti] *v* rely, count on, depend upon

pasiklysti [pasiklees'ti] *v* lose one's way

pasilinksminti [pasilinks'minti] *v* amuse oneself, enjoy oneself

pasimatymas [pasima'teemas] *n* meeting, appointment, rendezvous

pasimesti [pasimes'ti] *v* get lost, be mislaid

pasinaudoti [pasinaudo'ti] *v* profit, take advantage of, use

pasinerti [pasiner'ti] *v* dive, plunge, dip

pasipelnyti [pasipelnee'ti] *v* profit, make a fortune, become rich

pasipiktinęs [pasipik'tīnēs] *adj* indignant

pasipiršti [pasipirsh'ti] *v* propose, ask smb. to marry

pasipriešinti [pasiprie'shinti] *v* put up, offer, resistance, resist, oppose

pasipūsti [pasipoos'ti] *v* bloat, inflate, swell up

pasiraivyti [pasiraivee'ti] *v* stretch oneself

pasiremti [pasirem'ti] *v* lean, rest on

pasirengęs [pasiren'gēs] *adj* ready, prepared

pasirinkti [pasirink'ti] *v* choose, select, pick

pasiryžęs [pasiree'zhēs] *adj* determined, ready

pasirodyti [pasiro'deeti] *v* appear, show oneself, emerge

pasisekimas [pasiseki'mas] *n* success, good luck

pasiskolinti [pasisko'linti]*v* borrow

pasišiaušti [pasishiaush'ti] *v* bristle up, stand on end

pasišlykštėti [pasishleekshtė'ti] *v* loathe, have an aversion

pasišvęsti [pasishvēs'ti] *v* devote oneself, dedicate oneself

pasitarimas [pasitari'mas] *n* conference, meeting, consultation

pasiteirauti [pasiteirau'ti] *v* inquire, ask

pasiteisinti [pasitei'sinti] *v* justify oneself, make excuses

pasitenkinimas [pasiten'kinimas] *n*
satisfaction, gratification, contentment
pasitikėti [pasitikė'ti] *v* confide, trust, rely
pasitikti [pasitik'ti] *v* meet
pasitraukti [pasitrauk'ti] *v* withdraw, retreat
pasitvirtinti [pasitvir'tinti]*v* be confirmed,
be corroborated
pasiūlyti [pasioo'leeti] *v* offer, suggest,
propose
pasiųsti [pasioos'ti] *v* send, dispatch
pasiūti [pasioo'ti] *v* sew, make
pasivaikščiojimas [pasivaiksh'chioyimas] *n*
walk, airing, stroll
pasižadėti [pasizhadė'ti] *v* engage,
undertake, pledge
paskaita [paskaita'] *n* lecture
paskala [paskala'] *n* gossip, scandal
paskambinti [paskam'binti]*v* ring, call up
paskatinti [paska'tinti]*v* stimulate, induce,
impel
paskelbti [paskel'bti] *v* declare, announce,
publish, proclaim
paskiau [paskiau'] *adv* then, later on
paskirstyti [paskirs'teeti] *v* allot, distribute,
apportion

paskirti [paskir'ti] *v* fix, set, appoint, prescribe

paskirtis [paskirtis'] *n* purpose, destination

pasklisti [pasklis'ti] *v* spread, get about

paskola [paskola'] *n* loan

paskui [paskui'] *adv* after, afterwards, later on

paskutinis [paskuti'nis] *adj* last, final

paslapčia [paslapchia'] *adv* secretly, in secret, by stealth

paslaptingas [paslaptin'gas] *adj* mysterious, enigmatic

paslaptis [paslaptis'] *n* mystery

paslauga [paslauga'] *n* service, favor, good turn

paslėpti [paslėp'ti] *v* hide, conceal, cover

paslysti [paslees'ti] *v* slip, slide

pasmerkti [pasmerk'ti] *v* condemn, doom, convict

pasodinti [pasodin'ti] *v* seat, plant

paspringti [paspring'ti] *v* choke with

pastaba [pastaba'] *n* remark, observation

pastatas [pas'tatas] *n* building, structure, edifice

pastebėti [pastebė'ti] *v* notice, remark, observe

pastogė [pasto'gė] *n* garret, roof, shelter, home

pastovus [pasto'vus'] *adj* constant, stable, steady

pasveikinti [pasvei'kinti]*v* greet, welcome, salute, congratulate

pašalinti [pasha'linti]*v* dismiss, expel, exclude, eliminate

pašaras [pa'sharas] *n* foddcr, forage, provender

pašėlęs [pashė'ɛs] *adj* furious, wild, frantic

pašiūrė [pashioo'rė] *n* shed, penthouse

pašnekesys [pashnekesees'] *n* talk, conversation, chat

paštas [pash'tas] *n* post, mail

pašvaistė [pashvais'tė] *n* glow

pašvęsti [pashvēs'ti] *n* celebrate, sanctify

pataikyti [patai'keeti] *v* hit

pataisyti [pataisee'ti] *v* correct, set right,reform

patalas [pa'talas] *n* bed

patalynė [patalee'nė] *n* bedding, bedclothes

patalpa [patalpa'] *n* lodging, room, living quarters

patarlė [patar'lė] *n* proverb, saying

patarnauti [patarnau'ti] *v* serve, do a good turn

patarti [patar'ti] *v* advise, counsel

patefonas [patefo'nas] *n* gramophone, phonograph

pateikti [pateik'ti] *v* present, produce, adduce

patekti [patek'ti] *v* get into, find oneself

patelė [pate'lė] *n* female

patenkinti [paten'kinti] *v* satisfy, content

patėvis [patė'vis] *n* stepfather

patiekalas [patie'kalas] *n* disk, course

patiekti [patiek'ti] *v* supply, stock, bring, serve

patiesti [paties'ti] *v* spread, lay, stretch

patikėti [patikė'ti] *v* believe, trust, confide

patikimas [pa'tikimas] *adj* reliable, dependable, trustworthy

patikrinti [patik'rinti] *v* verify, check

patikti [patik'ti] *v* please, like

patinas [pa'tinas] *n* male

patyrimas [pateeri'mas] *n* experience, know-how

patogus [patogus'] *adj* comfortable, convenient

patrauklus [patrauklus'] *adj* attractive, winning, engaging, alluring

pats [pats'] *prn* myself, yourself

patvarus [patvarus'] *adj* steadfast, steady, stable

patvirtinti [patvir'tinti] *v* confirm, ratify, corroborate, seal

paukštis [pauksh'tis] *n* bird

pavadinimas [pavadi'nimas] *n* name, appelation, denomination

pavaduoti [pavaduo'ti] *v* act, substitute, take the place of

pavaišinti [pavaishin'ti] *v* treat to, regale with, entertain

pavasaris [pava'saris] *n* spring, springtime

paveikslas [paveiks'las] *n* painting, picture, canvas

paveldėti [pavel'dėti] *v* inherit

pavėluoti [pavėluo'ti] *v* be late, be overdue

paversti [pavers'ti] *v* convert, transform, turn, reduce

pavidalas [pavi'dalas] *n* shape, form, semblance

pavydas [pavee'das] *n* envy, jealousy

pavyduliauti [paveeduliau'ti] *v* be jealous

paviršius [pavir'shius] *n* surface, superficies

pavyzdys [paveezdees'] *n* instance, example
pavojingas [pavoyin'gas] *adj* dangerous, perilous
pažadas [pa'zhadas] *n* promise
pažanga [pazhanga'] *n* progress
pažeminti [pazhe'minti] *v* humiliate, abase, demote, reduce
pažymėjimas [pazheemė'yimas] *n* certificate, marking
pažinti [pazhin'ti] *v* know, be acquainted
pečiai [pechiai'] *n* shoulders
pėda [pė'da] *n* foot
peikti [peik'ti] *v* blame, censure
peilis [pei'lis] *n* knife, carver
pelė [pelė'] *n* mouse
pelėda [pelė'da] *n* owl
pelėsis [pelė'sis] *n* mould
pelkė [pel'kė] *n* bog, swamp, marsh, morass
pelnas [pel'nas] *n* profit, gain, return
penėti [penė'ti] *v* feed, nurse, fatten
penki [penki'] *num* five
penkiasdešimt [pen'kiasdė'shimt] *num* fifty
penkiolika [penkio'lika] *num* fifteen
per [per'] *prp* through, across, on, over
perdėti [per'dėti] *v* exaggerate, magnify, overdo, relay

perduoti [per'duoti] *v* pass, give over, hand over

pereiti [per'eiti] *v* cross, get across, get over

perėjimas [per'ėyimas] *n* passage, transition, crossing

pergalė [per'galė] *n* victory, triuph

perkūnas [perkoo'nas] *n* thunder

perlaida [per'laida] *n* remittance

perlas [per'las] *n* pearl, gem

permaina [per'maina] *n* change, alteration

pernelyg [perneleeg'] *adv* too, too much

perniek [perniek'] *adv* in vain, to no purpose

persekioti [per'sekioti] *v* persecute, prosecute, victimize

persikas [per'sikas] *n* peach

perspėti [per'spėti] *v* warn, caution against

peršalti [per'shalti] *v* catch cold, take a chill

peršėti [pershė'ti] *v* itch, smart

pertrauka [per'trauka] *n* interval, break, intermission

pertraukti [per'traukti]*v* tear apart, break, interrupt

perversmas [per'versmas] *n* revolution, upheaval, overturn

pėsčiomis [pėschiomis'] *adv* go on foot, walk

pešti [pesh'ti] *v* pull, pluck

peteliškė [petelish'kė] *n* butterfly
piemuo [piemuo'] *n* shepherd, cowboy
pienas [pie'nas] *n* milk
pieninė [pie'ninė] *n* dairy, creamery
piešti [piesh'ti] *v* draw, sketch, picture
pietauti [pietau'ti] *v* eat dinner, dine
pietūs [pie'toos] *n* dinner, south
pieva [pie'va] *n* meadow, grassland
pigus [pigus'] *adj* cheap, low
piktas [pik'tas] *adj* angry, cross, wicked, fierce, savage
pykti [peek'ti] *v* be in a bad mood, be angry
pyktis [peek'tis] *n* spite, malice, anger
piktnaudžiauti [piktnaudzhiau'ti] *v* abuse, overindulge
piktžolė [pikt'zholė] *n* weed
pildyti [pil'deeti] *v* carry out, fulfill, execute
pilietis [pilie'tis] *n* citizen, subject
pilkas [pil'kas] *adj* gray
pilnametis [pilname'tis] *adj* adult, of age
pilnas [pil'nas] *adj* full, brimful, stout, plump
pilti [pil'ti] *v* pour
pilvas [pil'vas] *n* stomach
pinigas [pi'nigas] *n* coin, money
piniginė [pinigi'nė] *n* purse, wallet

pinklės [pink'lės] *n* trap, snare, intrigues, schemes

pinti [pin'ti] *v* weave, twine, braid, plait

pipiras [pipi'ras] *n* pepper

pypkė [peep'kė] *n* pipe

pyragaitis [peeragai'tis] *n* pastry cake

pyragas [peera'gas] *n* pie, cake, tart

pirkti [pirk'ti] *v* buy, purchase

pirmadienis [pirma'dienis] *n* Monday

pirmaeilis [pirmaei'lis] *adj* paramount, immediate

pirmas [pir'mas] *num* first

pirmenybė [pirmenee'bė] *n* preference, priority

pirmiau [pirmiau'] *adv* before, formerly, first

pirmyn [pirmeen'] *adv* forward, ahead

pirminis [pirmi'nis] *adj* primary

pirštas [pirsh'tas] *n* finger, toe

pirštinė [pirsh'tinė] *n* glove, mitten, gauntlet

pirtis [pirtis'] *n* bathe, bath house

pjauti [pyau'ti] *v* cut, knife, carve, slice

plačiai [plachiai'] *adv* wide, widely, broadly

plakti [plak'ti] *v* flog, thrash, lash, pulsate, whip, whisk

plasnoti [plasno'ti] *v* flap, flutter, fly

platus [platus′] *adj* wide, broad, extensive
plaučiai [plau′chiai] *n* lungs
plaukas [plau′kas] *n* hair
plaukti [plauk′ti] *v* swim, float, drift
plauti [plau′ti] *v* wash, rinse, swill, bathe
plentas [plen′tas] *n* highway, highroad
plepėti [plepė′ti] *v* chatter, jabber, prate
plėšikas [plėshi′kas] *n* robber, burglar, brigand
plėšti [plėsh′ti] *v* tear, rend, bark
pliažas [plia′zhas] *n* beach
plienas [plie′nas] *n* steel
plikas [pli′kas] *adj* bald, naked, nude, bare
plyšti [pleesh′ti] *v* fear, split, crack
plyta [plee′ta] *n* brick
plokščias [ploksh′chias] *adj* flat, plain
plonas [plo′nas] *adj* thin, fine, slender, slim
ploti [plo′ti] *v* clap, applaud
plotis [plo′tis] *n* width, breadth
plunksna [pluns′na] *n* feather, plume, quill
plušėti [plushė′ti] *v* toil, labor
pluta [pluta′] *n* crust, rind
po [po′] *prp* in, about, on, over
poilsis [po′ilsis] *n* rest, repose, relaxation, recreation
pojūtis [po′yootis] *n* sensation

pokštas [poksh'tas] *n* trick, prank, joke
pomidoras [pomido'ras] *n* tomato
ponas [po'nas] *n* gentleman, master, sir, Mr.
ponia [ponia'] *n* lady, Mrs., madame
popierius [po'pierius] *n* paper
popietis [po'pietis] *n* afternoon
pora [pora'] *n* pair, couple
poreikis [po'reikis] *n* need,want, requirement
posakis [po'sakis] *n* expression, locution, phrase
posėdis [po'sėdis] *n* meeting, conference, session
potvarkis [po'tvarkis] *n* decree, order
povas [po'vas] *n* peacock
poveikis [po'veikis] *n* influence
požymis [po'zheemis] *n* sign, indication
požiūris [po'zhiooris] *n* standpoint, point of view
prabanga [prabanga'] *n* luxury, splendor
pradėti [pradė'ti] *v* begin, start, commence
pradžia [pradzhia'] *n* beginning, outset, commencement
praeitas [pra'eitas] *adj* last, past
praeitis [praeitis'] *n* the past
pragaras [pra'garas] *n* hell, inferno

prakaitas [pra'kaitas] *n* sweat, perspiration
prakeikti [prakeik'ti] *v* curse, damn, call down curses
pralaimėti [pralaimė'ti] *v* lose, be defeated
pramoga [pramoga'] *n* amusement, distraction
pramonė [pra'monė] *n* industry
pranašumas [pranashu'mas] *n* advantage, superiority
pranešti [pranesh'ti] *v* inform, report, announce
prarasti [praras'ti] *v* lose, be deprived
prasmė [prasmė'] *n* sense, meaning, purport
prastai [prastai'] *adv* badly, not well
prašymas [pra'shymas] *n* request, application, petition
pratarmė [pratarmė'] *n* preface, foreword
pratinti [pra'tinti]*v* train, habituate, accustom
prekė [pre'kė] *n* goods, wares, commodity
prekiauti [prekiau'ti] *v* deal in, trade, sell, be engaged in commerce
prie [prie'] *prp* at, by, near
priedas [prie'das] *n* addition
priekaištas [prie'kaishtas] *n* reproach, reproof, rebuke

priekis [prie′kis] *n* front, forefront
priemiestis [prie′miestis] *n* suburb, outskirts
priemonė [prie′monė] *n* means
priesaika [prie′saika] *n* vow, oath
prieskoniai [prie′skoniai] *n* spicery,
seasoning
prieš [priesh′] *prp* before, in front of,
opposite
priešas [prie′shas] *n* enemy
priešingai [prie′shingai] *adv* the other way,
contrary
prieštarauti [prieshtarau′ti] *v* contradict,
gainsay
prietaisas [prie′taisas] *n* apparatus, device,
instrument
prietaras [prie′taras] *n* superstition,
prejudice
prievarta [prie′varta] *n* compulsion,
contraint, coercion
priežastis [priezhastis′] *n* cause, reason
priimti [priim′ti] *v* take, accept, admit
prinokęs [prino′kēs] *adj* ripe, mature
pripratęs [pripra′tēs] *adj* accustomed, used to
prisipažinti [prisipazhin′ti] *v* confess, own,
avow, admit

prisitaikyti [prisitai'keeti] *v* adjust oneself, adapt oneself

prislėgtas [pri'slėgtas] *adj* depressed, dispirited, despondent

pritarti [pritar'ti] *v* approve, assent

privalomas [priva'lomas] *adj* obligatory, compulsory

priversti [privers'ti] *v* compel, force, constrain

pro [pro'] *prp* through

proga [proga'] *n* occasion, chance, opportunity

protas [pro'tas] *n* mind, intelligence, wit

protingas [protin'gas] *adj* clever, intelligent, reasonable

pūga [pooga'] *n* snowstorm, blizzard

puikiai [pui'kiai] *adv* splendidly, perfectly, excellently, fine

puikus [puikus'] *adj* brilliant, splendid, excellent

pūkas [poo'kas] *n* down, pubescence, pile, fluff

pūliavimas [poolia'vimas] *n* fester, suppuration

pulkas [pul'kas] *n* flock, flight, crowd, regiment

pulti [pul'ti] *v* attack, assault, advance

pumpuras [pum'puras] *n* bud

punktas [punk'tas] *n* point, item, station

puodas [puo'das] *n* pot, saucepan, stewpan

puokštė [puoksh'tė] *n* bunck, posy, bouquet

puošti [puosh'ti] *v* adorn, decorate, ornament

puota [puota'] *n* feast, banquet, ball

pupelė [pupe'lė] *n* bean

purkšti [purksh'ti] *v* spray

purtyti [pur'teeti] *v* shake

purvas [pur'vas] *n* mud, dirt, filth

pusbačiai [pus'bachiai] *n* loafers, shoes

pusė [pu'sė] *n* half, part

puslapis [pus'lapis] *n* page

pūslė [puuslė'] *n* blister, vesicle, bladder

pusnis [pusnis'] *n* snowdrift, snowbank

pusryčiai [pus'reechiai] *n* breakfast, luncheon

pušis [pushis'] *n* pine-tree

puta [puta'] *n* scum, spume, froth

pūti [poo'ti] *v* rot, decay, putrefy, decompose

R

ragana [ra'gana] *n* witch, vixen, hag, harridan

raganosis [ragano'sis] *n* rhinoceros

ragas [ra'gas] *n* horn, antler

ragauti [ragau'ti] *v* taste, try food, sample

raginti [ra'ginti] *v* incite, urge, encourage

raidė [raidė'] *n* letter, character

rainas [rai'nas] *adj* streaky, tabby

raišas [rai'shas] *adj* lame, limping

raitas [rai'tas] *adj* horseback, mounted

raityti [raitee'ti] *v* roll, turn up, curl, twist

raivytis [raivee'tis] *v* stretch oneself

raižyti [rai'zheeti] *v* carve, engrave, cut

rajonas [rayo'nas] *n* district, ward, region, area

rakinti [rakin'ti] *v* lock

rakštis [rakshtis'] *n* splinter

raktas [rak'tas] *n* key, clue

ramiai [ramiai'] *adv* quietly, calmly, peacefully

ramus [ramus'] *adj* calm, quiet, composed, placid

randas [ran'das] *n* scar, wale, welt

ranka [ranka'] *n* hand, arm

rankena [ran'kena] *n* handle, grip, knob

rasa [rasa'] *n* dew
rąstas [raas'tas] *n* log, block, timber
rašalas [ra'shalas] *n* ink
rašyti [rashee'ti] *v* write, spell
raštas [rash'tas] *n* writing
ratas [ra'tas] *n* wheel
rauda [rauda'] *n* lament, wail
raudonas [raudo'nas] *adj* red, ruddy
raudoti [raudo'ti] *v* sob, weep, lament
raukšlė [rauksh'lė] *n* wrinkle, pucker
raumuo [raumuo'] *n* muscle, lean meat
rauti [rau'ti] *v* pull up, tear up
regėjimas [regė'yimas] *n* sight, vision
reikalas [rei'kalas] *n* affair, business, matter
reikalauti [reikalau'ti] *v* demand, claim, urge
reikėti [reikė'ti] *v* need, require
reikšmingas [reikshmin'gas] *adj* significant, meaningful, important
reiškinys [reishkinees'] *n* phenomenon, occurrence
rėkauti [rė'kauti] *v* shout, bawl, yell
reklama [reklama'] *n* advertisement, publicity
rėkti [rėk'ti] *v* cry, shout, shriek, bawl

remontuoti [remontuo'ti] *v* repair, refit, recondition

remti [rem'ti] *v* support, prop up, shore up

rengti [reng'ti] *v* prepare, equip, arrange, dress

replės [rep'lės] *n* tongs, pincers

retai [retai'] *adv* sparsely, seldom, rarely

riba [riba'] *n* limit, boundary

riebalai [riebalai'] *n* fat, grease, adipose

riebus [rie'bus] *adj* fat, obese, corpulent

riedėti [riedė'ti] *v* roll, trundle

riekė [riekė'] *n* slice, hunk, chunk

riesti [ries'ti] *v* curve, bend, turn up

riešas [rie'shas] *n* wrist, carpus

riešutas [rie'shutas] *n* nut

ryklys [reeklees'] *n* shark

rimtai [rimtai'] *adv* seriously, earnestly, gravely

rinkti [rink'ti] *v* gather, collect

ryšys [reeshees'] *n* connection

ryškiai [reesh'kiai] *adv* distinctly, brightly

rišti [rish'ti] *v* bind, tie

rytai [reetai'] *n* the east

rytas [ree'tas] *n* morning

ryti [ree'ti] *v* swallow, gulp, gobble

rytoj [reetoy'] *adv* tomorrow

ryžiai [ree'zhiai] *n* rice

ryžtis [reezh'tis] *v* resolve, decide, bring oneself

rodyklė [rodeek'lė] *n* pointer, indicator, hand

rodyti [ro'deeti] *v* show, indicate, point

rogės [ro'gės] *n* sledge, sleigh

rojus [ro'yus] *n* paradise

ropė [ro'pė] *n* turnip

roploti [roplo'ti] *v* creep, crawl

rotušė [ro'tushė] *n* town hall

rožė [ro'zhė] *n* rose

rūbai [roo'bai] *n* clothes, clothing, garb

rūbinė [roo'binė] *n* cloakroom

rūda [rooda'] *n* ore

rudas [ru'das] *adj* brown, red, ruddy

rūdys [roo'dees] *n* rust

ruduo [ruduo'] *n* autumn, fall

rugiagėlė [rugia'gėlė] *n* cornflower, bluebottle

rugys [rugees'] *n* rye

rugpjūtis [rugpyoo'tis] *n* August

rugsėjis [rugsė'yis] *n* September

rūgštynė [roogshtee'nė] *n* sorrel

rūgštus [roogshtus'] *adj* sour

rūgti [roog'ti] *v* turn sour, ferment

rūkyti [rookee'ti] *v* smoke, bloat, cure in smoke

rūkas [roo'kas] *n* mist, fog, haze

rūmai [roo'mai] *n* palace, mansion

rungtynės [rungtee'nės] *n* competition, contest, match, game

runkelis [run'kelis] *n* beet

ruošti [ruosh'ti] *v* prepare, do

rūpestis [roo'pestis] *n* anxiety, trouble

rūpėti [roopė'ti] *v* be worried, care

rupūžė [rupoo'zhė] *n* toad

rūsys [roosees'] *n* cellar, basement, pit

rūstus [roostus'] *adj* wrathful, angry, stern, rigorous

rūšis [rooshis'] *n* quality, grade, sort, kind, variety

rūta [roo'ta] *n* rue

rutulys [rutulees'] *n* ball, sphere

S

saga [saga'] *n* button

saikas [sai'kas] *n* measure

saitas [sai'tas] *n* tie, leash, lead, tether

sakalas [sa'kalas] *n* falcon, hawk

sakinys [sakinees'] *n* sentence

sakyti [sakee'ti] *v* say, tell, speak

sakmė [sakmė'] *n* story, legend

saldainis [saldai'nis] *n* sweet, bon-bon, candy

salė [sa'lė] *n* hall

sala [sala'] *n* island, isle

sąlyga [saa'leega] *n* condition, term

salonas [salo'nas] *n* living room, saloon

salota [salo'ta] *n* lettuce, salad

samana [sa'mana] *n* moss

samdyti [samdee'ti] *v* hire, employ, engage, rent

sąmyšis [saa'meeshis] *n* confusion, disarray

sąmojis [saa'moyis] *n* wit, wittiness, joke

sąmokslas [saa'mokslas] *n* plot, conspiracy

sąmonė [saa'monė] *n* consciousness

samprotauti [samprotau'ti] *v* reason

samtis [sam'tis] *n* ladle, scoop, dipper

sąnarys [saanarees'] *n* joint, articulation

sandariai [sandariai'] *adv* tightly, hermetically

sandėlis [san'dėlis] *n* store, warehouse, larder, pantry

sandėris [san'dėris] *n* transaction, bargain, deal

sanitarė [sanita'rė] *n* hospital attendant, nurse

santaika [san'taika] *n* concord, harmony
santykis [san'teekis] *n* relation, relationship, intercourse
santuoka [san'tuoka] *n* marriage, wedlock
santūrus [santoorus'] *adj* restrained, reserved, moderate
santvarka [san'tvarka] *n* system, order
sapnas [sap'nas] *n* dream
sąrašas [saa'rashas] *n* list
sargas [sar'gas] *n* watchman
sargyba [sargee'ba] *n* watch, guard
sąsiuvinis [saa'siuvinis] *n* exercisebook, notebook
sąskaita [saas'kaita] *n* bill, account
saugoti [sau'goti] *v* take care, preserve, protect
saugus [saugus'] *adj* safe
saulė [sau'lė] *n* sun
saulėgrąža [saulė'graazha] *n* sunflower
sausainis [sausai'nis] *n* biscuit, cracker, rusk
sausakimšas [sausa'kimshas] *adj* packed, crammed
sausas [sau'sas] *adj* dry, arid
sausis [sau'sis] *n* January
sausra [sausra'] *n* draught, dry
savaime [savai'me] *adv* of one's own accord

savaip [savaip'] *adv* in one's own way

savaitė [savai'tė] *n* week

savanoris [savano'ris] *n* volunteer

savarankiškas [savaran'kishkas] *adj* independent, self-dependent

savas [sa'vas] *adj* one's own

savęs [savēs'] *prn* myself, yourself

savybė [savee'bė] *n* characteristic, quality, feature

savininkas [sa'vininkas] *n* owner, holder, proprietor

savitas [sa'vitas] *adj* distinctive, original, peculiar

savitvarda [savi'tvarda] *n* self-control, self-possession

savižudybė [savizhudee'bė] *n* suicide

sąvoka [saa'voka] *n* notion, concept

sąžinė [saa'zhinė] *n* conscience

sėdėti [sėdė'ti] *v* sit

segti [seg'ti] *v* fasten, do up, button, hook

seilės [sei'lės] *n* saliva, spittle, slobber

sekluma [sekluma'] *n* shoal

sekmadienis [sekma'dienis] *n* Sunday

sėkmė [sėkmė'] *n* success, luck, fortune

sekti [sek'ti] *v* watch, observe, track, spy, follow

semti [sem'ti] *v* draw, scoop, ladle
senas [se'nas] *adj* old, ancient, aged
senbernis [sen'bernis] *n* old bachelor, old resident, old-timer
senelė [sene'lė] *n* old woman, grandma
senelis [sene'lis] *n* old man, grandpa
seniai [seniai'] *adv* long ago, for ages
senis [se'nis] *n* old man
senmergė [sen'mergė] *n* old maid, spinster
septyni [septeeni'] *num* seven
septyniasdešimt [septee'niasde'shimt] *num* seventy
septyniolika [septeenio'lika] *num* seventeen
septintas [septin'tas] *num* seventh
serbentas [serben'tas] *n* currant
sėsti [sės'ti] *v* sit down
sesuo [sesuo'] *n* sister, nurse
sėti [sė'ti] *v* sow
siaubas [siau'bas] *n* terror, horror
siauras [siau'ras] *adj* narrow, tight
sidabras [sidab'ras] *n* silver
siela [siela'] *n* soul, heart
sielotis [sielo'tis] *v* grieve, sorrow
sielvartas [siel'vartas] *n* grief, sorrow, heartbreak
siena [sie'na] *n* wall

sijonas [siyo'nas] *n* skirt
sykis [see'kis] *n* time
silkė [sil'kė] *n* herring
silpnas [silp'nas] *adj* weak, faint, delicate
sirgti [sirg'ti] *v* be ill, be down, ail
siūbuoti [sioobuo'ti] *v* swing, sway, rock
siūlas [sioo'las] *n* thread, yarn
siūlyti [sioo'lceti] *v* offer, tender
siunta [slunta'] *n* dispatch, parcel
siurbti [siurb'ti] *v* suck, soak, absorb
siųsti [sioos'ti] *v* send, dispatch
siūti [sioo'ti] *v* sew, make
skaičiuoti [skaichiuo'ti] *v* count, compute
skaičius [skai'chius] *n* number, quantity
skaityti [skaitee'ti] *v* read
skalauti [skalau'ti] *v* rinse, swill, gargle
skalbti [skalb'ti] *v* wash, launder
skaldyti [skal'deeti] *v* split, strike
skambėti [skambė'ti] *v* sound, ring, resound, clink, jingle
skambutis [skambu'tis] *n* bell
skandinti [skandin'ti] *v* sink
skanus [skanus'] *adj* delicious, nice, tasty, dainty
skara [skara'] *n* wrap, shawl

skausmas [skaus'mas] *n* pain, pang, smart, ache

skelbti [skelb'ti] *v* announce, proclaim, declare

skėtis [skė'tis] *n* umbrella, parasol

skylė [skeelė'] *n* hole, rent, gap, opening

skilti [skil'ti] *v* split, cleave

skinti [skin'ti] *v* pluck, pick, cut

skyrius [skee'rius] *n* chapter, section, department

skirti [skir'ti] *v* separate, part, detach, divide

skirtingas [skirtin'gas] *adj* different, diverse, various

skystis [skees'tis] *n* liquid, fluid

skleisti [skleis'ti] *v* spread, diffuse, propagate

sklidinas [skli'dinas] *adj* full to the brim, brimful

sklypas [sklee'pas] *n* plot, lot, parcel

skola [skola'] *n* debt

skolingas [skolin'gas] *adj* owing, indebted

skolinti [sko'linti]*v* lend

skonis [sko'nis] *n* taste

skraidyti [skraidee'ti] *v* fly, flutter

skriauda [skriauda'] *n* offence, wrong

skrybėlė [skreebėlė'] *n* hat, bonnet

skruzdėlė [skruzdėlė'] *n* ant
skubėti [skubė'ti] *v* hurry, hasten, speed
skuduras [sku'duras] *n* rag, clout
skundas [skun'das] *n* complaint
skurdas [skur'das] *n* poverty, want, misery, penury
skusti [skus'ti] *v* shave, scrape, scour, peel
skųsti [skoos'ti] *v* report on, inform against
slaptas [slap'tas] *adj* secret, covert, confidential
slaugė [slau'gė] *n* nurse
slėgti [slėg'ti] *v* press, weigh down, oppress
slėnys [slė'nees] *n* valley, vale, dale
slėpti [slėp'ti] *v* hide, conceal, harbor
slidės [sli'dės] *n* skis
slidinėti [slidinė'ti] *v* slide, ski, go skiing
slidus [slidus'] *adj* slippery
sliekas [slie'kas] *n* earthworm
slyva [slee'va] *n* plum
sloga [sloga'] *n* head cold
slopinti [slopin'ti] *v* smother, stifle, muffle, deaden
smagus [smagus'] *adj* pleasant, cheerful, merry
smaigalys [smaigalees'] *n* point, spike, tip
smailus [smailus'] *adj* sharp, pointed, acute

smakras [smak'ras] *n* chin
smalsus [smalsus'] *adj* curious, inquisitive
smarkiai [smar'kiai] *adv* violently, hard, very much
smaugti [smaug'ti] *v* strangle, stifle, throttle
smegenys [sme'genees] *n* brain, cerebrum
smėlis [smė'lis] *n* sand
smerkti [smerk'ti] *v* condemn, censure
smilkinys [smilkinees'] *n* temple
smirdėti [smirdė'ti] *v* stink, reek
smūgis [smoo'gis] *n* blow, stroke, thrust, stab
smuikas [smui'kas] *n* violin
smulkus [smulkus'] *adj* small, fine, petty, detailed
smurtas [smur'tas] *n* violence
snaigė [snai'gė] *n* snowflake
snapas [sna'pas] *n* beak, bill, peak
snausti [snaus'ti] *v* drowse, doze, slumber
sniegas [snie'gas] *n* snow
snukis [snu'kis] *n* muzzle, snout, face
sodas [so'das] *n* garden, orchard
sodinti [sodin'ti] *v* plant, pot, put
sotus [so'tus] *adj* satiated, replete
spalis [spa'lis] *n* October
spalva [spalva'] *n* color, coloration

spanguolė [span'guolė] *n* cranberry
spardyti [spar'deeti] *v* kick
sparnas [spar'nas] *n* wing, flank, vane, sail
spartus [spartus'] *adj* quick, rapid, speedy
spąstai [spaas'tai] *n* snare, trap, pitfall
spausdinti [spaus'dinti] *v* print, type, publish
spausti [spaus'ti] *v* press, squeeze, wring
spėlioti [spėlio'ti] *v* guess, surmise, conjecture
spėti [spė'ti] *v* guess, suppose
spiegti [spieg'ti] *v* squeal, screech, shriek
spyna [speena'] *n* lock, padlock
spindulys [spindulees'] *n* ray, beam
spinta [spin'ta] *n* cupboard, wardrobe
spirti [spir'ti] *v* kick
spjaudyti [spyau'deeti] *v* spit
spręsti [sprēs'ti] *v* judge, decide
sprogdinti [sprogdin'ti] *v* blow up, explode, detonate
sprogimas [sprogi'mas] *n* explosion, outburst, burst
spuogas [spuo'gas] *n* pimple, blotch
sraigė [srai'gė] *n* snail
sraigtas [sraig'tas] *n* screw, helix
srautas [srau'tas] *n* stream, torrent
sritis [sritis'] *n* region, area, province

sriuba [sriuba'] *n* soup

srovė [srovė'] *n* current, stream, torrent, flow

stabdyti [stabdee'ti] *v* stop, make smb. stop, brake

staiga [staiga'] *adv* suddenly, by surprise

stalas [sta'las] *n* table

staltiesė [stal'tiesė] *n* tablecloth

stambus [stambus'] *adj* large, big

standus [standus'] *adj* stiff, rigid

statyba [statee'ba] *n* building, construction

statyti [statee'ti] *v* put, set, stand, build, construct

stebėti [stebė'ti] *v* observe, watch, supervise

stebuklas [stebuk'las] *n* miracle, wonder, prodigy

steigti [steig'ti] *v* found, establish, set up

stengtis [steng'tis] *v* try, endeavor, strive, seek

styga [steega'] *n* string, chord

stiklas [stik'las] *n* glass

stiklinė [stikli'nė] *n* glass, tumbler, glassful

stiprus [stiprus'] *adj* strong, firm, powerful, fierce

stirna [stir'na] *n* roe

stoka [stoka'] *n* lack, shortage, deficiency

storas [sto'ras] *adj* thick, heavy, fat, corpulent, deep

stoti [sto'ti] *v* stand, join, enter, stop

stotis [stotis'] *n* station

stovėti [stovė'ti] *v* stand, stop

straipsnis [straips'nis] *n* article

strėnos [strė'nos] *n* loins, the small of the back

stropus [stropus'] *adj* diligent, studious, industrious

stuburas [stu'buras] *n* spinal column, spine, backbone

stulbinti [stul'binti] *v* stun, startle, strike

stulpas [stul'pas] *n* post, pole, pillar

stumdyti [stum'deeti] *v* push, shove, order about

stverti [stver'ti] *v* snatch, catch, seize

su [su'] *prp* with

suburti [subur'ti] *v* unite, rally

sudaryti [sudaree'ti] *v* form, make, create, work out

sudėti [sudė'ti] *v* put together, pack up, pile, heap

sudėtingas [sudėtin'gas] *adj* complicated, complex, intricate

sudie [sudie'] *int* goodbye, farewell

sūdyti [su'deeti] *v* salt, pickle, corn
sudužti [suduzh'ti] *v* break, smash
sugundyti [sugun'deeti] *v* tempt, entice, seduce
suimti [suim'ti] *v* arrest, take up, apprehend
sujungti [suyung'ti] *v* connect, link up, couple, join, unite
sukalbamas [su'kalbamas] *adj* compliant, tractable
sukčiauti [sukchiau'ti] *v* swindle, cheat
suknelė [sukne'lė] *n* dress, gown, frock
suktas [suk'tas] *adj* sly, cunning, wily, artful
sukti [suk'ti] *v* twist, twirl, twine
sulig [su'lig] *prp* up to, from, since
sultinys [sultinees'] *n* stock, broth, beef tea
sultys [sul'tees] *n* juice, sap
sumanus [sumanus'] *adj* quick-witted, intelligent, bright
sumišęs [sumi'shēs] *adj* confused, embarrassed, perplexed
sumuštinis [sumushti'nis] *n* sandwich
sūnėnas [soonė'nas] *n* nephew
sunkus [sunkus'] *adj* heavy, hard, difficult
sūnus [soonus'] *n* son
suolas [suo'las] *n* bench, desk

suprasti [supras'ti] *v* understand, realize, comprehend

supti [sup'ti] *v* muffle, wrap, surround, rock, swing

surasti [suras'ti] *v* find, discover, detect

sūris [soo'ris] *n* cheese

sūrus [soorus'] *adj* salt, salty

susijęs [susi'yēs] *adj* connected, related, bound

susikaupti [susikaup'ti] *v* concentrate, accumulate, conglomerate

susipažinti [susipazhin'ti] *v* make the acquaintance of, become acquainted

susitikti [susitik'ti] *v* meet, come across, encounter

sustingęs [sustin'gēs] *adj* stiff, torpid, numb

sutartis [sutartis'] *n* agreement, contract, pact, treaty

sutema [sutema'] *n* twilight, dusk, nightfall

suvažiavimas [suvazhia'vimas] *n* congress, convention

sužadinti [suzha'dinti] *v* rouse, waken, excite, stimulate

sužinoti [suzhino'ti] *v* learn, get to know, hear

svaigti [svaig'ti] *v* feel giddy, be dizzy

svaja [svaya'] *n* dream

svarbus [svarbus'] *adj* important, significant, valid

svarstyklės [svarsteek'lės] *n* balance, scale

svarstyti [svarstee'ti] *v* consider, discuss

svečias [sve'chias] *n* guest, visitor

sveikas [svei'kas] *adj* healthy, strong, sound, robust

sveikata [sveikata'] *n* health

sveikinti [svei'kinti]*v* greet, hail, welcome, salute

sverti [sver'ti] *v* weigh

svetainė [svetai'nė] *n* sitting-room, salon, drawing-room

svetimas [sve'timas] *adj* other people's, another's

svetimšalis [svetimsha'lis] *n* foreigner

svetingas [svetin'gas] *adj* hospitable

sviedinys [sviedinees'] *n* ball

sviestas [svies'tas] *n* butter

sviesti [svies'ti] *v* fling, throw, sling, hurl

svogūnas [svogoo'nas] *n* onion, bulb

svoris [svo'ris] *n* weight

Š

šachmatai [shakh'matai] *n* chess

šaipytis [shaipee'tis] *v* mock, sneer, jeer, scoff

šaižus [shaizhus'] *adj* sharp, keen, penetrating

šaka [shaka'] *n* branch, limb, bough, twig

šaknis [shaknis] *n* root

šakotas [shako'tas] *adj* branchy, branched

šaldyti [shal'dccti] *v* freeze, congeal, make cool, chill

šalia [shalia'] *prp* by, near, next to

šaligatvis [shali'gatvis] *n* pavement, sidewalk

šalikas [sha'likas] *n* scarf, muffler, shawl

šalin [shalin'] *adv* away, off

šalinti [sha'linti]*v* remove, eliminate, send away

šalis [shalis'] *n* side, land, country

šalmas [shal'mas] *n* helmet, headpiece

šalna [shalna'] *n* frost

šaltakraujis [shaltakrau'yis] *adj* cold-blooded, cool, composed

šaltas [shal'tas] *adj* cold, cool, light

šalti [shal'ti] *v* freeze, congeal

šaltinis [shalti'nis] *n* spring, source, origin

šarka [shar'ka] *n* magpie

šaudyti [shau′deeti] *v* shoot, fire
šaukštas [shaush′tas] *n* spoon
šaukti [shauk′ti] *v* cry, shout, bawl, clamor
šautuvas [shau′tuvas] *n* gun, rifle
šeima [sheima′] *n* family
šeimininkas [sheiminin′kas] *n* master, boss, owner, host
šelpti [shelp′ti] *v* aid, support, dole
šen [shen′] *adv* here
šerkšnas [sherksh′nas] *n* hoarfrost, rime
šermukšnis [shermuksh′nis] *n* mountain ash, rowan-tree
šerti [sher′ti] *v* feed, fodder
šešėlis [sheshė′lis] *n* shade, shadow
šeši [sheshi′] *num* six
šešiasdešimt [she′shiasde′shimt] *num* sixty
šešiolika [sheshio′lika] *num* sixteen
šeškas [shesh′kas] *n* polecat
šiaip [shiaip′] *adv* so, this way
šiąnakt [shiaa′nakt] *adv* tonight, this night
šiandien [shian′dien] *adv* today
šiaudas [shiau′das] *n* straw, thatch
šiaurė [shiau′rė] *n* north
šiemet [shie′met] *adv* this year
šienas [shie′nas] *n* hay
šikšnosparnis [shikshno′sparnis] *n* bat

šykštus [sheekshtus'] *adj* stingy, niggardly, miserly

šilas [shi'las] *n* pine, forest, pinewood

šildyti [shil'deeti] *v* give out warmth

šilkas [shil'kas] *n* silk

šiltas [shil'tas] *adj* warm, cordial

šimtas [shim'tas] *num* hundred

šypsena [sheep'sena] *n* smile, grin

širdis [shirdis'] *n* heart

širšė [shir'shė] *n* hornet

šis [shis'] *prn* this, the present

šįsyk [shee'scck] *adv* for once, this time

šiukšlės [shiuksh'lės] *n* sweepings, rubbish

šiurkštus [shiurkshtus'] *adj* rough, coarse, rude, gross

šiurpas [shiur'pas] *n* shudder, shiver

šiurpus [shiurpus'] *adj* horrible, terrible, ghastly

šlaitas [shlai'tas] *n* slope

šlamštas [shlamsh'tas] *n* garbage, trash, junk

šlapdriba [shlapdriba'] *n* sleet, snowy rain

šlapias [shla'pias] *adj* wet, moist, soggy

šlaunis [shlaunis'] *n* thigh, hip

šleikštus [shleikshtus'] *adj* sickening, nauseating

šleivas [shlei'vas] *adj* bandy, bandy-legged, bow-legged

šlepetė [shlepe'tė] *n* slipper

šliaužti [shliauzh'ti] *v* crow, creep

šlieti [shlie'ti] *v* lean against, rest against

šlykštynė [shleekshtee'nė] *n* filth, muck, nasty thing

šliužas [shliu'zhas] *n* slug

šlovė [shlovė] *n* glory, honor

šlubas [shlu'bas] *adj* lame, limping

šluostyti [shluos'teeti] *v* wipe, wipe dry

šluota [shluo'ta] *n* broom

šmeižti [shmeizh'ti] *v* calumniate, slander, smear, libel

šmėkla [shmėk'la] *n* ghost, specter, spook

šnabždėti [shnabzhdė'ti] *v* whisper

šnekėti [shnekė'ti] *v* talk, speak, converse

šnipas [shni'pas] *n* snout, spy

šokinėti [shokinė'ti] *v* jump, leap, bob, skip

šokis [sho'kis] *n* dance

šokti [shok'ti] *v* jump, leap, dance, spring, rush

šonas [sho'nas] *n* side, flank

šonkaulis [shon'kaulis] *n* rib

špyga [shpee'ga] *n* fig

šriftas [shrif'tas] *n* print, type

štai [shtai'] *adv* here
šukė [shu'kė] *n* splinter, fragment, shiver
šūkis [shoo'kis] *n* slogan, motto, device, call
šukos [shu'kos] *n* comb
šukuosena [shukuo'sena] *n* coiffure, hairdo, haircut
šulinys [shulinees'] *n* well
šuo [shuo'] *n* dog
šuolis [shuo'lis] *n* jump, bound, leap
švaistyti [shvaistee'ti] *v* squander, waste, scatter
švarkas [shvar'kas] *n* coat, jacket
švarus [shvarus'] *adj* clean, neat, tidy
šveisti [shveis'ti] *v* scour, scrub
švelnus [shvelnus'] *adj* soft, tender, delicate, mild, smooth
šventas [shven'tas] *adj* sacred, holy, saint
šventė [shven'tė] *n* holiday, feast, festival, festivity
šventikas [shventi'kas] *n* priest, clergyman
šveplas [shvep'las] *adj* lisping
švęsti [shvēs'ti] *v* celebrate, observe, hold
šviesa [shviesa'] *n* light
šviesti [shvies'ti] *v* shine, give smb. a light
šviesus [shviesus'] *adj* light, bright, fair, lucid

šviežias [shvie′zhias] *adj* fresh
švilpti [shvilp′ti] *v* whistle, pipe, howl
švinas [shvi′nas] *n* lead
švyturys [shveeturees′] *n* lighthouse, beacon

T

tačiau [tachiau′] *cnj* however, but, though
tada [tada′] *adv* then, at that time
tai [tai′] *prn* it, this, that
taigi [tai′gi] *mod* so, now then, then, thus
taika [taika′] *n* peace
taikyti [tai′keeti] *v* aim at, take aim at, point at
taip [taip′] *mod* yes
taisyti [taisee′ti] *v* correct, repair, mend
takas [ta′kas] *n* path, walk, lane
talija [ta′liya] *n* waist
talka [talka′] *n* assistance, help
talonas [talo′nas] *n* coupon, check
tamsa [tamsa′] *n* dark, darken
tankus [tan′kus] *adj* thick, dense, close, compact
tapyti [tapee′ti] *v* paint
tapti [tap′ti] *v* become, get, grow
tarakonas [tarako′nas] *n* cockroach, blackbeetle

tardymas [tar'deemas] *n* investigation, inquest

taryba [taree'ba] *n* council

tarimas [tari'mas] *n* pronunciation, articulation

tarytum [taree'tum] *cnj* as if, as though

tarkuoti [tarkuo'ti] *v* grate

tarmė [tarmė'] *n* dialect

tarnaitė [tarnai'tė] *n* servant, maidservant, maid

tarnauti [tarnau'ti] *v* serve, be employed

tarp [tarp'] *adv* between, among, amidst

tarpas [tar'pas] *n* interval, distance, gap, space

tarptautinis [tarptau'tinis] *adj* international

tarti [tar'ti] *v* pronounce, utter, say

tartis [tar'tis] *v* consult, ask advice, negotiate, treat for

tas, ta [tas', ta'] *prn* that, that one, this

taškas [tash'kas] *n* point, dot, spot

tau [tau'] *prn* you

taukai [taukai'] *n* fat, grease, lard, drippings

taupyti [taupee'ti] *v* save, economize, lay up

taurė [tau'rė] *n* goblet, glass, wineglass

tauta [tauta'] *n* people, nation

tautybė [tautee'bė] *n* nationality

tavo [ta'vo] *prn* your, yours
tebūnie [teboonie'] *v* let it be
teigiamas [tei'giamas] *adj* affirmative, positive
teigti [teig'ti] *v* affirm, assert, maintain
teirautis [teirau'tis] *v* inquire, ask for
teisė [tei'sė] *n* right, law
teisėjas [teisė'yas] *n* judge, referee, umpire
teisybė [teisee'bė] *n* truth, justice
teismas [teis'mas] *n* trial, court
teisingai [teisin'gai] *adv* right, correctly, fairly
teisinti [tei'sinti] *v* justify, vindicate
tekėti [tekė'ti] *v* flow, run, stream, marry
telkti [telk'ti] *v* recruit, concentrate, rally, assemble
tempti [temp'ti] *v* pull, draw, haul, drag, stretch
temti [tem'ti] *v* grow dark
ten [ten'] *adv* there
tenkinti [ten'kinti] *v* satisfy, meet
tepalas [te'palas] *n* grease, oil, lubricant
tepti [tep'ti] *v* oil, smear, spread, daub
teptukas [teptu'kas] *n* brush
terlioti [terlio'ti] *v* soil, dirty, blot, daub

tęsti [tēst'ti] *v* continue, go on, carry on, proceed

tešla [teshla'] *n* dough, paste, batter

tėtis [tė'tis] *n* dad, papa

tėvai [tėvai'] *n* parents

tėvas [tė'vas] *n* father, parent

tyčia [tee'chia] *adv* purposely, on purpose, for fun, intentionally

tiek [tiek'] *adv* so much, so many

tiekti [tiek'ti] *v* supply, furnish, provide, purvey

tiesa [tiesa'] *n* truth

tiesiai [tie'siai] *adv* straight, right, right out

tiesti [ties'ti] *v* stretch, build, lay

tiesus [tiesus'] *adj* straight, right, upright, erect

tik [tik'] *prt* only, merely, solely

tikėti [tikė'ti] *v* believe, have faith, trust

tykoti [teeko'ti] *v* lie in wait, watch, lurk

tikrai [tikrai'] *adv* sure, surely, certain, indeed

tikras [tik'ras] *adj* real, true, sure, certain

tikrinti [tik'rinti] *v* verify, check, control, test

tikrovė [tikro'vė] *n* reality, fact

tikslas [tiks'las] *n* aim, purpose, object, end

tikslus [tikslus'] *adj* exact, precise, accurate, punctual

tikti [tik'ti] *v* be fit, suit

tyla [teela'] *n* silence, still, quiet, calm

tiltas [til'tas] *n* bridge

tylus [teelus'] *adj* soft, low, quiet, silent, still

tinginys [tinginees'] *n* idler, lazy person, sluggard

tinkamai [tin'kamai] *adv* properly, suitably, duly

tyras [tee'ras] *adj* pure, clear, honest

tirpti [tirp'ti] *v* melt, thaw, fuse, grow numb

tirštas [tirsh'tas] *adj* thick, dense

tobulas [to'bulas] *adj* perfect

todėl [todėl'] *cnj* therefore, so, that is why

toks [toks'] *prn* such, so

tol [tol'] *prp* until, till

tolesnis [toles'nis] *adj* further, farther, subsequent

toli [toli'] *adv* far, in the distance

toliau [toliau'] *adv* further, then, continue

tolimas [to'limas] *adj* distant, remote

tolti [tol'ti] *v* move away, go away

tomas [to'mas] *n* volume, tome

tortas [tor'tas] *n* cake

tramdyti [tram'deeti] *v* tame, suppress

trapus [trapus'] *adj* fragile, brittle, friable, crumbly

trasa [trasa'] *n* route, track

trauka [trauka'] *n* gravitation, attraction

traukinys [traukinees'] *n* train

traukti [trauk'ti] *v* pull, draw, tug, lug

trečiadienis [trechia'dienis] *n* Wednesday

trečias [tre'chias] *num* third

trenkti [trenk'ti] *v* crash, bang, strike, hit, knock

trepsėti [trepsė'ti] *v* stamp, tramp

trykšti [treeksh'ti] *v* gush, spurt, spout, play

trylika [tree'lika] *num* thirteen

trynys [treenees'] *n* yolk

trinti [trin'ti] *v* rub, grind, chafe

trys [trees'] *num* three

trisdešimt [tris'deshimt] *num* thirty

triukas [triu'kas] *n* trick, stunt

triukšmauti [triukshmau'ti] *v* make noise, row

triūsas [trioo'sas] *n* toil, labor

triušis [triu'shis] *n* rabbit, bunny rabbit

triuškinti [triush'kinti] *v* crush, smash, shatter

trokšti [troksh'ti] *v* feel thirsty, choke, desire, wish

troškimas [troshki'mas] *n* desire, wish, thirst for

troškulys [troshkulees'] *n* thirst

trukdyti [trukdee'ti] *v* hinder, hamper, impede, prevent

trukmė [trukmė'] *n* length, duration, continuance

trūkti [trook'ti] *v* lack, burst, break

trūkumas [troo'kumas] *n* lack, shortage, deficit, shortcoming

trumpas [trum'pas] *adj* short, brief, terse

trupinys [trupinees'] *n* crumb

truputis [trupu'tis] *adv* a little, a bit, some

tu [tu'] *prn* you

tualetas [tuale'tas] *n* toilet, lavatory, WC

tūkstantis [tooks'tantis] *num* thousand

tuoj [tuoy'] *adv* at once, immediately

tuomet [tuomet'] *adv* at that time, then

tupėti [tupė'ti] *v* perch, sit, roost

turbūt [turboot'] *mod* probably, very likely

turėti [turė'ti] *v* have, possess, own

turgus [tur'gus] *n* market, bazaar

turinys [turnees'] *n* content, substance, matter

tūris [too'ris] *n* volume, size

turtas [tur'tas] *n* riches, wealth, resources

turtingas [turtin'gas] *adj* rich, wealthy

tuščias [tush'chias] *adj* empty, hollow, vacant, blank

tvaikas [tvai'kas] *n* fumes, stink, stench

tvankus [tvankus'] *adj* stuffy, close

tvarka [tvarka'] *n* order, manner, procedure

tvarkingas [tvarkin'gas] *adj* orderly, neat, tidy, accurate

tvarkyti [tvarkee'ti] *v* put in order, regulate

tvenkinys [tvenkinees'] *n* pond, reservoir

tvirkinti [tvir'kinti] *v* corrupt, deprave

tvirtas [tvir'tas] *adj* strong, firm, tough, hard, solid

tvora [tvora'] *n* fence

U

ugdyti [ugdee'ti] *v* bring up, rear, raise

ūgis [oo'gis] *n* height, stature

ugnikalnis [ugni'kalnis] *n* volcano

ugnis [ugnis'] *n* fire, live wire

ūkininkas [oo'kininkas] *n* farmer, landowner

ūkis [oo'kis] *n* economy, farm

ūkiskaita [ookis'kaita] *n* self-supporting, self- financing

ūksmė [ooksmė'] *n* shade

ūmai [oomai'] *adv* suddenly, immediately

ūmus [oomus'] *adj* quick-tempered, hasty, peppery

ungurys [ungurees'] *n* eel

uodega [uodega'] *n* tail, train, brush, scut

uoga [uo'ga] *n* berry, soft fruit

uola [uola'] *n* rock, crag, cliff

uolus [uolus'] *adj* zealous, diligent, assiduous

uosis [uo'sis] *n* ash-tree

uoslė [uoslė'] *n* smell, scent

uostas [uos'tas] *n* port, harbor

uosti [uos'ti] *v* smell, sniff, scent

uošvė [uosh'vė] *n* mother-in-law

uošvis [uosh'vis] *n* father-in-law

ūpas [oo'pas] *n* mood, spirits

upė [u'pė] *n* river, stream

upėtakis [upė'takis] *n* trout

upokšnis [upoksh'nis] *n* brook, rill, creek

uraganas [uraga'nas] *n* hurricane, tornado

urgzti [urgz'ti] *v* growl, snarl, rumble

urmu [ur'mu] *adv* in a crowd, wholesale

urvas [ur'vas] *n* cave, burrow, hole, cavern

ūsas [oo'sas] *n* moustache, whisker, feeler

usnis [us'nis] *n* thistle

utėlė [utėlė'] *n* louse

už [uzh'] *prp* behind, over, at, out of, in, later, by, for

užbaigti [uzhbaig'ti] *v* finish, end, complete, conclude

užbėgti [uzhbėg'ti] *v* drop in, run up

užburtas [uzhbur'tas] *adj* charmed, bewitched, spell-bound

uždaras [uzh'daras] *adj* closed, close, reserved

uždarbis [uzh'darbis] *n* earnings, wages

uždavinys [uzhdavinees'] *n* problem, sum

uždegimas [uzhdegi'mas] *n* ignition, inflammation

uždegti [uzhdeg'ti] *v* light up, set fire, kindle

uždirbti [uzhdirb'ti] *v* earn, gain

uždrausti [uzhdraus'ti] *v* forbid, interdict, prohibit

uždusęs [uzhdu'sēs] *adj* out of breath, breathless

užeiti [uzhei'ti] *v* call at, drop in on, call on

ūžesys [oozhesees'] *n* noise, sound, murmur

užgauti [uzhgau'ti] *v* hurt, bruise, insult, offend

užgesinti [uzhgesin'ti] *v* put out, extinguish, stall

užgožti [uzhgosh'ti] *v* grow over, choke, deaden, drown

užgrobti [uzhgrob'ti] *v* seize, capture, usurp, occupy

užguitas [uzhgui'tas] *adj* downtrodden, oppressed, maltreated

užimtas [uzh'imtas] *adj* busy, engaged, hired

užimti [uzhim'ti] *v* take up, occupy, hold, entertain

užjausti [uzhyaus'ti] *v* sympathize, feel for, take compassion

užkimęs [uzhki'mēs] *adj* hoarse, husky

užprenumeruoti [uzhprenumeruo'ti] *v* subscribe

užsakyti [uzhsakee'ti] *v* order, book

užsienis [uzh'sienis] *n* foreign countries

užuolaida [uzhuo'laida] *n* curtain, blind

užuomina [uzhuo'mina] *n* hint, allusion

užuot [uzhuot'] *prp* instead of

V

vabalas [va'balas] *n* beetle

vadas [va'das] *n* leader, chief

vadinti [vadin'ti] *v* call

vagis [vagis'] *n* thief

vagonas [vago'nas] *n* carriage, coach, car

vaidinti [vaidin'ti] *v* play, act, perform

vaidmuo [vaidmuo'] *n* role, part, lines

vaiduoklis [vaiduok'lis] *n* ghost, specter

vaikas [vai'kas] *n* child, the young

vaikinas [vaiki'nas] *n* lad, boy

vaikščioti [vaiksh'chioti] *v* walk, pace

vairas [vai'ras] *n* steering wheel, rudder, helm

vairuoti [vairuo'ti] *v* drive, steer

vaisius [vai'sius] *n* fruit, results

vaistas [vais'tas] *n* medicine, remedy

vaistinė [vais'tinė] *n* drugstore

vaišinti [vaishin'ti] *v* entertain, treat smb.

vaivorykštė [vaivo'reekshtė] *n* rainbow

vaizdas [vaiz'das] *n* view, sight, scene, prospect

vakar [va'kar] *adv* yesterday

vakaras [va'karas] *n* evening

vakarienė [vakarie'nė] *n* supper

valanda [valanda'] *n* hour

valdyti [valdee'ti] *v* govern, rule over

valdžia [valdzhia'] *n* power, authority, rule

valgykla [valgykla'] *n* dinning room, restaurant, canteen

valgis [val'gis] *n* dish, food

valgyti [val'geeti] *v* eat, have, take

valia [valia'] *n* will
valyti [valee'ti] *v* clean, brush
valiuta [valiuta'] *n* currency
valstybė [valstee'bė] *n* State
valstietis [valstie'tis] *n* peasant
vanagas [va'nagas] *n* hawk
vandenynas [vandenee'nas] *n* ocean
vanduo [vanduo'] *n* water
vardas [var'das] *n* name
vargas [var'gas] *n* hardship, misery, hard life
vargu [vargu'] *adv* hardly, scarcely
variklis [varik'lis] *n* motor, engine
varis [va'ris] *n* copper
varyti [varee'ti] *v* drive, turn out, compel
varlė [varlė'] *n* frog
varna [var'na] *n* crow, raven
varnėnas [varnė'nas] *n* starling
varpa [var'pa] *n* ear
varpas [var'pas] *n* bell
varškė [varshkė'] *n* curd, curds
vartai [var'tai] *n* gate, gates, goal
vartoti [varto'ti] *v* use, take, apply
varžybos [varzhee'bos] *n* contest, competition, emulation
vasara [va'sara] *n* summer

vasaris [vasa'ris] *n* February

vata [vata'] *n* wadding, cotton wool

važiuoti [vazhiuo'ti] *v* go, drive, ride

veidas [vei'das] *n* face

veidrodis [veid'rodis] *n* looking glass, mirror

veikla [veikla'] *n* activities, activity, work

veikti [veik'ti] *v* do, act, operate, work

vėjas [vė'jas] *n* wind

vėl [vėl'] *adv* again, anew, once again

vėliava [vė'liava] *n* flag, banner

Velykos [velee'kos] *n* Easter

velnias [vel'nias] *n* devil, deuce

vėlus [vėlus'] *adj* late, tardy

vengti [veng'ti] *v* avoid, evade, shun

verkti [verk'ti] *v* cry, weep, shed tears

vertė [vertė'] *n* value

vertėjas [vertė'yas] *n* translator

vertinti [ver'tinti] *v* value, estimate, appreciate

veržti [verzh'ti] *v* tighten, draw, hurt, pinch

vesti [ves'ti] *v* lead, install, direct, conduct, marry

vestuvės [vestu'vės] *n* wedding

vėsus [vėsus'] *adj* cool, fresh, chilly

vėžlys [vėzhlees'] *n* tortoise, turtle

vežti [vezh'ti] *v* convey, carry, cart

vidinis [vidi′nis] *adj* inside, interior, inner, internal

vidurys [vidurees′] *n* middle, midst

vidurnaktis [vidur′naktis] *n* midnight

vien [vien′] *prt* only, but

vienas [vie′nas] *num* one

vienišas [vie′nishas] *adj* alone, lonely, lonesome, single

vienuolika [vienuo′lika] *num* eleven

viešas [vie′shas] *adj* public

viešbutis [viesh′butis] *n* hotel

viešpats [viesh′pats] *n* lord, ruler, God, the Lord

vieta [vieta′] *n* place, spot, locality

vietoj [vie′toy] *adv* instead of

vykdyti [veek′deeti] *v* implement, carry out, fulfill, execute, realize

vikrus [vikrus′] *adj* nimble, agile, swift, deft

vilioti [vilio′ti] *v* attract, allure, decoy

vilkas [vil′kas] *n* wolf

vilna [vil′na] *n* wool

viltis [viltis′] *n* hope

vynas [vee′nas] *n* wine

vinis [vinis′] *n* nail, tack, peg

vynuogė [vee′nuogė] *n* grape

vyras [vee′ras] *n* man, male, husband

virėjas [virė'jas] *n* cook

virpėti [virpė'ti] *v* tremble, quiver, shake, vibrate

viršininkas [vir'shininkas] *n* head, chief, superior

viršuj [virshuy'] *adv* above, over, upstairs

viršūnė [virshoo'nė] *n* top, summit, peak, apex

virti [vir'ti] *v* boil, bubble, cook

virtuvė [virtu've] *n* kitchen

virvė [vir've] *n* rope, cord, string

visada [visada'] *adv* always

visai [visai'] *adv* quite, completely, entirely, absolutely

visas [vi'sas] *adj* all, whole, entire

viskas [vis'kas] *n* everything, all

vyskupas [vees'kupas] *n* bishop

visuomenė [visuo'menė] *n* society

viščiukas [vishchiu'kas] *n* chicken, chick

vyšnia [veesh'nia] *n* cherry

višta [vishta'] *n* hen, fowl, chicken

vogti [vog'ti] *v* steal, pilfer

vokas [vo'kas] *n* eyelid, envelope, cover

vonia [vonia'] *n* bath

voras [vo'ras] *n* spider

vos [vos'] *adv* hardly

voverė [voveré'] *n* squirrel

Z

zirzti [zirz'ti] *v* hum, buzz, drone, whine, snivel
zuikis [zui'kis] *n* hare

Ž

žadėti [zhadė'ti] *v* promise
žadinti [zha'dinti] *v* wake, awaken, arouse
žagsėti [zhagsė'ti] *v* hiccup, hiccough
žaibas [zhai'bas] *n* lightning
žaislas [zhais'las] *n* toy, child's play
žaisti [zhais'ti] *v* play, sport, frisk, romp
žaizda [zhaizda'] *n* wound
žala [zhala'] *n* harm, hurt, injury, damage
žalias [zha'lias] *adj* green, raw, uncooked
žaliava [zhaliava'] *n* raw material
žaltys [zhaltees'] *n* grass-snake
žandas [zhan'das] *n* cheek
žandikaulis [zhandi'kaulis] *n* jaw
žarna [zharna'] *n* gut, intestine, hose
žąsis [zhaasis'] *n* goose
žemai [zhemai'] *adj* low, below, underneath
žemas [zhe'mas] *adj* low
žemė [zhe'mė] *n* earth, land

žeminti [zhe'minti] *v* humble, humiliate, abase

žemuogė [zhe'muogė] *n* strawberry

žengti [zheng'ti] *v* step, walk, march, pace

ženklas [zhenk'las] *n* omen, sign, token, mark

žentas [zhen'tas] *n* son-in-law

žėrėti [zhėrė'ti] *v* shine, sparkle, twinkle

žiaurus [zhiaurus'] *adj* cruel, brutal, savage

žibintas [zhibin'tas] *n* lantern, lamp, flashlight, flash

žydėti [zheedė'ti] *v* flower, bloom, blossom, prosper

žydra [zheedra'] *adj* blue spot, azure, sky-blue

žiedas [zhie'das] *n* blossom, flower, ring

žiema [zhiema'] *n* winter

žievė [zhievė'] *n* crust, cortex, peel, rind, bark

žygis [zhee'gis] *n* march, trip, cruise, hike

žilas [zhi'las] *adj* grey

žymus [zheemus'] *adj* considerable

žingsnis [zhings'nis] *n* step, stride

žinia [zhinia'] *n* news, information, knowledge

žinyba [zhinee'ba] *n* department

žinoti [zhino'ti] *v* know

žiogas [zhio'gas] *n* grasshopper

žioplas [zhiop'las] *adj* foolish, gullible, gaper, gull

žiovauti [zhio'vauti] *v* yawn

žirklės [zhirk'lės] *n* scissors, shears

žirnis [zhir'nis] *n* pea

žiūrėti [zhioorė'ti] *v* look at

žiurkė [zhiur'kė] *n* rat

žlugti [zhlug'ti] *v* fail, fall through, be a failure

žmogiškas [zhmo'gishkas] *adj* human

žmogus [zhmogus'] *n* man, person

žmogžudystė [zhmogzhudees'tė] *n* murder

žmona [zhmona'] *n* wife

žmonės [zhmo'nės] *n* people

žnybti [zhneeb'ti] *v* pinch, nip, tweak

žodynas [zhodee'nas] *n* dictionary, vocabulary

žodis [zho'dis] *n* word

žolė [zholė] *n* grass

žudyti [zhudee'ti] *v* kill, murder

žūti [zhoo'ti] *v* perish, fall, die

žuvauti [zhuvau'ti] *v* fish, catch fish

žuvėdra [zhuvėd'ra] *n* seagull

žuvis [zhuvis'] *n* fish

žvaigždė [zhvaigzhdė] *n* star

žvairas [zhvai'ras] *adj* squint, squinting

žvakė [zhva'kė] *n* candle, plug

žvalgytis [zhvalgee'tis] *v* be looking round, exchange glances

žvalus [zhvalus'] *adj* cheerful, brisk, bright, smart

žvelgti [zhvclg'ti] *v* look, glance, cast a glance

žvėris [zhvėris'] *n* beast

žvilgsnis [zhvilgs'nis] *n* look, gaze, stare, glare

žvirgždas [zhvirgzh'das] *n* rough sand, gravel

ENGLISH-LITHUANIAN
DICTIONARY

A

aback [abak] *adv* atgal´, už´pakalyje
abandon [ebanden] *v* palik´ti, apleis´ti, atsisaky´ti
abase [ebeis] *v* paže´minti
abash [ebash] *v* sugė´dinti, sukonfū´zyti
abbreviate [ebreevieit] *v* sutrum´pinti
abdicate [abdikeit] *v* atsisaky´ti, išsižadė´ti
abduct [ebdukt] *v* pagrob´ti, smurtu´ nusives´ti
abet [ebet] *v* kurstyti
abhor [ebhōl] *v* bjaurė´tis
abide [ebīd] *v* bū´ti, gyven´ti
ability [ebiliti] *n* galė´jimas, sugebė´jimas, gabu´mai
abject [abjekt] *adj* niekin´gas, paže´mintas
able [eibl] *adj* gabus´, sumanus´, galis´
abolish [ebolish] *v* panaikin´ti
abound [ebaund] *v* per´tekti, knibždė´ti
about [ebaut] *prp* apie´, aplink´, po´, prie´
above [ebuv] *prp* ant´, virš´
abrade [ebreid] *v* trin´ti, išskus´ti, nulup´ti
abreast [ebrest] *adv* šalia´, greta´
abridge [ebrij] *v* trum´pinti, apribo´ti
abroad [ebrōd] *adv* plačiai´, visur´
abrupt [ebrupt] *adj* status´, staigus´, ūmus´

absence [absens] *n* nebuvi'mas,
neatvyki'mas

absolve [abzolv] *v* atleis'ti, dovano'ti,
ištei'sinti

absorb [absōrb] *v* suger'ti

abstain [abstein] *v* susilaiky'ti

abstruse [abstroos] *adj* neaiš'kus,
nesupran'tamas, gilus'

absurd [absėrd] *adj* bepras'miškas, kvai'las,
absur'diškas

abuse [ebyooz] *v* piktnaudžiau'ti, įžeis'ti,
išplūs'ti

accede [akseed] *v* sutik'ti, pradė'ti,
prisijung'ti

accept [aksept] *v* priim'ti, sutik'ti

access [akses] *n* priėjimas, prie'puolis

accident [aksident] *n* nelaimin'gas
atsitiki'mas, į'vykis, ava'rija

accomodate [ekomedeit] *v* pritai'kyti,
sude'rinti, aprū'pinti

accomplish [ekomplish] *v* atlik'ti, užbaig'ti,
to'bulinti

accord [ekōrd] *n* sutiki'mas, sutari'mas

accost [ekost] *v* kreip'tis, svei'kinti,
prakal'binti

account [ekaunt] *n* sąs'kaita, atas'kaita

accumulate [ekyoomyeleit] *v* sukaup'ti, krau'ti

accurate [akyerit] *adj* tikslus, tvarkin'gas

accustom [ekustem] *v* pripra'tinti

ache [eik] *v* skaudė'ti

achieve [echeev] *v* pasiek'ti, laimė'ti, atlik'ti

acquaint [ekweint] *v* supažin'dinti, praneš'ti

acquaintance [ekweintens] *n* pažintis'

acquire [ekwīer] *v* įgy'ti, pasiek'ti

acquit [ekwit] *v* ištei'sinti

acrid [akrid] *adj* aštrus', aitrus', kandus'

across [ekros] *adv* skersai', kryžmais', per'

act [akt] *n* veiki'mas, dar'bas, nutari'mas

actuate [akchooeit] *v* ju'dinti, ža'dinti, ska'tinti

acute [ekyoot] *adj* smailus', aštrus', smarkus'

adapt [edapt] *v* pritai'kyti

add [ad] *v* pridė'ti, sudė'ti, pridur'ti, prijung'ti

addict [edikt] *v* atsiduo'ti, atsidėti, *n* narkoma'nas

addle [adl] *adj* suge'dęs, supu'vęs, tuš'čias

address [edres] *v* adresuo'ti, kreip'tis *n* ad'resas

adequate [adekwit] *adj* atitin'kamas, ly'gus, pakan'kamas

adit [adit] *n* priėji'mas, anga', kori'dorius

adjective [ajiktiv] *adj* priklau'somas, papil'domas, būd'vardis

adjourn [edjėrn] *v* atsidė'ti, padary'ti per'trauką

adjust [ejust] *v* pritai'kyti, sutvarky'ti, sude'rinti

admire [admīer] *v* žavė'tis, grožė'tis, gėrė'tis

admit [admit] *v* prileis'ti, leis'ti

admonish [admonish] *v* įtikinė'ti, ra'ginti, įspė'ti

adolescent [edolesent] *n* jaunuo'lis

adopt [edopt] *v* įsū'nyti, priim'ti, parink'ti

adore [edōr] *v* gar'binti, die'vinti

adorn [edōrn] v puoš'ti, gra'žinti

adult [edult] *adj* pilname'tis, suau'gęs

advance [advans] *v* paaukš'tinti, iškel'ti, ge'rinti, iš anks'to mokė'ti

advantage [advaantij] *n* nauda, pranašu'mas

adventure [advencher] *n* nuo'tykis, avantiū'ra, į'vykis

advertisement [advėrtisment] *n* skelbi'mas, reklama'

advice [advīz] *n* patari'mas, praneši'mas

affable [afebl] *adj* malonus', meilus'

affair [efier] *n* rei'kalas, daly'kas

affect [efekt] *v* dė'tis, mėg'ti, veik'ti, jau'dinti

affirm [efėrm] patvir'tinti

affix [efix] *v* pritvir'tinti, pridė'ti

afford [efōrd] *v* išgalė'ti, įsteng'ti, pajėg'ti

affray [efrei] *n* kivir'čas, mušty'nės

affront [efrunt] *v* užgau'ti, įžeisti

afoot [efūt] *adv* pėsčia', ju'dant

afraid [efreid] *adj* išgąs'dintas

afresh [efresh] *adv* vėl', iš nau'jo

after [after] *conj* po to', kai

again [egen] *adv* dar' kar'tą, vėl'

against [egenst] *prep* prieš', į', ant'

age [eij] *n* am'žius, me'tai

agile [ejīl] *adj* vikrus', judrus'

ago [egou] *adv* prieš'

agree [egree] *v* sutik'ti, sutar'ti, atitik'ti

ahead [ehed] *adv* priešaky', pirmyn'

aid [eid] *n* pagal'ba, padėjė'jas

ail [eil] *v* skaudė'ti, sukel'ti skaus'mą

aim [eim] *n* taikinys', tiks'las, keti'nimas

air [ier] *n* o'ras, vė'jas

ale [eil] *n* alus'

alert [elėrt] *adj* budrus', atsargus'

alien [eilyen] *adj* sve'timas, kitoks', to'limas

alike [elīk] *adj* panašus'

aliment [alement] *n* mais´tas, išlai´kymas
alive [elīv] *adj* gy´vas, žvalus´, budrus´
all [ōl] *adj* vi´sas, visi´, vis´kas
allay [elei] *v* nuramin´ti, numalšin´ti
allot [elot] *v* padaly´ti, paskirs´tyti, paskir´ti
allow [elau] *v* leis´ti, sutik´ti, tvir´tinti
allude [elood] *v* užsimin´ti
allure [elūr] *v* vilio´ti, ma´sinti, gun´dyti
allusion [eloozhen] *n* užuo´mina,
nuro´dymas
ally [elī] *v* sujung´ti, suvie´nyti
almost [ōlmoust] *adv* beveik´
alone [eloun] *adj* vie´nas, vie´nišas
along [elong] *adv* išilgai´, pa´lei
aloof [eloof] *adv* nuošaliai´, atokiai´
aloud [elaud] *adv* bal´siai, gar´siai
already [ōlredee] *adv* jau´
also [ōlsou] *adv* taip pat´
although [ōlthou] *cnj* nors´, nežiū´rint
alter [ōlter] *v* keis´ti
always [ōlweiz] *adv* visuomet´, visada´
amateur [ametėr] *n* mėgė´jas
amazing [emeizing] *adj* nuostabus´,
nepap´rastas
amber [amber] *n* gin´taras
amend [emend] *v* page´rinti, ištaisy´ti

amenity [emenitee] *n* malonu'mas,
meilu'mas

amerce [emėrs] *v* nubaus'ti

amiable [eimyebel] *adj* malonus',
drau'giškas, patrauklus'

among [emung] *prp* tarp'

amount [emaunt] *n* kie'kis, skai'čius, suma'

ample [ampel] *adj* erdvus', gausus'

amuse [emyooz] *v* links'minti

ancient [einshent] *adj* seno'vinis

and [and] *cnj* ir', bei'

anew [ennyoo] *adv* iš nau'jo

anger [anger] *v* pyk'tis

angle [angel] *v* meškerio'ti *n* kam'pas

angry [angree] *adj* supy'kęs, pik'tas

animal [anemel] *n* gyvulys'

anniversary [anevėrseree] *n* me'tinės,
jubilie'jus

announce [cnauns] *v* paskelb'ti

annoy [enoi] *v* py'kinti, įkyrė'ti

annual [anyooel] *adj* kasmeti'nis, me'tinis

another [enuther] *prn* ki'tas

answer [anser] *v* atsaky'ti, laiduo'ti

ant [ant] *n* skruzdėlė'

anxiety [angzīitee] *n* susirū'pinimas,
ne'rimas

any [enee] *prn* kas nors′, koks nors′, bet koks′

apart [epaart] *adv* išsky′rus, be to′, nuošaliai′

apologize [epolejīz] *v* atsiprašy′ti, pasitei′sinti

appall [epōl] *v* gąs′dinti

appalling [epōling] *adj* baisus′

appeal [epeel] *v* šauk′tis, kreip′tis

appear [epeer] *v* ro′dytis, atro′dyti, pasiro′dyti

append [epend] *v* pridur′ti, prijung′ti

apple [apel] *n* obuolys′

appoint [epoint] *v* paskir′ti, nustaty′ti, įreng′ti

appraise [epreiz] *v* įver′tinti

appreciate [epreeshieit] *v* ver′tinti, supras′ti, pripažin′ti

apprehend [aprihend] *v* suvok′ti, numaty′ti

approach [eprouch] *v* ar′tintis, kreip′tis

approve [eproov] *v* patvir′tinti, pritar′ti, pasireikš′ti

approximate [eproksemit] *v* apy′tikris, ar′timas

approximate [eproksemeit] *v* ar′tintis

apricot [eiprekot] *n* abriko′sas

April [eiprel] *n* balan'džio mė'nuo
apt [apt] *adj* tikė'tinas, spė'jamas
archbishop [aarchbishep] *n* arkivys'kupas
are [aar] *v* yra'
argue [aargyoo] *v* gin'čytis, svarsty'ti, įrodinė'ti
arise [erīz] *v* kil'ti, atsiras'ti
arm [aarm] *n* ranka', gink'las
armchair [aarm chier] *n* krės'las, fo'telis
around [eraund] *prep* apie', aplink'
arouse [erauz] *v* ža'dinti, kel'ti
arrange [ereinj] *v* tvarkyti, susitar'ti
array [erei] *v* išrikiuo'ti, sutvarky'ti
arrest [erest] *v* suim'ti, sulaiky'ti
arrive [erīv] *v* atvyk'ti, pasiek'ti
arrogant [aregent] *adj* išdidus', išpui'kęs, aki'plėšiškas
arrow [arou] *n* strėlė'
art [aart] *n* dailė', me'nas
artful [aartfel] *adj* gudrus', apsukrus'
article [aartikel] *n* straips'nis
artificial [aartefishel] *adj* dirbti'nis
as [az] *adv* kaip'
ascend [esent] *v* kop'ti, kil'ti, pasikel'ti
ascertain [esertein] *v* nustaty'ti, įsiti'kinti
ashamed [esheimd] *adj* susigė'dęs

ash can [ash kan] *n* šiukš′lių dėžė′

ashtray [ash trei] *n* peleni′nė

aside [esīd] *adv* šalia, šalin′

ask [ask] *v* klaus′ti, teirau′tis, prašy′ti, kvies′ti

asleep [esleep] *adj* mie′gantis

asp [asp] *n* gyva′tė, e′pušė, drebulė′

aspect [aspekt] *n* iš′vaizda, po′žiūris

aspen [aspen] *n* epušė′, drebulė′

ass [as] *n* a′silas, kvailys′

assay [esei] *v* bandy′ti, mėgin′ti

assent [esent] *n* pritari′mas, sutiki′mas

assert [esėrt] *v* tvir′tinti, gin′ti

assign [esīn] *v* paskir′ti, asignuo′ti

assist [esist] *v* padė′ti, dalyvau′ti

assume [esoom] *v* prisiim′ti, pasisa′vinti

assure [eshūr] *v* užtik′rinti, garantuo′ti

astonish [estonish] *v* nuste′binti

astound [estaund] *v* nuste′binti, abstul′binti

astute [estyoot] *adj* įžvalgus′, gudrus′, suk′tas

asunder [esunder] *adv* atskirai′, pusiau′

asylum [esīlem] *n* prie′glauda, psichiat′rinė ligo′ninė

at [at] *prp* prie′

athwart [ethwōrt] *adv* skersai′, prie′šingai

atone [etoun] *v* atly'ginti, susitai'kyti

atop [etop] *adv* viršuje

atrocious [etroushes] *adj* žiaurus', baisus', bjaurus'

attach [etach] *v* pririš'ti, pritvir'tinti, pritaisy'ti

attack [etak] *v* pul'ti, atakuo'ti

attain [etein] *v* pasiek'ti, gau'ti

attaint [eteint] *n* gė'da, nešlovė'

attempt [etempt] *v* mėgin'ti, pasikėsin'ti

attend [etend] *v* kreip'ti dė'mesį, lanky'tı, rū'pintis

attention [etenshen] *n* dėmesys'

attest [etest] *v* liu'dyti, pažymė'ti, atestuo'ti

attitude [atityood] *n* padėtis', po'žiūris, po'za

attract [etrakt] *v* pritrauk'ti, pritrauk'ti, vilio'ti

attribute [atrebyoot] *n* savy'bė, pažiminys'

audit [ōdit] *n* revi'zija

August [ōgest] *n* rugpjū'tis

aunt [aant] *n* teta

aurally [ōrelee] *adv* žodžiu', iš klausos'

austere [ōsteer] *adj* griež'tas, aštrus'

author [ōther] *n* au'torius, kūrė'jas

autumn [ōtem] *n* ruduo

avail [eveil] *v* padė′ti, bū′ti naudin′gam
avaricious [averishes] *adj* godus′, šykštus′
avenge [evenj] *v* ker′šyti
avenue [avenyoo] *n* plati′ gat′vė, prospek′tas
average [avrij] *adj* viduti′nis
avert [evėrt] *v* nukreip′ti
avid [avid] *adj* godus
avoid [evoid] *v* išveng′ti, panaikin′ti
avouch [evauch] *v* tvir′tinti, užtik′rinti, garantuo′ti
awake [eweik] *v* bu′dinti, ža′dinti, atsibus′ti
award [ewōrd] *v* priteis′ti, suteik′ti
away [ewei] *adj* nesąs′, neatė′jęs
awful [ōfel] *adj* baisus′
awhile [ewhīl] *adv* valandė′lei, neilgam′
awkward [ōkwerd] *adj* nerangus′, nejaukus′, nepatogus′
awry [erī] *adv* kreivai′, įstrižai′
axe [aks] *n* kir′vis
azure [eizher] *adj* žyd′ras

B

baby [beibee] *n* kū′dikis
bachelor [bacheler] *n* viengun′gis, bakalau′ras
back [bak] *n* nugara′, užpakali′nė dalis′

bacon [beiken] *n* beko'nas, kiaulie'na
bad [bad] *adj* blo'gas, nege'ras, suge'dęs
baffle [bafel] *v* suardy'ti, kliudy'ti
bag [bag] *n* mai'šas, krepšys', lagami'nas
bake [beik] *v* kep'ti
bald [bōld] *adj* pli'kas, apnuo'gintas
bale [beil] *v* suriš'ti, supakuo'ti
ball [bōl] *n* rutulys', kamuolys', sviedinys'
ballot [balet] *v* balsuo'ti *n* balsa'vimas, balsa'vimo korte'lė
ban [ban] *v* uždraus'ti, prakeik'ti
band [band] *n* kas'pinas, raištis, būrys', gauja', orkes'tras
bang [bang] *v* trenk'ti, smog'ti
banish [banish] *v* ištrem'ti, išvary'ti
banner [baner] *n* vė'liava
baptism [baptizem] *n* krikš'tas, krikšty'nos
bar [baar] *n* ga'balas, kliūtis', ba'ras, barje'ras
barber [baarber] *n* kirpė'jas
bare [bier] *adj* nuo'gas, pli'kas, pa'prastas
bargain [baagin] *n* san'dėris, pirkinys'
bark [baak] *n* me'džio žievė', *v* lo'ti
barley [barlee] *n* mie'žiai
barren [baren] *adj* nederlin'gas, skurdus', neturtin'gas

barring [baaring] *prp* išsky'rus
barter [baarter] *v* mainy'ti
base [beis] *n* ba'zė, pa'grindas, pa'matas
basin [beisen] *n* tvenkinys', basei'nas
basket [baaskit] *n* krepšys'
basketball [baaskit bōl] *n* krepši'nis
bastard [basterd] *adj* netik'ras, padirb'tas
baste [beist] *v* muš'ti, bels'ti, pertrauk'ti
bat [bat] *n* šikšno'sparnis, te'niso rake'tė,
lazda'
batch [bach] *n* par'tija, gru'pė
bath [baath] *n* pirtis', maudyk'lė, vonia
bathe [beith] *v* mau'dytis
bathrobe [baathroub] *n* chala'tas
bathroom [baathroom] *n* vonios' kambarys'
bating [beiting] *prp* išsky'rus
batter [bater] *v* plak'ti, muš'ti, daužy'ti
battle [batl] *n* mū'šis, kova'
bauble [boubel] *n* maž'možis, menk'niekis
bawdy [bōdee] *adj* nepado'rus
bay [bei] *n* į'lanka, užu'tekis, laurų' me'dis
bazaar [bezaar] *n* tur'gus
be [bee] *v* bū'ti, egzistuo'ti, gyven'ti
beach [beech] *n* paplūdimys', plia'žas,
pajū'ris
beam [beem] *n* rąs'tas, spindulys', ašis'

bean [been] *n* pupa'

bear [bier] *n* lokys', meška'

bear [bier] *v* gimdy'ti, kur'ti, neš'ti, pakęs'ti, rem'tis

beard [beerd] *n* barzda'

beast [beest] *n* žvėris', gyvulys'

beat [beet] *v* muš'ti, dauži'ti, kal'ti, sukčiau'ti

beautiful [byootefel] *adj* gražus'

becalm [bikaam] *v* nuramin'ti

because [bıkoz] *conj* nes', todėl', kad', kadan'gi

becloud [biklaud] *v* užtem'dyti, apsiniauk'ti

become [bikum] *v* tap'ti, pavirs'ti, nutik'ti

bed [bed] *n* lo'va, guo'lis, lys'vė

bedew [bidyoo] *v* apraso'ti, aptašky'ti

bedim [bidim] *v* užtem'dyti, aptrauk'ti

bedroom [bed room] *n* miegama'sis kambarys'

bee [bee] *n* bi'tė

beef [beef] *n* jautie'na

beer [beer] *n* alus'

beet [beet] *n* run'kelis

beetle [beetl] *n* va'balas

beetroot [beetroot] *n* buro'kas

befall [bifo] *v* atsitik'ti, įvyk'ti

befool [bifool] *v* apkvai'linti

before [bifōr] *prp* prieš', *adv* prie'šais, anksčiau'

befriend [bifrend] *v* padė'ti, palaiky'ti

beg [beg] *v* prašy'ti, mels'ti, elgetau'ti

beggar [beger] *n* el'geta

begin [bigin] *v* pradė'ti

beguile [bigīl] *v* apgau'ti, klaidin'ti, links'minti

behalf [bihaaf] *n* nauda', la'bas

behave [biheiv] *v* elg'tis, laiky'tis

behind [bihīnd] *adv* po', paskui', užpakalyje', už'

behold [bihould] *v* maty'ti, pastebė'ti

being [beeing] *n* būtis', gyve'nimas

belch [belch] *v* atsirau'gėti

belie [bilī] *v* apšmeiž'ti, prieštarau'ti

believe [bileev] *v* tikė'ti, many'ti

bell [bel] *n* var'pas, skambu'tis

bellow [belou] *v* staug'ti, rėk'ti

belong [bilong] *v* priklausy'ti, kil'ti

below [bilou] *adv* žemiau', po', apačioj'

belt [belt] *n* dir'žas, juos'ta, zo'na

bench [bench] *n* suo'las, stak'lės

bend [bend] *v* lenk'ti, ries'ti

beneath [bineeth] *adv* apačioj', po', žemai'

beneficence [benefisens] *n* labdara′

beneficial [benefishel] *adj* naudin′gas

benefit [benefit] *n* nauda′, malo′nė

benevolent [benevelent] *adj* palankus′

berry [beree] *n* uo′ga

beseech [biseech] *v* maldau′ti, prašy′ti

beside [bisīd] *adv* šalia′, prie′, arti′

besides [bisīdz] *adv* be to′, *prp* be′, išsky′rus

besom [beczzcm] *v* šluo′ti *n* šluo′ta

best [best] *adj* geriau′sias

bet [bet] *v* la′žintis, ei′ti lažy′bų

betray [bitrei] *v* išduo′ti

better [beter] *adj* geres′nis, sveikes′nis

betting [beting] *n* lažy′bos

between [bitween] *prep* tarp′

beware [biwier] *v* sau′gotis

bewilder [biwilder] *v* suklaidin′ti, suglu′minti

bewitch [biwich] *v* apkerė′ti, sužavė′ti

beyond [biyond] *adv* ana′pus, už′, virš′

bicycle [bīsikel] *n* dvi′ratis

bid [bid] *v* liep′ti, įsaky′ti, siū′lyti

big [big] *adj* di′delis, platus′, svarbus′

bight [bīt] *n* į′lanka, vin′gis

bijou [beezhoo] *n* brangeny′bė, nieku′tis

bilberry [bilberee] *n* mėly′nė

bind [bīnd] *v* riš'ti, suriš'ti, įpareigo'ti

birch [bėrch] *n* ber'žas

bird [bėrd] *n* paukš'tis

birth [bėrth] *n* gimi'mas, kilmė'

bishop [bishep] *n* vys'kupas

bit [bit] *n* gabalė'lis, kąsne'lis, trupu'tis

bitch [bich] *n* kalė', kek'šė

bite [bīt] *v* kąsti, gel'ti, kib'ti

bitter [biter] *adj* kartus', aitrus'

blab [blab] *v* plepė'ti, taukš'ti

black [blak] *adj* juo'das, tamsus', niūrus'

blade [bleid] *n* aš'menys, laiške'lis

blame [bleim] *v* peik'ti, kal'tinti

bland [bland] *adj* meilus', švelnus', mandagus'

blank [blangk] *adj* tuš'čias, sumi'šęs, vi'siškas

blanket [blangkit] *v* apklo'ti

blaze [bleiz] *v* žėrė'ti, žibė'ti

bleach [bleech] *v* bal'tinti, bal'ti

bleak [bleek] *adj* išba'lęs, niūrus', šal'tas

blear [bleer] *adj* tamsus', apsiblau'sęs

bleed [bleed] *v* kraujuo'ti

blessing [blesing] *n* palai'minimas, gamtos' dovana'

blind [blīnd] *adj* ak'las, neaiš'kus, tamsus'

bliss [blis] *n* palai′ma
blockhead [blokhed] *n* kvailys′
blood [blud] *n* krau′jas, kilmė′, giminys′tė
bloom [bloom] *n* žie′das, žydė′jimas
blossom [blosem] *v* žydė′ti
blot [blot] *n* dėmė′, sutepi′mas
blouse [blauz] *n* palaidinu′kė, bliuze′lė
blow [blou] *v* pūs′ti, trimituo′ti, nusišnypš′ti
blue [bloo] *adj* mė′lynas, žyd′ras
bluff [bluf] *n* apgavys′tė, įbaugi′nimas,
ble′fas
blush [blush] *v* raudonuo′ti, paraus′ti
board [bōrd] *n* lenta′, sta′las, bor′tas,
valdy′ba
boast [boust] *v* gir′tis, didžiuo′tis
boat [bout] *n* val′tis, lai′vas
body [bodee] *n* kū′nas, lavo′nas, liemuo′,
kor′pusas
bogus [bouges] *adj* netik′ras, fikty′vus
boil [boil] *v* vir′ti, vi′rinti, pyk′ti
bold [bould] *adj* drąsus′, įžūlus′
bone [boun] *n* kau′las
book [būk] *n* knyga′
boost [boost] *v* pakel′ti, palaiky′ti
boot [boot] *n* ba′tas, pus′batis, nauda′
border [bōrder] *n* sie′na, kraš′tas, riba′

bore [bōr] *v* gręž'ti, te'kinti, įkyrė'ti

boring [bōring] *adj* įkyrus', gre̜'žiamas

borrow [borou] *v* pasisko'linti

bosom [boozem] *n* krūti'nė, širdis', užan'tis, gel'mės

boss [bos] *n* šeiminin'kas, į'monininkas

both [bouth] *pron* abu'

bother [bother] *v* varg'ti, trukdy'ti, įkyrė'ti

bottle [botl] *n* bu'telis

bottom [botem] *n* dug'nas, žemuti'nė dalis', pag'rindas

bough [bau] *n* šaka'

bound [baund] *n* riba', sie'na, šuo'lis

boundless [baundlis] *adj* beri'bis

bounteous [baunties] *adj* dosnus', gausus'

bouquet [boukei] *n* puokš'tė

bout [baut] *n* kar'tas, sy'kis

bow [bau] *v* lenk'ti, pasilenk'ti

bowl [boul] *n* tau'rė, vaza'

box [boks] *n* dėžė', lo'žė, kir'tis, smū'gis

boy [boi] *n* berniu'kas, vaiki'nas

brace [breis] *v* suriš'ti, suverž'ti, sutvir'tinti

brag [brag] *v* gir'tis

brain [brein] *n* sme'genys, pro'tas

branch [braanch] *n* šaka', sky'rius, atšaka'

brass [braas] *n* bron'za, žal'varis

brave [breiv] *adj* drąsus', narsus', šaunus'

brawl [brōl] *v* bar'tis, triukšmau'ti, *n* triukš'mas

bread [bred] *n* duo'na

break [breik] *v* lauž'ti, skin'ti, švis'ti

breakfast [brekfest] *n* pus'ryčiai

breast [brest] *n* krūti'nė, krūtis'

breath [breth] *n* kva'pas, kvėpa'vimas

breathe [breeth] *v* kvėpuo'ti, pūs'ti, atsidus'ti

brawn [brōn] *n* rau'menys

breathless [brethlis] *adj* uždu'sęs, be kva'po

breed [breed] *v* veis'tis, dau'gintis, gimdy'ti

brevity [brevitee] *n* trumpu'mas

bribe [brīb] *n* ky'šis, papirki'mas

brick [brik] *n* ply'ta

bride [brīd] *n* nuo'taka

bridge [brij] *n* til'tas, bri'džas

brief [breef] *adj* trum'pas, su'glaustas, sutrauk'tas

bright [brīt] *adj* šviesus, skaistus', gied'ras, ryškus'

brilliant [brilyent] *adj* puikus', bliz'gantis

brim [brim] *n* kraš'tas, briauna'

bring [bring] *v* atneš'ti, atves'ti, pristaty'ti

brisk [brisk] *adj* links'mas, smagus', vikrus'

brittle [britl] *adj* trapus, dūž'tamas

broad [brōd] *adj* platus', aiš'kus

broadcast [brōdkaast] *v* transliuo'ti

broker [brouker] *n* mak'leris, tar'pininkas

brook [brūk] *v* pakęs'ti, ištver'ti

broom [broom] *n* šluo'ta

broth [broth] *n* sriuba', buljo'nas

brother [bruthėr] *n* bro'lis

brow [brau] *n* an'takis, kakta', kraš'tas

brown [braun] *adj* ru'das, rus'vas, įde'gęs sau'lėje

bruit [broot] *n* gan'das, gar'sas

brush [brush] *n* šepetys', teptu'kas, va'lymas

brute [broot] *adj* žiaurus', nuožmus'

bud [bud] *n* pum'puras

buffoon [befoon] *n* juokdarys'

bug [bug] *n* bla'kė

build [bild] *v* staty'ti, kur'ti

bulge [bulj] *n* panašu'mas

bull [būl] *n* bu'lius, jau'tis

bullet [būlit] *n* kulka'

bump [bump] *n* smū'gis, gum'bas

bunch [baunch] *n* puokš'tė, ke'kė, ryše'lis, krūva'

bundle [bundl] *n* ryšulys'

burglar [bėrgler] *n* vagis', įsilau'žėlis

burial [beriel] *n* šer'menys, lai'dotuvės

burn [bėrn] *v* deg´ti, sude´ginti

burst [bėrst] *v* trūk´ti, plyš´ti, sprog´ti, pratrūk´ti

bury [beree] *v* lai´doti, paslėp´ti

bus [bus] *n* autobu´sas

bush [būsh] *n* krū´mas

business [biznis] *n* rei´kalas, užsiėmi´mas, komer´cinė veikla´

busy [bizee] *adj* užim´tas, gy´vas

but [hut] *prp* be´, išsky´rus

butcher [būcher] *n* mė´sininkas, skerdi´kas

butter [buter] *n* svies´tas

butterfly [buterflī] *n* druge´lis, peteliš´kė

button [butn] *n* saga´

buy [bī] *v* pirk´ti

by [bī] *prp* prie´, šalia´, greta´

bypass [bīpass] *v* apei´ti, apsup´ti

byword [bīwėrd] *n* prie´žodis

C

cabbage [kabij] *n* kopūs´tas

cab [kab] *n* kabina´, taksi´, automobi´lis

cabin [kabin] *n* trobe´lė, kaju´tė

cable [keibel] *n* ka´belis, lai´das, telegrama´

cache [kash] *v* slėp´ti

cachet [kashei] *n* ant´spaudas

cad [kad] *n* storžie′vis, stačio′kas, cha′mas

cafe [kafei] *n* kavi′nė

cage [keij] *n* narve′lis, kalė′jimas, kabina′

cake [keik] *n* pyragai′tis, kek′sas

calamity [kelamitee] *n* nelai′mė, ne′gandas

calculate [kalkyeleit] *v* apskaičiuo′ti, numaty′ti, many′ti

calf [kaaf] *n* ver′šis, blauzda′

call [kōl] *v* šauk′ti, vadin′ti, skelb′ti, užei′ti į′ svečius′

callow [kalou] *adj* nepaty′ręs, neįgu′dęs

calm [kaam] *adj* ramus′

camel [kamel] *n* kupranuga′ris

camera [kamere] *n* fotoapara′tas

camp [kamp] *n* stovykla′, la′geris

can [kan] *v* galiu′, mo′ku, turiu′ tei′sę

cancel [kansel] *v* išbrauk′ti, anuliuo′ti, panaikin′ti

cancer [kanser] *n* vėžys′ (liga′)

candid [kandid] *adj* tiesus′, at′viras, tik′ras

candle [kandel] *n* žva′kė

candy [kandee] *n* ledinu′kas, saldai′nis

canned [kand] *adj* konservuo′tas

canteen [kanteen] *n* krau′tuvė, ba′ras, bu′fetas

canvas [kanves] *n* stora′ dro′bė, brezen′tas, paveiks′las

cap [kap] *n* kepu′rė, gaub′tas

capable [keipebel] *adj* gabus′, sugebąs′

capacity [kepasitee] *n* gabu′mas, sugebė′jimas

capital [kapitl] *n* sos′tinė, kapita′las, *adj* pagrindi′nis, svarbiau′sias

caption [kapshen] *n* ant′raštė, a′reštas, sulai′kymas

captious [kapshes] *adj* priekabus

captivate [kapteveit] *v* sužavė′ti, patrauk′ti

captive [kaptiv] *n* belais′vis

capture [kapcher] *n* užgrobi′mas, gro′bis, pagavi′mas

carcass [kaarkes] *n* lavo′nas, griau′čiai, griuvė′siai

card [kaard] *n* kor′ta, bi′lietas, skelbi′mas

cardigan [kaardegen] *n* nerti′nis, megzti′nis

cardinal [kaardenel] *adj* svarbiau′sias, pagrindi′nis, *n* kardino′las

care [kier] *n* rū′pestis, globa′, atidu′mas, apdairu′mas

careful [kierfel] *adj* rūpestin′gas, atidus′, atsargus′

caress [keres] *v* glamonė′ti, glos′tyti

carpet [kaarpit] *n* ki'limas, patie'salas
carriage [karij] *n* veži'mas, vago'nas, per've žimas
carrot [karet] *n* mor'ka
carry [karee] *v* gaben'ti, neš'ti, vež'ti, pardavinė'ti
cartoon [kaartoon] *n* karikatū'ra
carve [kaarv] *v* pjaus'tyti, rai'žyti, pjau'ti
case [keis] *n* at'vejis, atsitiki'mas, dėžė', lagami'nas
cash [kash] *n* gryni' pinigai'
casing [keising] *n* ap'mušalas, pa'danga
cast [kaast] *v* mes'ti, svies'ti, nulie'ti, suskaičiuo'ti
castigate [kastegeit] *v* baus'ti, bar'ti
castle [kaasel] *n* pilis'
casual [kazhooel] *adj* atsitikti'nis, nepastovus', nenumaty'tas
cat [kat] *n* katė', ka'tinas
catch [kach] *v* gau'dyti, pagau'ti, supras'ti, sulaiky'ti
cater [keiter] *v* aprū'pinti maistu', steng'tis įtik'ti
catgut [katgut] *n* styga'
cattle [katl] *n* raguo'čiai

cause [kōz] *n* priežastis´, pa´grindas, argu´mentas

caution [kōshen] *n* atsargu´mas, įspėji´mas

cave [keiv] *n* ur´vas, ola´, įdubi´mas

caviar [kaveeaar] *n* ik´rai

cavity [kavitee] *n* įdubi´mas, tuštuma´

cease [sees] *v* nusto´ti, per´traukti

cede [seed] *v* nusileis´ti, užleis´ti, atsisaky´ti

ceiling [seeling] *n* lu´bos

celebrate [selebreit] *v* švęs´ti, šlo´vinti

cellar [seler] *n* rūsys´, po´grindis

cemetery [semiteree] *n* ka´pinės, kapai´

century [sencheree] *n* šimt´metis, am´žius

cereal [seereel] *n* ko´šė, kruo´pos

certain [sėrten] *adj* tik´ras, tam tik´ras, kažkoks´

certainly [sėrtenlee] *adv* ži´noma,

certify [sėrtefī] *v* pažymė´ti, paliu´dyti

chafe [cheif] *v* trin´tis, ner´vintis

chaff [chaaf] *v* er´zinti

chaffer [chafer] *v* derė´tis, išderė´ti

chagrin [shegrin] *n* siel´vartas

chain [chein] *n* grandi´nė, grandinė´lė, saitai´

chair [chier] *n* kėdė´, ka´tedra, pir´mininkas

chalk [chōk] *n* kreida´, kre´ditas, skola´

chamber [cheimber] *n* kambarys', konto'ra, ka'mera

champ [champ] *v* kramty'ti, čepsė'ti

chance [chaans] *n* atsitiktinu'mas, proga', galimy'bė, šan'sas

chancel [chaansel] *n* alto'rius

chandelier [shandeleer] *n* siety'nas, lius'tra

change [cheinj] *n* per'maina, pasikeiti'mas, grąža', *v* keis'ti

chant [chaant] *n* daina', giesmė'

chap [chap] *n* vaiki'nas, vyru'kas

chapel [chapel] *n* bažnytė'lė, koply'čia

chapter [chapter] *n* sky'rius, tema', siuže'tas

characterize [karikterīz] *v* apibrėž'ti, apibū'dinti, charakterizuo'ti

charge [chaarj] *n* pareiga', pavedi'mas, užduotis'

charity [charitee] *n* labdara'

charm [chaarm] *n* bur'tai, žavesys'

charwoman [chaarwūmen] *n* valy'toja

chary [chieree] *adj* atsargus', santūrus', šykštus'

chase [cheis] *v* vy'tis, medžio'ti

chaste [cheist] *adj* griež'tas, santūrus', skaistus'

chat [chat] *n* pasikalbė'jimas, šneka', plepalai'

cheap [cheep] *adj* pigus', blo'gas

cheat [cheet] *v* apgaudinė'ti, sukčiau'ti, išveng'ti

check [chek] *v* sustabdy'ti, patik'rinti, atitik'ti

cheek [cheek] *n* skruos'tas

cheer [cheer] *v* padrą'sinti, para'ginti

cheese [cheez] *n* sū'ris

chequer [cheker] *n* šaš'kės

cherish [cherish] *v* puo'selėti, globo'ti, sau'goti, mylė'ti

cherry [cheree] *n* vyš'nia

chess [ches] *n* šach'matai

chestnut [chesnut] *n* kašto'nas

chest [chest] *n* dėžė', krūti'nė, krūti'nės ląsta'

chew [choo] *v* kramty'ti, gro'muliuoti

chicken [chiken] *n* viščiu'kas, paukščiu'kas

chief [cheef] *n* va'das, galva', vir'šininkas

child [chīld] *n* vai'kas

chill [chil] *n* šal'tis, vėsuma', drugys'

chimney [chimnee] *n* ka'minas, židinys'

chin [chin] *n* smak'ras

china [chīne] *adj* porcelia'ninis, ki'niškas

chink [chink] *n* plyšys', praraja'
choice [chois] *n* pasirinki'mas, alternaty'va
choke [chouk] *v* dus'ti, smaug'ti
choose [chooz] *v* pasirink'ti, beve'lyti
chop [chop] *v* kapo'ti, pjau'ti, keis'ti
Christmas [krismes] *n* Kalė'dos
chuck [chuk] *v* svies'ti, paleis'ti
chuckle [chukl] *v* juok'tis, kiken'ti,
kudakuo'ti
chum [chum] *n* ge'ras drau'gas, bičiu'lis
chump [chump] *n* rąst'galis, mul'kis, mėsa'
filė'
church [chėrch] *n* bažny'čia
cinder [sinder] *n* pelenai'
cinema [sineme] *n* ki'nas, kinoteat'ras,
kinofil'mas
circle [sėrkel] *n* apskriti'mas, sfe'ra, sritis',
cik'las
circular [sėrkyeler] *adj* apvalus', aps'kritas
circumstance [sėrkemstens] *n* at'vejis,
aplinky'bė
circus [sėrkes] *n* cir'kas
city [sitee] *n* di'delis mies'tas
claim [kleim] *n* reikala'vimas, tei'sė,
preten'zija
clammy [klamee] *adj* lipnus', drėg'nas

clamor [klamer] *v* protestuo'ti, šauk'ti, reikalau'ti

clang [klang] *v* skam'binti, žvangė'ti

clap [klap] *v* plo'ti, plekšno'ti, trenk'ti

clarify [klarefī] *v* paaiš'kinti, paaiškė'ti, išvaly'ti

clasp [klasp] *v* suseg'ti, paspaus'ti, apkabin'ti

class [klaas] *n* kla'sė, rūšis', katego'rija

clause [klōz] *n* straips'nis, para'grafas

claw [klō] *n* na'gas, le'tena

clay [klei] *n* mo'lis, dul'kės, že'mė

clean [kleen] *adj* švarus'

clear [kleer] *adj* švarus', aiš'kus, supran'tamas

cleave [kleev] *v* per'skelti, skros'ti

clement [klement] *adj* gailestin'gas, minkš'tas

clench [klench] *v* suspaus'ti, sukąs'ti

clergyman [klėrjeemen] *n* dva'sininkas, ku'nigas

clerk [klėrk] *n* val'dininkas, sekreto'rius, raš'tininkas

clever [klever] *adj* gudrus', protin'gas, gabus', gerašir'dis

cliff [klif] *n* stati' uola'

climb [klīm] *v* lip'ti, kop'ti

cloak [klouk] *n* apsiaus'tas, danga', dingstis', preteks'tas

clock [klok] *n* laik'rodis

clod [klod] *n* grums'tas

close [klouz] *adj* už'daras, sandarus', ar'timas

cloth [kloth] *n* au'deklas, gelum'bė, stal'tiesė

clothe [klouth] *v* apvilk'ti, uždeng'ti

cloud [klaud] *n* de'besys, dangus'

clump [klump] *n* grums'tas, ga'balas

clumsy [klumzee] *adj* nevikrus', nerangus', netak'tiškas

cluster [kluster] *n* ke'kė, gru'pė, puokš'tė

coal [koul] *n* anglis'

coarse [kōrs] *adj* šiurkštus', blo'gas, neapdirb'tas

coast [koust] *n* pajū'ris, pakran'tė

coat [kout] *n* apsiaus'tas, švar'kas

coax [kouks] *v* meilikau'ti, įkalbinė'ti, įsiteik'ti

cobweb [kobweb] *n* vora'tinklis

cock [kok] *n* gaidys'

coddle [kodl] *v* prižiūrė'ti, slaugy'ti, le'pinti, pataikau'ti

coeval [koueevel] *adj* vienme'tis,
am'žininkas, tuometi'nis

coerce [kouėrs] *v* privers'ti

coffee [kofee] *n* kava'

coffin [kofin] *n* kars'tas

cognac [konyek] *n* konja'kas

cognate [kogneit] *adj* giminin'gas, panašus'

coin [koin] *n* moneta'

coincidence [kouinsidens] *n* sutapi'mas

cold [kould] *adj* šal'tas, abejin'gas

collaborate [kelabereit] *v* bendradarbiau'ti

collar [koler] *n* apy'kaklė, ant'kaklis,
kakla'saitis

collect [kelekt] *v* surink'ti, sukoncentruo'ti

college [kolij] *n* universite'tas, kole'gija

colloquial [keloukwiel] *adj* šnekama'sis

colon [koulen] *n* dvi'taškis

colonel [kėnel] *n* pul'kininkas

color [kuler] *n* spalva', dažai', kolori'tas

column [kolem] *n* kolo'na, pamink'las,
stul'pas, skiltis'

comb [koum] *n* šu'kos

come [kum] *v* atei'ti, atvyk'ti, atvažiuo'ti

comfort [kumfert] *n* paguo'da, parama',
patogu'mai

comfortable [kumfetebel] *adj* pato'gus, rami'nantis

command [kemaand] *v* įsaky'ti, komanduo'ti, valdy'ti

commence [kemens] *v* pradė'ti

commend [kemend] *v* gir'ti, rekomenduo'ti, paves'ti

commerce [komers] *n* preky'ba

commit [kemit] *v* atlik'ti, įvyk'dyti, paves'ti

commodity [kemoditee] *n* pre'kė

common [komen] *adj* bend'ras, pa'prastas, įprasti'nis

commotion [kemoushen] *n* siau'tėjimas, sukrėti'mas

communicate [kemyoonikeit] *v* praneš'ti, bendrau'ti, susisiek'ti

compact [kempakt] *adj* glaudus', tan'kus, kompak'tiškas

compare [kempier] *v* paly'ginti

compassion [kempashen] *n* gai'lestis, užuo'jauta

compel [kempel] *v* privers'ti, prispir'ti

competition [kompitishen] *n* lenkty'nės, rungty'nės, varžy'bos

complain [kemplein] *v* skųs'tis

complete [kempleet] *adj* pil'nas, už'baigtas

comply [kemplī] *v* sutik'ti, nusileis'ti, įvyk'dyti

compose [kempouz] *v* sudary'ti, sukur'ti, nuramin'ti

compound [kempaund] *adj* sudurti'nis, sudėti'nis

comprehend [komprihend] *v* supras'ti, aprėp'ti

compulsion [kempulshen] *n* prie'varta

comrade [kumrid] *n* drau'gas

conceal [kenseel] *v* slėp'ti, nutylė'ti

conceive [kenseev] *v* įsivaizduo'ti, supras'ti, sugalvo'ti

concept [konsept] *n* mintis', są'voka

concern [kensėrn] *v* lies'ti, do'minti, *n* į'monė

concise [kensīs] *adj* su'glaustas, trum'pas, konkrctus', aiš'kus

conclude [kenklood] *v* užbaig'ti, padary'ti iš'vadą, nutar'ti

concord [konkōrd] *n* san'tarvė, sutari'mas, sude'rinimas

concrete [konkreet] *n* beto'nas, *adj* konkretus'

condemn [kendem] *v* nuteis'ti, pasmerk'ti, brokuo'ti, išduo'ti

condition [kendishen] *n* są'lyga
condole [kendoul] *v* užjaus'ti
condone [kendoun] *v* dovano'ti, atleis'ti
conduct [kendukt] *v* elg'tis
confectionery [kenfeksheneree] *n*
kondite'rijos parduotu've, kondite'rijos
gaminiai'
confess [kenfes] *v* prisipažin'ti, išpažin'ti
confident [konfident] *adj* įsiti'kinęs, tik'ras,
pasi'tikintis savimi'
confine [kenfīn] *v* įka'linti, apribo'ti
confirm [kenfėrm] *v* patvir'tinti
conform [kenfōrm] *v* de'rinti, atitik'ti
confusion [kenfyoozhen] *n* netvarka',
maišatis', painiava'
confute [kenfyoot] *v* paneig'ti
congeal [kenjeel] *v* užšal'dyti, susting'ti
congenial [kenjeenyel] *adj* giminin'gas,
ar'timas, tin'kamas
congest [kenjest] *v* per'krauti, per'pildyti
congratulate [kengracheleit] *v* svei'kinti
congregate [kongregeit] *v* susirink'ti
conjecture [kenjekcher] *n* spėji'mas,
prie'laida
conjoin [kenjoin] *v* susijung'ti
connate [koneit] *adj* įgimtas

connect [kenekt] *v* riš'ti, jung'ti, asocijuo'ti

connive [kenīv] *v* pataikau'ti, nuolaidžiau'ti

conquer [konker] *v* užkariau'ti, nugalė'ti, pasiek'ti tiks'lą

conscience [konshens] *n* są'žinė

conscious [konshes] *adj* supran'tantis, są'moningas

consent [kensent] *v* sutik'ti, nusileis'ti

consequence [konsekwens] *n* iš'vada, padarinys'

consider [kensider] *v* many'ti, skaity'tis, svarsty'ti, apgalvo'ti

consist [kensist] *v* susidė'ti, susidary'ti, pasireikš'ti

console [kensoul] *v* ramin'ti, guos'ti

consolidate [kensolideit] *v* stip'rinti, tvir'tinti, suvie'nyti

constant [konstent] *adj* pastovus', iš'tikimas, tvir'tas

constitute [konstityoot] *v* įsteig'ti, sudary'ti, paskir'ti, išleis'ti

constrain [kenstrein] *v* privers'ti, varžy'ti

constrict [kenstrikt] *v* sutrauk'ti, suspaus'ti

construct [kenstrukt] *v* staty'ti, kur'ti, konstruo'ti

consult [kensult] *v* tar'tis, konsultuo'tis, atsižvelg'ti

contain [kentein] *v* turė'ti savyje', talpin'ti, laiky'ti

contemn [kentem] *v* nie'kinti

contempt [kentempt] *n* panieka', že'minimas

contend [kentend] *v* kovo'ti, varžy'tis

content [kentent] *adj* paten'kintas

contest [kentest] *n* gin'čas, varžy'bos, lenkty'nės

continue [kentinyoo] *v* tęs'ti, truk'ti

contort [kentōrt] *v* iškreip'ti, sudarky'ti

contract [kentrakt] *n* sutartis', kontrak'tas

contradict [kontredikt] *v* prieštarau'ti, paneig'ti

contrary [kontreree] *adj* prie'šingas, nepalankus'

contribute [kentribyoot] *v* padė'ti, įmokė'ti, auko'ti, įneš'ti

contravene [kontreveen] *v* gin'čyti, prieštarau'ti

convene [kenveen] *v* sušauk'ti, surink'ti

convenient [kenveenyent] *adj* patogus', tin'kamas

convention [kenvenshen] *n* suvažia'vimas, sutartis'

conversation [konverseishen] *n* pasikalbė′jimas, kalba′

convey [kenvei] *v* gaben′ti, per′duoti, reikš′ti

convict [kenvikt] *v* nuteis′ti, pripažin′ti kaltu′

convince [kenvins] *v* įti′kinti

cook [kūk] *v* vir′ti, kep′ti, *n* virė′jas

cool [kool] *adj* vėsus′, ramus′, šaltakrau′jis

cop [kop] *v* sugau′ti

cope [koup] *v* pajėg′ti susidoro′ti, kovo′ti

copper [koper] *n* va′ris, ka′tilas, vari′nis pi′nigas

copy [kopee] *v* nurašy′ti, kopijuo′ti, sek′ti

cord [kōrd] *n* vir′vė, styga′

cork [kōrk] *n* kamš′tis, plū′dė

corn [kōrn] *n* grū′das, javai′, kviečiai′, kukurū′zai

corner [kōrner] *n* kam′pas

cornflower [kōrn flauer] *n* rugia′gėlė

corpse [kōrps] *n* lavo′nas

correct [kerekt] *adj* tik′ras, teisin′gas, tikslus′

correspond [korispond] *v* atitik′ti, susirašinė′ti

corrode [keroud] *v* rūdy′ti

corrupt [kerupt] *adj* pagadin'tas, ištvir'kęs, pa'perkamas

cost [kost] *n* kai'na

cosy [kouzee] *adj* jaukus', malonus', plati' so'fa

cotton [kotn] *n* med'vilnė, vata'

couch [kauch] *n* guo'lis, so'fa, kuše'tė

cough [kof] *v* ko'sėti, *n* kosulys'

council [kaunsel] *n* tary'ba, pasitari'mas

count [kaunt] *v* skaičiuo'ti, apskaičiuo'ti, išskaičiuo'ti

country [kuntree] *n* šalis', tėvy'nė, kai'mas

county [kauntee] *n* apy'garda

couple [kupel] *n* pora', elemen'tas

courage [kurij] *n* drąsa', drąsu'mas

course [kōrs] *n* kur'sas, eiga'

court [kōrt] *n* teis'mas, kie'mas

courteous [kōrteees] *adj* mandagus'

cousin [kuzin] *n* pus'brolis, pus'seserė

covenant [kuvenent] *n* sutartis'

cover [kuver] *v* deng'ti, slėp'ti, aprėp'ti

cow [kau] *n* kar'vė

coward [kauerd] *n* bailys'

coy [koi] *adj* drovus', kuklus'

crack [krak] *n* traškė'jimas, plyšys', smū'gis

cradle [kradel] *n* lpšys', pradžia', vaikys'tė

crafty [kraaftee] *adj* gudrus', gabus', nagin'gas

cram [kram] *v* prikimš'ti, įgrūs'ti, penė'ti, įkal'ti į gal'vą

cranberry [kranberee] *n* span'guolė

cranny [kranee] *n* plyšys'

crash [krash] *n* trenks'mas, bankro'tas, ava'rija

crave [kreiv] *v* geis'ti, trokš'ti, maldau'ti, prašy'ti

craven [kreiven] *n* bailys', *adj* ir tą', ir kitą'

crawl [krōl] *v* šliauž'ti, rėplio'ti

crayfish [kreifish] *n* vėžys'

crazy [kreizee] *adj* bepro'tiškas, pami'šęs

creak [kreek] *v* girgždė'ti

cream [kreem] *n* kre'mas, grietinė'lė

crease [krees] *n* raukš'lė, klos'tė

create [krieit] *v* kur'ti, sudary'ti

creature [kreecher] *n* būty'bė, pa'daras, sutvėri'mas

credit [kredit] *n* pasitikė'jimas, garbė', kre'ditas

creed [kreed] *n* tiky'ba, pa'žiūros

creek [kreek] *n* upokš'nis

creep [kreep] *v* šliauž'ti, sė'linti, krūp'čioti

crew [kroo] *n* lai'vo į'gula, koman'da, brigada', gauja'

crib [krib] *v* nusirašinė'ti

crime [krīm] *n* nusižengi'mas, nusikalti'mas

crimp [krimp] *v* garbano'ti, gofruo'ti

cripple [kripel] *v* suluo'šinti, sužalo'ti

crisp [krisp] *adj* traškus', gy'vas, garbano'tas

crook [krūk] *n* kablys', lazda'

crop [krop] *n* der'lius, pjūtis', javai'

cross [kros] *n* kry'žius, or'dinas

crow [krou] *n* var'na

crowd [kraud] *n* minia', žmonių' būrys'

crown [kraun] *n* vaini'kas, karū'na, kro'na

crucial [krooshel] *adj* spren'džiamas, le'miamas, kri'tiškas

crucify [kroosefī] *v* nukryžiuo'ti

crude [krood] *adj* ža'lias, neprino'kęs, nesubren'dęs

cruel [krooel] *adj* žiaurus', baisus'

cruise [krooz] *v* plau'kioti

crumb [krum] *n* trupinė'lis, dalely'tė

crush [krush] *v* triuš'kinti, naikin'ti, min'džioti

crust [krust] *n* pluta', žievė, danga'

cry [krī] *v* šauk'ti, rėk'ti, verk'ti

cucumber [kyookumber] *n* agur'kas

cult [kult] *n* kul'tas

cultivate [kultiveit] *v* dirb'ti, la'vinti, kultivuo'ti

culture [kulcher] *n* kultū'ra, veisi'mas

cunning [kuning] *adj* gudrus', klastin'gas, vikrus', patrauklus'

cup [kup] *n* puode'lis, puo'das, tau'rė

curd [kėrd] *n* varškė'

cure [kyūr] *n* vais'tai, gy'dymas, keistuo'lis

curious [kyūries] *adj* smalsus', keis'tas, re'tas

curl [kėrl] *v* suk'tis, garbano'tis

currant [kurent] *n* serben'tai

currency [kurensee] *n* pinigų' apy'varta, valiuta'

current [kurent] *adj* ei'namas, einama'sis

curse [kėrs] *v* keik'tis, prakeik'ti, plūs'tis

curtain [kėrtin] *n* užuo'laida, už'danga

curve [kėrv] *v* lenk'ti, išsilenk'ti

cushion [kūshen] *n* pagalvė'lė

custody [kustedee] *n* sau'gojimas, lai'kymas, globa'

custom [kustem] *n* paprotys', į'protis, mui'tas

cut [kut] *v* pjau'ti, kirs'ti, kirp'ti

cute [kyoot] *adj* gudrus', sumanus', meilus', są'mojingas

cycle [sīkel] *n* cik'las, ra'tas, dvi'ratis

D

dabble [dabel] *v* tašky'tis, pliuš'kintis

daddy [dadee] *n* tė'tis

daft [daaft] *n* be'protis, silpnapro'tis, pai'kas

daily [deilee] *adv* kasdien'

dairy [dieree] *n* pie'ninė

dally [dalee] *v* gaiš'ti lai'ką, dels'ti, flirtuo'ti

dam [dam] *n* už'tvanka

damage [damij] *n* nuos'tolis, žala'

damn [dam] *v* keik'ti

damp [damp] *adj* drėg'nas

dance [daans] *v* šok'ti

dandelion [dandelīen] *n* kiaul'pienė

danger [deinjer] *n* pavo'jus, grėsmė'

dare [dier] *v* išdrįs'ti, rizikuo'ti

dark [daark] *adj* tamsus', niūrus', slap'tas

darling [daarling] *adj* brangu'sis, miela'sis, mylima'sis

darn [daarn] *v* ady'ti

dart [daart] *n* ie'tis, geluo'nis *v* mes'ti

dash [dash] *v* pul'ti, šok'ti, verž'tis

dastard [dasterd] *n* bailys', niek šas

data [deite] *n* duo menys, ži nios, fak tai

daughter [dōter] *n* duktė'

daunt [dōnt] *v* išgąs dinti, įbaugin ti

dawdle [dōdl] *v* dykinė ti, slampinė ti

dawn [dōn] *v* auš ti, švis ti, prasidė ti, *n* aušra'

day [dei] *n* diena'

daze [deiz] *v* nuste binti, apstul binti

dazzle [dazel] *v* apa kinti

dead [ded] *adj* mi ręs, negy vas

deaden [dedn] *v* netek ti jėgų', slopin ti

deadlock [dedlok] *n* bevil tiška padėtis, akla vietė

deaf [def] *adj* kur čias, apy kurtis

deal [deel] *v* turė ti reikalų', elg tis, paskir ti

dear [dear] *adj* brangu sis, miela sis, my limas

dearth [dėrth] *n* trū kumas, ba das

death [deth] *n* mirtis'

debase [dibeis] *v* paže minti, men kinti

debate [dibeit] *v* svarsty ti, gin čytis

debauch [dibōch] *v* tvir kinti, suvilio ti, gadin ti, suvedžio ti

debt [det] *n* skola'

decay [dikei] *v* pū ti, ges ti, smuk ti, ir ti

deceive [diseev] *v* apgau ti, klaidin ti

December [disember] *n* gruo'dis
deception [disepshen] *n* apgavys'tė, me'las
decide [disīd] *v* ryž'tis, nuspręs'ti, nutar'ti
decision [disizhen] *n* nuos'prendis,
sprendi'mas, pasiryži'mas
deck [dek] *n* de'nis, vago'no sto'gas
declare [diklier] *v* pareikš'ti, paskelb'ti,
deklaruo'ti
decline [diklīn] *v* link'ti, nukryp'ti, mažė'ti,
blogė'ti
decorate [dekereit] *v* puoš'ti, dekoruo'ti
decoy [dikoi] *n* spąs'tai, ma'salas
decrease [dikrees] *v* mažė'ti, kris'ti
decree [dikree] *n* nuo'sprendis, po'tvarkis,
į'sakas
deed [deed] *n* veiks'mas, po'elgis, fak'tas
deep [deep] *adj* gilus', tamsus'
deer [deer] *n* el'nias
default [difōlt] *n* trū'kumas, nepri'teklius
defeat [difeet] *n* pralaimė'jimas, žlugi'mas
defect [difekt] *n* trū'kumas, yda', defek'tas
defense [difens] *n* gyny'ba, apsauga',
gyni'mas
defer [difėr] *v* atidė'ti, dels'ti
definite [defenit] *adj* apibrėž'tas,
nustaty'tas, aiš'kus, tikslus'

defray [difrei] *v* apmokė'ti

deft [deft] *adj* vikrus', sumanus', apsukrus'

defy [difī] *v* ignoruo'ti, nesiskaity'ti, nie'kinti

degree [digree] *n* laips'nis

delay [dilei] *v* dels'ti, gaiš'ti,

delete [dileet] *v* išbrauk'ti, panaikin'ti
sulaiky'ti, atidė'ti

deliberate [dilibereit] *v* apgalvo'ti, svarsty'ti

delicate [delekit] *adj* švelnus', meilus',
opus', glež'nas

delicious [dilishes] *adj* žavin'gas, puikus',
skanus'

delight [dilīt] *n* pasigėrė'jimas, žavesys',
malonu'mas

delirious [dileeries] *adj* klie'dintis, įnir'šęs,
pami'šęs

deliver [diliver] *v* pristaty'ti, atgaben'ti,
įtcik'ti

delude [dilood] *v* apgau'ti, klaidin'ti

deluge [delyooj] *n* pot'vynis, liūtis'

delve [delv] *v* kas'ti, kapsty'ti, įsigi'linti

demand [dimaand] *n* reikala'vimas,
po'reikis

demerit [deemerit] *n* trū'kumas, yda',
defek'tas

demolish [dimolish] *v* griau'ti, prary'ti

demur [dimė́r] *v* abejo'ti, svyruo'ti, prieštarau'ti

demure [dimyūr] *adj* rim'tas, kuklus'

dense [dense] *adj* tan'kus, tirš'tas, bukapro'tis

deny [dinī́] *v* neig'ti, atsisaky'ti

departure [dipaarcher] *n* išvyki'mas, išvažia'vimas

department [dipaartment] *n* ministe'rija

depend [dipend] *v* priklausy'ti

depict [dipikt] *v* pieš'ti, vaizduo'ti, aprašy'ti

deport [dipōrt] *v* išsiųs'ti, liu'dyti, ištrem'ti

depose [dipouz] *v* paša'linti, nuvers'ti,

deposit [dipozit] *n* in'dėlis, už'statas, sluoks'nis

depot [deepou] *n* geležin'kelio stotis'

deprave [dipreiv] *v* tvir'kinti, gadin'ti

depress [dipres] *v* slopin'ti, spaus'ti, liū'dinti, ma'žinti

depth [depth] *n* gilu'mas, gy'lis, giluma'

deride [dirī́d] *v* išjuok'ti, pajuok'ti

descend [disend] *v* nusileis'ti, nulip'ti, užgriū'ti

describe [diskrī́b] *v* aprašy'ti, atvaizduo'ti, išreikš'ti

descry [diskrī́] *v* pastebė'ti, išskir'ti

desert [dezert] *n* dykuma', negyve'nama vieta'

deserve [dizẻrv] *v* nusipelny'ti, bū'ti vertam'

design [dizīn] *v* skir'ti, ketin'ti, planuo'ti, projektuo'ti

desire [dizīer] *n* troški'mas, no'ras, aistra'

desk [desk] *n* rašoma'sis sta'las, mokyk'los suo'las, redak'cija

despair [dispier] *n* nusivyli'mas, beviltišku'mas

desperate [desperit] *adj* bevil'tiškas, baisus'

despite [dispīt] *n* pyk'tis

despoil [dispoil] *v* grob'ti, atim'ti

despond [dispond] *v* netek'ti vilties', nusimin'ti

destine [destin] *v* paskir'ti, lem'ti

destiny [destinee] *n* liki'mas, lemtis'

destroy [distroi] *v* griau'ti, naikin'ti

detach [ditach] *v* atskir'ti, atriš'ti, atkabin'ti

detail [deeteil] *n* smulk'mena, deta'lė

detain [ditein] *v* užlaiky'ti, sulaiy'ti, trudy'ti

detect [ditekt] *v* atras'ti, išaiš'kinti,

deter [ditẻr] *v* atbaidy'ti, sulaiky'ti susek'ti

determined [ditẻrmind] *adj* ryžtin'gas

detest [ditest] *v* neapkęs'ti, bjaurė'tis

detour [deitye] *n* lanks′tas, aplinki′nis ke′lias

detract [ditrakt] *v* ma′žinti, že′minti

devastate [devesteit] *v* nunioko′ti, nusiaub′ti

develop [divelep] *v* vys′tytis, la′vintis, išaiš′kinti

device [divīs] *n* prie′monė, bū′das, pla′nas, devi′zas

devil [devil] *n* vel′nias, nelaba′sis

devote [divout] *v* atsiduo′ti, atsidė′ti

devout [divaut] *adj* nuolankus′, pagarbus′, nuoširdus′

dew [dyoo] *n* rasa′, šviežu′mas, skaistu′mas

dewlap [doolap] *n* pagurk′lis, paliau′kis

diary [dīeree] *n* dieno′raštis, dieny′nas

dictionary [diksheneree] *n* žody′nas

die [dī] *v* mir′ti

differ [difer] *v* skir′tis, nesutar′ti

different [diferent] *adj* skirtin′gas, ki′tas

difficult [difikelt] *adj* sunkus′, var′ginantis

dig [dig] *v* kas′ti, suras′ti, išsijuo′sus, dirb′ti

digest [dijest] *n* virš′kinti, supras′ti

dignity [dignitee] *n* oru′mas, kilnu′mas, diduo′menė

dike [dīk] *n* py′limas, už′tvanka, griovys′

diligent [dilijent] *adj* stropus´, uolus´, rūpestin´gas

dill [dil] *n* kra´pas

dilute [diloot] *v* skies´ti, silp´ninti

dim [dim] *adj* neaiš´kus, miglo´tas, blankus´

din [din] *n* ūžesys´, bildesys´

dine [dīn] *v* pietau´ti

dinner [diner] *n* pie´tūs

dip [dip] *v* merk´ti, paner´ti, sem´ti

dipper [diper] *n* sam´tis, kau´šas

direct [direkt] *adj* tiesus´, tiesio´ginis, tikslus´

dirt [dėrt] *n* pur´vas, že´mė, dirva´, grun´tas

dirty [dėrtee] *adj* pur´vinas, nešvarus´

disabled [diseibeld] *adj* sužalo´tas

disaccord [disekōrd] *v* nesutar´ti

disaffirm [discfėrm] *v* paneig´ti, panaikin´ti

disagree [disegree] *v* nesutik´ti, nesutar´ti, prieštarau´ti

disappear [disepeer] *v* išnyk´ti, ding´ti, prapul´ti

disappoint [disepoint] *v* apvil´ti, apgau´ti

disapprove [diseproov] *v* nepritar´ti

disarray [diserei] *n* netvarka´, suiru´tė

disaster [dizaaster] *n* nelai´mė, ne´gandas

disavow [disevau] *v* neig´ti, atsisaky´ti, išsigin´ti

disbelieve [disbileev] *v* nepasitikė'ti, abejo'ti

disburse [disbėrs] *v* išmokė'ti, apmokė'ti

discern [disėrn] *v* išskir'ti, atskir'ti, pažinti

discharge [dischaarj] *v* atleis'ti, iškrau'ti, išleis'ti

disclaim [diskleim] *v* atsisaky'ti, atsižadė'ti

disclose [disklouz] *v* atskleis'ti, paro'dyti, demaskuo'ti

discontent [diskentent] *n* nepasiten'kinimas, ap'maudas

discover [diskuver] *v* atras'ti, atskleis'ti, išaiš'kinti

discrete [diskreet] *adj* ats'kiras, pavie'nis

discretion [diskreshen] *n* atsargu'mas, nuo'žiūra

discuss [diskus] *v* svarsty'ti, diskutuo'ti

disdain [disdein] *n* panieka', išdidu'mas, pasipūti'mas

disease [dizeez] *n* liga'

disengage [disengeij] *v* išvaduo'ti, atpalaiduo'ti, nusikraty'ti

disgrace [disgreis] *n* nemalo'nė, negarbė', gė'da

disgust [disgust] *n* pasibjaurė'jimas

dish [dish] *n* dubuo', lėkštė', val'gis, patie'kalas

dishevelled [disheveld] *adj* pasišiau ́šęs

dismal [dizmel] *adj* niūrus ́, liūd ́nas,
prislėg ́tas

dismay [dismei] *n* bai ́mė, iš ́gąstis

dismiss [dismis] *v* atleis ́ti, paleis ́ti,
nutrauk ́ti, atidė ́ti

disorder [disōrder] *n* netvarka ́, liga ́,
bruzdė ́jimas

disown [disoun] *v* atsisaky ́ti, nepripažin ́ti

dispel [dispel] *v* išsklaidy ́ti, išblašky ́ti

dispensable [dispensebel] *adj* nebū ́tinas

dispensary [dispenseree] *n* ambulato ́rija

dispense [dispens] *v* išdaly ́ti, atleis ́ti,
atpalaiduo ́ti

display [displei] *v* paro ́dyti, išdėlio ́ti,
išstaty ́ti

dissipated [disepeited] *adj* išblašky ́tas,
ištvir ́kęs, pasilei ́dęs

distance [distens] *n* nuo ́tolis, atstu ́mas

distinct [distinkt] *adj* ryškus ́, aiš ́kus,
ats ́kiras, ypatin ́gas

distinguish [distingwish] *v* atskir ́ti, išskir ́ti

distort [distōrt] *v* iškreip ́ti, iškraipy ́ti

distract [distrakt] *v* atitrauk ́ti, išblašky ́ti,
suglu ́minti

distribute [distribyoot] *v* skirs'tyti, dalin'ti, pla'tinti

district [distrikt] *n* sritis', apy'garda, rajo'nas

disturb [distėrb] *v* trukdy'ti, ardy'ti

ditch [dich] *n* griovys', *v* patir'ti ava'riją

dive [dīv] *v* ner'ti, įsiskverb'ti, įkiš'ti

diverse [divėrs] *adj* įvairus', skirtin'gas

divide [divīd] *v* daly'ti, smul'kinti, atskir'ti

divorce [divōrs] *n* skyry'bos, atsiskyri'mas

dizzy [dizee] *adj* svaigi'nantis

do [doo] *v* dary'ti, veik'ti, atlik'ti

dog [dog] *n* šuo'

dole [doul] *n* pašalpa'

doll [dōl] *n* lėlė'

dollar [doler] *n* do'leris

dolt [doult] *n* kvailys', bukapro'tis

domestic [demestik] *adj* nami'nis, šeimy'ninis, prijaukin'tas

donkey [donkee] *n* a'silas

doom [doom] *n* lemtis', liki'mas, pražūtis'

door [dōr] *n* du'rys

dormitory [dōrmitouree] *n* studen'tų bendra'butis

dot [dot] *n* taš'kas

double [dubel] *adj* dvi'gubas, dvejo'pas *adv* du'kartus'

doubt [daut] *n* abejo'nė

dough [dou] *n* tešla', pas'ta

dove [duv] *n* balan'dis

down [daun] *prp* žemyn'

downy [daunee] *adj* pūkuo'tas, minkš'tas, gudrus'

doze [douz] *v* snaus'ti

drab [drab] *n* apsilei'dėlė, ne'vala

draff [draf] *n* at'matos, pa'mazgos, pa'dugnės

draft [draaft] *n* būrys', skers'vėjis, trauka'

drag [drag] *v* vilk'ti, trauk'ti

drain [drein] *v* sau'sinti, išsem'ti

draw [drō] *v* pieš'ti, braižy'ti, išrašy'ti

drawback [drōbak] *n* trū'kumas, kliūtis'

drawing room [drōing room] *n* svečių' kambarys'

dread [dred] *v* bijo'ti

dream [dreem] *n* svajo'nė, sap'nas

dreary [drearee] *adj* liūd'nas, niūrus'

dress [dres] *v* apsireng'ti, pasipuoš'ti, *n* drabu'žiai, sukne'lė, rū'bai

dressmaker [dresmeiker] *n* siuvė'ja

drift [drift] *n* srovė', plauki'mas, kryptis', pusnis'

drill [dril] *v* gręž'ti

drink [drink] *v* ger'ti, girtau'ti, *n* gurkš'nis

drip [drip] *v* varvė'ti, lašė'ti

drive [drīv] *v* vary'ti, per'sekioti, važiuo'ti, vairuo'ti

driver [drīver] *n* vairuo'tojas, mašinis'tas, šo'feris

drizzle [drizel] *v* lyno'ti, dulk'ti

drop [drop] *n* la'šas

drought [draut] *n* sausra

drown [draun] *v* skęs'ti, skandin'ti

drug [drug] *n* vais'tas, narko'tikas

drum [drum] *n* būg'nas, būgne'lis

drunk [drunk] *adj* gir'tas, apsvai'gęs

dry [drī] *adj* sau'sas, nuobodus'

dual [dyooel] *adj* dvily'pis, dvejo'pas

duck [duk] *n* an'tis

due [dyoo] *adj* priklausąs', pri'deramas, tin'kamas

dull [dul] *adj* bu'kas, kvai'las, nuobodus', niūrus'

duly [dyoolee] *adv* rei'kiamai, pri'deramai, laiku'

dumb [dum] *adj* nebylus', nekalbus', kvai'las

dump [dump] *n* šiukšly'nas, lau'žas
dune [dyoon] *n* ko'pa
dung [dung] *n* mėš'las, trąša'
during [dyooring] *prp* metu', per'
dusk [dusk] *n* prie'blanda, prie'tema
dust [dust] *n* dul'kės, pelenai'
duty [dyootee] *n* pareiga', prie'volė, budė'jimas
dwarf [dwōrf] *n* nykštu'kas, neuž'auga
dwell [dwel] *v* gyven'ti
dye [dī] *v* dažy'ti *n* spalva', dažai'

E

each [eech] *prn* kiekvie'nas
eager [eeger] *adj* karštai', uo'liai
eagle [eegel] *n* ere'lis
ear [ear] *n* ausis', klausa'
early [ėrlee] *adv* anksti', laiku'
earn [ėrn] *v* uždirb'ti, nusipelny'ti
earnest [ėrnist] *adj* rim'tas, svarbus', nuoširdus', uolus'
earring [earing] *n* aus'karas
earth [ėrth] *n* že'mė, že'mės rutulys', sausuma'
east [eest] *n* rytai'
Easter [eester] *n* Vely'kos

easy [eezee] *adj* leng'vas, pato'gus

eat [eet] *v* val'gyti, ės'ti

echo [ekou] *n* ai'das, pamėg'džiojimas

edge [ej] *n* aš'menys, kraš'tas, briauna'

edit [edit] *v* ruoš'ti spau'dai, redaguo'ti

edition [idishen] *n* leidi'mas

editor [editer] *n* redak'torius

educate [edyūkeit] *v* auk'lėti, mo'kyti, švies'ti

eel [eel] *n* ungurys'

efface [ifeis] *v* nutrin'ti, išbrauk'ti, išdil'dyti

effect [ifekt] *n* veiks'mas, pasekmė', efek'tas

effort [efert] *n* pastanga', ban'dymas, jėgų' įtempi'mas

effuse [ifyooz] *v* lie'ti, skleis'ti

egg [eg] *n* kiauši'nis

eglantine [eglenteen] *n* erškė'tis

egregious [igreejes] *adj* nepa'prastas, negirdė'tas

eight [eit] *num* aštuoni'

eighteen [eiteen] *num* aštuonio'lika

eighty [eitee] *num* aštuoniasde'šimt

either [īther] *prn* vie'nas iš' dviejų', tas' ar ki'tas, ar'ba

eject [ijekt] *v* išvary'ti, iškraus'tyti, išmes'ti

elaborate [ilabereit] *v* detaliai′ paruoš′ti, vys′tyti, to′bulinti

elbow [elbou] *n* alkū′nė

elder [elder] *adj* vyres′nis

elect [ilekt] *v* išrink′ti

elephant [elefent] *n* dramb′lys

eleven [ileven] *num* vienuo′lika

eliminate [ilimineit] *v* paša′linti,išskir′ti, panaikin′ti

elk [elk] *n* brie′dis

else [els] *adv* dar′, be to′, kitaip′, prie′šingu at′veju

elude [ilood] *v* veng′ti, apei′ti, išsisuk′ti

embassy [embesee] *n* pasiuntiny′bė

embog [imbog] *v* įklimp′ti

embolden [embouldn] *v* padrą′sinti, ska′tinti

embowel [embauel] *v* išdarinė′ti, išmėsinė′ti

embrace [imbreis] *v* apkabin′ti, pripažin′ti, suvok′ti, apim′ti

embroider [imbroider] *v* išsiuvinė′ti, pagra′žinti

emerald [emereld] *n* smarag′das

emerge [imėrj] *v* pasiro′dyti, iškil′ti, atei′ti

emit [imit] *v* spinduliuo′ti, skleis′ti, išleis′ti

emotion [imoushen] *n* jau′dinimasis, emo′cija

emperor [emperer] *n* impera'torius

empire [empīer] *n* impe'rija

employ [emploi] *v* samdy'ti, naudo'ti, varto'ti

empower [empauer] *v* įgalio'ti

empty [emptee] *adj* tuš'čias

enable [eneibel] *v* įga'linti, duoti' tei'sę

enact [enakt] *v* įsaky'ti, nutar'ti, skelb'ti, vaidin'ti

encase [enkeis] *v* pakuo'ti

enchant [enchaant] *v* sužavė'ti

enclose [enklouz] *v* apim'ti, įdė'ti, aptver'ti

encourage [enkurij] *v* padrą'sinti, parem'ti, ra'ginti

encroach [enkrouch] *v* įsiverž'ti, pasikėsin'ti

end [end] *n* ga'las, pabaiga',

endue [endyoo] *v* įgalio'ti, suteik'ti riba'

endurance [endyūrens] *n* ištvermingu'mas, kantry'bė

enemy [enemee] *n* prie'šas, prie'šininkas

engage [engeij] *v* išnuomo'ti, pasamdy'ti, įjung'ti, užim'ti

engine [enjen] *n* mašina', garvežys', varik'lis

enigma [enigme] *n* mįslė'

enjoy [enjoi] *v* gėrė'tis, patik'ti

enmesh [enmesh] *v* įpai'nioti

enormous [inōrmes] *adj* didžiu'lis, baisus'

enough [inuf] *adv* pakan'ka, gana'

enrage [enreij] *v* siu'tinti

enrapture [enrapcher] *v* žavė'ti

enrobe [enroub] *v* apreng'ti

enrol [enroul] *v* registruo'ti, įsto'ti

ensure [enshūr] *v* garantuo'ti, užtik'rinti

entangle [entengel] *v* įpai'nioti, įtrauk'ti, pagau'ti

enter [enter] *v* įei'ti, įsto'ti

enterprise [enterpīz] *n* į'monė, iniciaty'va, apsukru'mas

entertain [entertein] *v* priim'ti, vaišin'ti, links'minti

entice [entīs] *v* gun'dyti, vilio'ti

entire [entīer] *adj* vi'sas, pil'nas, iš'tisas

entrance [entrens] *n* įėji'mas

entreat [entreet] *v* maldau'ti

envelope [enveloup] *n* vo'kas, ap'valkalas

envious [envies] *adj* pavydus'

envy [envee] *n* pavy'das

equal [eekwel] *adj* ly'gus, vieno'das, atitin'kamas

equip [ikwip] *v* aprū'pinti, apginkluo'ti, teik'ti

erase [ireis] *v* itrin'ti, išskus'ti, išdil'dyti

erect [irekt] *v* įreng'ti, pastaty'ti, ištes'ti
err [er] *v* klys'ti
erupt [irupt] *v* išsiverž'ti, prasikal'ti
escape [eskeip] *v* pabég'ti, išveng'ti,
ištrūk'ti, išsigel'béti
escort [eskōrt] *n* apsauga', sargy'ba
especial [espeshel] *adj* ypatin'gas, specialus'
especially [espeshelee] *adv* y'pač
essay [esei] *n* apy'braiža, rašinys
establish [establish] *v* įkur'ti, įsteig'ti,
įsikur'ti
esteem [esteem] *v* gerb'ti
estimate [estimeit] *n* ver'tinimas, są'mata
esurient [esūrient] *adj* al'kanas, godus'
eternal [itérnel] *adj* am'žinas, tvir'tas,
nesikeičiąs'
evade [iveid] *v* veng'ti, išsisuk'ti,
nepasiduo'ti
evaluate [ivalyooeit] *v* įver'tinti
eve [eev] *n* iš'vakarés
even [eeven] *adj* ly'gus, vieno'das, panašus',
adv net'
evening [eevning] *n* va'karas
evenminded [eevenmīndid] *adj* ramus',
šaltakrau'jis
event [ivent] *n* į'vykis, atsitiki'mas

ever [ever] *adv* kada' nors'

every [evree] *adj* kiekvie'nas

evict [ivikt] *v* išvary'ti, iškraus'tyti, iškel'ti

evident [evident] *adj* aiš'kus, akivaizdus'

evil [eevel] *n* blogy'bė, nelai'mė, nuodėmė'

evince [ivins] *v* paro'dyti, pareikš'ti

exact [igzakt] *adj* tikslus', tik'ras

exaggerate [igzajereit] *v* per'dėti

example [igzaampel] *n* pavyzdys'

exceed [ikseed] *v* vir'šyti, pralenk'ti

excellent [ekselent] *adj* puikus

except [iksept] *v* išskir'ti, *prp* iššky'rus, be'

excerption [eksėrpshen] *n* fragmen'tas, citata'

exchange [ikscheinj] *v* keis'ti, pakeis'ti

excite [iksit] *v* sukel'ti, jau'dintis, er'zinti

exciting [iksīting] *adj* jau'dinantis, įdomus'

exclaim [ikskleim] *v* sušuk'ti

exclude [iksklood] *v* išskir'ti, neprileis'ti

excrescence [ikskresens] *n* auglys', navi'kas

excuse [ikskyooz] *v* atsiprašy'ti, atleis'ti, dovano'ti

execute [eksekyoot] *v* įvyk'dyti, atlik'ti

exemplar [igzempler] *n* pavyzdys', egzemplio'rius

exempt [igzempt] *v* atleis'ti, išim'ti

exercise [eksersīz] *n* prati′mas, mankšta′
exert [igzėrt] *v* įsitemp′ti
exhale [igzeil] *v* įkvėp′ti, garuo′ti, ga′rinti
exhaust [igzōst] *v* išsek′ti, išsem′ti, išeikvo′ti
exhibition [eksebishen] *n* paroda′,
paro′dymas
exhort [igzōrt] *v* įkalbinė′ti, įti′kinti
exist [igzist] *v* bū′ti, egzistuo′tì
expect [ikspekt] *v* lauk′ti, tikė′tis, many′ti
expel [ikspel] *v* išvary′ti, ištrem′ti
expend [ikspend] *v* išeikvo′ti, išleis′ti
expense [ikspens] *n* iš′laidos, vertė′, kai′na
expensive [ikspensiv] *adj* brangus′
experience [ikspeeriens] *n* patyri′mas
expert [ekspėrt] *n* žino′vas, specialis′tas,
eksper′tas
expiate [ekspieit] *v* išpirk′ti, atpirk′ti
explain [iksplein] *v* aiš′kinti
explicit [iksplisit] *adj* aiš′kus, tikslus′,
api′brėžtas
explode [iksploud] *v* sprog′ti, pratrūk′ti
explore [ikspōr] *v* tir′ti, tyrinė′ti
explosion [iksplouzhen] *n* sprogi′mas
expose [ekspouzei] *v* išstaty′ti
exposition [ekspezishen] *n* išdės′tymas,
paroda′, išlai′kymas

expound [ikspaund] *v* išdės'tyti, išaiš'kinti
express [ikspres] *v* išreikš'ti, išspaus'ti
extend [ikstend] *v* ištęs'ti, il'ginti, išplės'ti
extent [ikstent] *n* il'gis, plo'tas, dy'dis
exterior [iksteerier] *n* iš'orė, iš'vaizda
external [ikstėrnl] *adj* išori'nis, užsieni'nis
extort [ikstōrt] *v* išplėš'ti, iškvos'ti
extract [ikstrakt] *v* ištrauk'ti, išim'ti
extraordinary [ikstrōrdneree] *adj*
nepa'prastas, ypatin'gas, keis'tas
extreme [ikstreem] *adj* kraštuti'nis,
paskuti'nis, prie'šingas, didžiau'sias
extricate [ekstrekeit] *v* išpai'nioti,
išnarp'lioti, išspręs'ti
extrude [ikstrood] *v* išstum'ti, išspaus'ti
exude [igzood] *v* sunk'tis
exult [igzult] *v* džiaug'tis, džiū'gauti
eye [ī] *n* akis', kilpe'lė
eyebrow [ībrau] *n* an'takis

F

fable [feibel] *n* pa'saka, me'las, siuže'tas
face [feis] *n* vei'das
facile [fasīl] *adj* leng'vas, lais'vas,
paviršuti'niškas
fact [fakt] *n* fak'tas, į'vykis, reiškinys'

fad [fad] *n* arkliu′kas, y′pač mėgs′tamas daly′kas, už′gaida

fade [feid] *v* vys′ti, bluk′ti, nyk′ti

fag [fag] *v* dirb′ti, triūs′ti, pails′ti, pavarg′ti

fail [feil] *v* stoko′ti, trūk′ti, nusilp′ti, nesugebė′ti

faint [feint] *adj* silp′nas, nusil′pęs

fair [fier] *adj* gražus′, pakan′kamas, gied′ras, šviesus′

faith [feith] *n* tikė′jimas, ištikimy′bė

fake [feik] *v* padirb′ti, suklasto′ti, *n* klasto′tė

falcon [fōlken] *v* sa′kalas

fall [fōl] *v* kris′ti, sugriū′ti, nusileis′ti, žū′ti

false [fōls] *adj* klaidin′gas, melagin′gas, dirbti′nis

family [familee] *n* šeima′, šeimy′na, giminė′

famine [famin] *n* ba′das, bada′vimas

famous [feimes] *adj* garsus′, ži′nomas, puikus′

fan [fan] *n* mėgė′jas, ša′lininkas, sirga′lius

fancy [fansee] *n* vaizduo′tė, už′gaidas, mėgs′tamas daly′kas, *adj* vaizdin′gas

fang [fang] *n* il′tis, danties′ šaknis′

far [faar] *adv* toli′, žy′miai

fare [fier] *n* mo′kestis už′ važia′vimą, kelei′vis

farm [faarm] *n* ū'kis, fer'ma

farther [faarther] *adj* toliau'

fascinate [fasineit] *v* žavė'ti

fashion [fashen] *n* mada', bū'das

fast [faast] *adj* stiprus', grei'tas, tvir'tas

fasten [faasen] *v* pririš'ti, pritvir'tinti, suspaus'ti, suseg'ti

fat [fat] *adj* riebus', taukuo'tas, sto'ras, nupenė'tas

fate [feit] *n* liki'mas, lemtis', pražūtis'

father [faather] *n* tė'vas, pra'dininkas, pro'tėvis

fatigue [feteeg] *n* nuo'vargis

fault [fōlt] *n* klaida', trū'kumas, yda', kaltė'

favor [feiver] *n* palanku'mas, malo'nė, simpa'tija, nauda'

fear [fear] *n* bai'mė, būkš'tavimas, nuogąsta'vimas

feast [feest] *n* šven'tė, puota', ba'lius, malonu'mas

feather [fether] *n* plunks'na, plunks'nų danga'

feature [feecher] *n* vei'do bruo'žai, ypaty'bė, savy'bė

February [febrooeree] *n* vasa'ris

feckless [feklis] *adj* silp'nas, bejė'gis, nenaudin'gas

fecund [feekend] *adj* derlin'gas, vaisin'gas

fee [fee] *n* atly'ginimas, mo'kestis, arbat'pinigiai

feed [feed] *v* maitin'ti, penė'ti, šer'ti, aprū'pinti

feel [feel] *v* jaus'ti, jus'ti, per'gyventi

feign [fein] *v* apsimes'ti, dė'tis, išsigalvo'ti

felicity [filisitee] *n* lai'mė, pasiseki'mas

fellow [felou] *n* drau'gas, bičiu'lis

felon [felen] *n* nusikal'tėlis

female [feemeil] *n* moteris', pate'lė

fence [fens] *n* tvora', už'tvara

fennel [fenl] *n* kra'pas

ferial [feariel] *adj* pap'rastas, kasdie'nis

fern [fėrn] *n* papar'tis

ferret [ferit] *n* šeš'kas *v* suuos'ti, raus'tis, ieško'ti

ferry [feree] *v* per'vežti, per'kelti

fertile [fėrtl] *adj* derlin'gas, našus', vaisin'gas

fester [fester] *v* pūliuo'ti

fetch [fech] *v* atnešti, atgaben'ti, atves'ti, trauk'ti

fever [feever] *n* karš'tis, karščia'vimas, karšt'ligė

few [fyoo] *adj* nedau'gelis, nedaug', ma'ža

fib [fib] *v* prasimany'ti, meluo'ti

fiction [fikshen] *n* prasima'nymas, beletris'tika, fik'cija

fiddle [fidl] *n* smui'kas

field [feeld] *n* lau'kas, pie'va, sritis', rajo'nas

fierce [fears] *adj* žiaurus', smarkus', nemalonus'

fifteen [fifteen] *num* penkio'lika

fifty [fiftee] *num* pen'kiasde'šimt

fight [fīt] *v* kovo'ti, kau'tis, grum'tis, kariau'ti

file [fīl] *n* eilė', greta', ap'lankas, byla'

fill [fil] *v* pripil'dyti, priso'tinti, paten'kinti

filthy [filthee] *adj* nešvarus', bjaurus', šlykštus', nešvankus'

final [fīnel] *adj* galuti'nis, baigiama'sis

find [fīnd] *v* rast'ti, susek'ti, išaiš'kinti

fine [fīn] *n* bauda', *adj* švelnus', puikus'

finger [finger] *n* pirš'tas

finish [finish] *v* baig'ti, nutrauk'ti, nusto'ti

fir [fėr] *n* eg'lė

fire [fīer] *n* ugnis', liepsna', gais'ras, lau'žas

firm [fėrm] *adj* stiprus', tvir'tas, atsparus', *n* fir'ma

first [fėrst] *num* pir'mas

fish [fish] *n* žuvis'

fist [fist] *n* kumš'tis, ranka'

fit [fit] *v* tik'ti, pritai'kyti

five [fīv] *num* penki'

fix [fiks] *v* pritvir'tinti, nustaty'ti, pritrauk'ti, užkietė'ti

flag [flag] *n* vė'liava, plokš'tė

flake [fleik] *n* snieguo'lės, snai'gės, dribs'niai

flame [fleim] *n* liepsna', mei'lė, aistra'

flap [flap] *v* nukar'ti, skrajo'ti, mosuo'ti, plasno'ti

flare [flier] *v* deg'ti, liepsno'ti

flash [flash] *v* spindė'ti, tvyks'telėti

flat [flat] *n* bu'tas, *adj* plokš'čias, lygus', seklus', vieno'das

flavor [fleiver] *n* sko'nis, kva'pas

flax [flaks] *n* linai', lini'niai dirbi'niai

flay [flei] *v* lup'ti, skus'ti

flea [flee] *n* blusa'

fleck [flek] *n* dėmė'

fleece [flees] *v* nulup'ti, nukirp'ti, prievartau'ti

flight [flīt] *n* skridi'mas, būrys', laip'tai

flimsy [flimzee] *adj* trapus', nepatvarus'

flinch [flinch] *v* išsisukinė'ti, atsitrauk'ti

fling [fling] *v* pul'ti, šok'ti, mes'ti, svies'ti, blokš'ti

flint [flint] *n* tit'nagas

flip [flip] *n* sprig'tas, pliaukš'telėjimas

flippant [flipent] *adj* nerim'tas, lengvabū'dis, įžūlus'

flirt [flėrt] *v* flirtuo'ti, koketuo'ti

float [flout] *v* plauk'ti, plūduriuo'ti, skrajo'ti

flock [flok] *n* būrys', banda', minia', pul'kas

flood [flud] *v* patvin'ti, siūb'telėti

floor [flōr] *n* grin'dys, aukš'tas, sa'lė

flour [flauer] *n* mil'tai, milte'liai

flout [flaut] *v* nie'kinti, ty'čiotis

flow [flou] *v* tekė'ti, sroven'ti, daugė'ti

flower [flauer] *n* žie'das, gėlė'

flu [floo] *n* gri'pas

fluent [flooent] *adj* sklandus', te'kantis, skys'tas

fluid [flooid] *n* skys'tis

flush [flush] *v* paplūs'ti, švirkš'ti, paraus'ti, siūb'telėti

fly [flī] *n* mu'sė *v* skris'ti, skubė'ti, dum'ti

foam [foum] *v* puto'ti

foe [fou] *n* prie'šas

fog [fog] *n* rū'kas, ū'kana, migla'

foist [foist] *v* įbruk'ti, įkiš'ti, įsiū'lyti

fold [fould] *v* sudė'ti, sulanksty'ti, suklos'tyti, apkabin'ti

folk [foulk] *n* liau'dis, žmo'nės

follow [folou] *v* sek'ti, ei'ti iš paskos', supras'ti

fond [fond] *adj* my'lintis, švelnus', meilus'

food [food] *n* mais'tas

fool [fool] *n* kvailys', be'protis, juokdarys'

foot [fūt] *n* ko'ja, pė'da

for [fōr] *prp* per', į', už', dėl'

forbid [fōrbid] *v* uždraus'ti

force [fōrs] *n* jėga'

forecast [fōrkaast] *v* numaty'ti

forehand [fōrhand] *adj* išanksti'nis

forefinger [fōrfinger] *n* smi'lius

forehead [forid] *n* kakta'

foreign [forin] *adj* užsieni'nis

foreknow [fōrnou] *v* numaty'ti

foreman [fōrmen] *n* meis'tras, darbų' vyk'dytojas

foremost [fōrmous] *adv* pirma', pirmiau'sia

forest [forist] *n* miš'kas, giria'

forever [fōrever] *adv* amžinai', visiems' laikams'

forget [ferget] *v* užmirš'ti, neprisimin'ti

forgive [fergiv] *v* atleis'ti, dovano'ti

fork [fōrk] *n* ša'kės, šaku'tės

form [fōrm] *n* for'ma, pavi'dalas, iš'vaizda

foreword [fōrwėrd] *n* į'žanga, pratarmė

former [fōrmer] *adj* bu'vęs, ankstes'nis

forsake [fōrseik] *v* apleis'ti, atsisaky'ti, palik'ti

fortnight [tortnit] *n* dvi' savai'tės

fortune [fōrchen] *n* lai'mė

forty [fōrtee] *num* ke'turiasde'šimt

forward [fōrwerd] *adv* pirmyn', į prie'kį, toliau'

four [fōr] *num* keturi'

fowl [faul] *n* nami'nis paukš'tis

fox [foks] *n* la'pė

fracture [frakcher] *n* įtrūki'mas, įskili'mas

fragile [frajel] *adj* trapus', dūž'tamas, silp'nas

frame [freim] *v* įrė'minti, apipavi'dalinti, kur'ti, staty'ti

frank [frank] *adj* at'viras, nuoširdus

fraud [frōd] *n* apgavi'kas, suk'čius

frazzle [frazel] *n* suiri'mas, skarmalai'

freak [freek] *n* už'gaidas, į'noris, išdai'ga
free [free] *adj* lais'vas, išlais'vintas
freedom [freedem] *n* lais've
freeze [freez] *v* šal'ti, pašal'ti, sting'ti
frequent [freekwent] *adj* daž'nas, dažnai' pasikarto'jantis
fresh [fresh] *adj* šviežias, nau'jas, švarus', gė'las, žvalus'
Friday [frīdee] *n* penkta'dienis
friend [frend] *n* drau'gas, drau'gė, bičiu'lis
fright [frīt] *n* iš'gąstis, baidyk'lė
frog [frog] *n* varlė'
from [from] *prp* iš', nuo'
front [frunt] *n* fasa'das, priešakys'
frost [frost] *n* šal'tis, spei'gas, šerkš'nas
frown [fraun] *v* susirauk'ti, bū'ti nepaten'kintam
fruit [froot] *n* vai'sius, vai'siai
frustration [frustreishen] *n* suar'dymas, žlugi'mas
fry [frī] *v* kep'ti
fuel [fyooel] *n* ku'ras
fulfil [fūlfil] *v* atlik'ti, įvyk'dyti, užbaig'ti
full [fūl] *adj* pil'nas, vi'sas
fume [fyoom] *n* dū'mai, garai'

fun [fun] *n* juo'kas, pokš'tas, malonu'mas, džiaugs'mas

funeral [fyoonerel] *n* lai'dotuvės

funny [funee] *adj* juokin'gas, keis'tas

furious [fyūries] *adj* įsiu'tęs, įdū'kęs

furniture [fėrnicher] *n* bal'dai, vi'sas apsta'tymas

further [fėrther] *adv* toliau', be to', toles'nis, se'kantis

fuss [fus] *n* sam'brūzdis, susirū'pinimas

fusty [fustee] *adj* tvankus', troškus'

future [fyoocher] *n* ateitis', bū'simas lai'kas, *adv* būsima'sis

G

gain [gein] *v* uždirb'ti, gau'ti, įsigy'ti, pasiek'ti, laimė'ti

gall [gōl] *n* tulžis', įžūlu'mas, akiplėšišku'mas

game [geim] *n* žaidi'mas, pramoga', par'tija, varžy'bos

gammon [gamen] *n* kum'pis, apgau'lė, nesą'monė

gander [gander] *n* žą'sinas, kvailys', ve'dęs vy'ras

gap [gap] *n* tar′pas, plyšys′, spraga′, skir′tumas

gape [geip] *v* žio′vauti, žiopso′ti, plačiai′ išsižio′ti

garden [gaarden] *n* so′das, par′kas, dar′žas

gargle [gaargel] *v* skalau′ti gerklę′

garlic [gaarlic] *n* česna′kas

garment [gaarment] *n* drabu′žis, drabu′žiai

garret [gɑrit] *n* pasto′gė, palė′pė

gas [gas] *n* du′jos, benzi′nas, degalai

gasp [gaasp] *v* uždus′ti, išsižio′ti iš nustebi′mo

gate [geit] *n* var′tai, varte′liai, už′tvara

gather [gather] *v* rink′ti, skin′ti, kaup′ti

gauge [geij] *n* ma′tas, maste′lis, dy′dis, kalib′ras

gawk [gōk] *n* pus′galvis

gay [gei] *adj* links′mas, *n* homoseksualis′tas

gaze [geiz] *v* atidžiai′ žiūrė′ti, spokso′ti

gender [jender] *n* giminė′

general [jenerel] *adj* bend′ras, pa′prastas, vyriau′sias

generate [jenereit] *v* pagimdy′ti, sukel′ti, gamin′ti

generous [jeneres] *adj* dosnus′, kilnus′

genesis [jenisis] *n* kilmė′

gentle [jentl] *adj* švelnus', ramus', kilmin'gas

get [get] *v* gau'ti, pasiek'ti, atei'ti, tap'ti

ghost [goust] *n* vaiduok'lis, dvasia', šešė'lis

giant [jīent] *n* mil'žinas

gift [gift] *n* dovana', ta'lentas

giggle [gigel] *v* kiken'ti

gin [jin] *n* degti'nė, dži'nas

Gipsy [jipsee] *n* čigo'nas

girl [gėrl] *n* mergai'tė, mergina'

give [giv] *v* duo'ti, atiduo'ti, dovano'ti, mokė'ti

glad [glad] *adj* paten'kintas, links'mas

glamor [glamer] *v* žavė'ti

glance [glaans] *v* žvilgtelėti, blykstelėti

glare [glier] *n* aštrus' žvilgs'nis, spindė'jimas

glass [glaas] *n* stik'las, stikli'nė, tau'rė

gleam [gleem] *n* silpna' šviesa', atspindys', pro'švaistė

glide [glīd] *v* slys'ti, praslys'ti

glitter [gliter] *v* blizgė'ti

gloom [gloom] *adj* nusimi'nęs, niūrus', liūd'nas

glory [glōree] *n* šlovė'

glove [gluv] *n* pirš'tinė

glue [gloo] *n* klijai' *v* klijuo'ti

gnat [nat] *n* uo'das

go [gou] *v* ei'ti, vaikš'čioti, važiuo'ti, vyk'ti

goal [goul] *n* tiks'las, var'tai, į'vartis

goat [gout] *n* ožys', ožka'

god [god] *n* die'vas

gold [gould] *n* auk'sas

good [gūd] *adj* ge'ras, malonus', gabus'

goods [gūdz] *n* pre'kės, daiktai', tur'tas, krovinys'

goose [goos] *n* žąsis'

gooseberry [goosberee] *n* agras'tas

gorge [gōrj] *n* gerklė', ryklė'

gossip [gosep] *v* liežuvau'ti

govern [guvern] *v* valdy'ti

gown [gaun] *n* mo'teriškas drabu'žis, sukne'lė

grab [grab] *v* grieb'ti, užgrob'ti

grace [greis] *n* gra'cija, grakštu'mas, palanku'mas, malo'nė

grade [greid] *n* laips'nis, rūšis', koky'bė, kla'sė

graduate [grajooeit] *v* baig'ti universite'tą ar mokyk'lą

grain [grein] *n* grū'das, javai', kruope'lė

grandchild [granchīld] *n* anū'kas

grandfather [granfaather] *n* sene'lis, diedu'kas

grandmother [granmuther] *n* močiu´tė,
bobu´tė

grape [greip] *n* vyn´uogė

grasp [graasp] *v* grieb´ti, pagau´ti, supras´ti

grass [graas] *n* žolė´, ganykla´

grate [greit] *v* trin´ti, griež´ti, er´zinti

gratitude [gratityood] *n* dėkingu´mas

grave [greiv] *n* ka´pas, *adj* liūd´nas, rim´tas,
sunkus´

gravel [greivel] *n* žvy´ras

gravy [greivee] *n* pa´dažas

gray [grei] *adj* pil´kas, ži´las

grease [grees] *n* taukai´, riebalai´

great [greit] *adj* di´delis, didy´sis, didžiu´lis

greedy [greedee] *adj* godus´

green [green] *adj* ža´lias, nesubren´dęs,
neprity´ręs

greet [greet] *v* svei´kinti

grief [greef] *n* var´gas, nelai´mė

grime [grīm] *n* suo´džiai, nešvaru´mas

grin [grin] *v* šaipy´tis, ro´dyti dantis

grind [grīnd] *v* mal´ti, griež´ti, galąs´ti

grip [grip] *v* suspaus´ti, pagrieb´ti

grocery [grouseree] *n* bakalė´jinių pre´kių
krau´tuvė

ground [graund] *n* že'mė, dirva', pa'grindas, dug'nas

group [groop] *n* gru'pė, fra'kcija

grow [grou] *v* aug'ti, didė'ti, tap'ti, dary'tis

guard [gaard] *n* sargy'ba, apsauga', sargy'binis

guess [ges] *v* atspėti, many'ti

guest [gest] *n* sve'čias, viešnia'

guide [gīd] *v* vadovau'ti, ves'ti

guilty [giltee] *adj* kal'tas

gulp [gulp] *v* go'džiai ry'ti *n* gurkš'nis

gum [gum] *n* dan'tenos, guma', *v* klijuo'ti

gun [gun] *n* šau'tuvas, patran'ka

gust [gust] *n* gū'sis, išsiverži'mas, pro'trūkis

gut [gut] *n* žarna', viduriai'

guy [gī] *n* vaiki'nas, baidyk'lė

H

haberdashery [haberdasheree] *n* galante'rija

habit [habit] *n* į'protis, paprotys', įprati'mas

hag [hag] *n* ra'gana

hair [hier] *n* plau'kas, plaukai'

half [haaf] *n* pu'sė

hall [hōl] *n* sa'lė, prieš'kambaris, vestibiu'lis

ham [ham] *n* kum'pis, šlaunis'

hammer [hamer] *n* plaktu'kas, kū'jis

hand [hand] *n* ranka', rodyk'lė, rašy'sena

handkerchief [hankercheef] *n* no'sinė, skepetai'tė

handle [handl] *n* ran'kena, proga', pre'tekstas

handsome [hansem] *adj* gražus', stuomenin'gas, žymus'

handy [handee] *adj* patogus', vikrus', apsukrus'

hang [hang] *v* kabė'ti, kabin'ti, kar'ti

happen [hapen] *v* atsitik'ti, įvyk'ti

happy [hapee] *adj* laimin'gas, paten'kintas

harbor [haarber] *n* uos'tas, prie'glauda

hard [haard] *adj* kie'tas, tvir'tas, sunkus'

hardly [haardlee] *adv* vos', ko'ne, vargu'

hare [hier] *n* kiš'kis

harm [haarm] *n* žala'

harvest [haarvist] *n* pjūtis', der'lius, vai'siai

haste [heist] *v* skubė'ti, sku'binti

hat [hat] *n* skrybėlė'

hate [heit] *v* neapkęs'ti

haul [hōl] *v* trauk'ti, per-vež-ti

haunch [hōnch] *n* šlaunis'

have [hav] *v* turė'ti, privalė'ti, saky'ti

haven [heiven] *n* uos'tas, prie'glauda

hawk [hōk] *n* va'nagas

hay [hei] *n* šie'nas

haze [heiz] *n* rū'kas, migla'

he [hee] *prn* jis'

head [hed] *n* galva', viršū'nė, va'das

headache [hedeik] *n* galvos' skaus'mas

health [helth] *n* sveikata'

heap [heep] *n* krūva', daugy'bė

hear [heer] *v* girdė'ti, išklausy'ti, sužino'ti

heart [haart] *n* širdis'

heat [heet] *n* kaitra', karš'tis, šiluma'

heaven [heven] *n* dangus'

heavy [hevee] *adj* sunkus', smarkus',
grioz'diškas

hedge [hej] *n* tvora', gyva'tvorė, kliūtis'

heed [heed] *n* dėmesys', atsargu'mas

heel [heel] *n* kul'nas

height [hīt] *n* aukš'tis, ū'gis, aukštuma'

hell [hel] *n* pra'garas

help [help] *v* padė'ti, pagel'bėti, vaišin'ti

hen [hen] *n* višta'

her [hėr] *prn* jos', jai', ją'

herb [hėrb] *n* au'galas, žolė'

here [heer] *adv* čia'

herring [hering] *n* sil'kė

herself [herself] *prn* pati', save'

hesitate [heziteit] *v* svyruo'ti, dvejo'ti, nesiryž'ti

hew [hyoo] *v* kapo'ti

hiccup [hikup] *v* žagsė'ti

hide [hīd] *v* slėp'ti, slapsty'ti

hideous [hīdies] *adj* baisus', bjaurus'

high [hī] *adj* aukš'tas, di'delis

hike [hīk] *v* keliau'ti pėsčiomis', valkatau'ti, žygiuo'ti

hill [hil] *n* kalva', krūva'

hint [hint] *n* aliu'zija, užuo'mina

hire [hīer] *v* samdy'ti, nuomo'ti

hiss [his] *v* šnypš'ti, nušvilp'ti

hit [hit] *v* smog'ti, kirs'ti, suduo'ti

hoar [hōr] *adj* ži'las *n* šerkš'nas, migla', senat'vė

hoarse [hōrs] *adj* kimus', užki'męs

hog [hog] *n* mei'tėlis, šer'nas, kiau'lė

hold [hould] *v* laiky'ti, išlaiky'ti, užim'ti

hole [houl] *n* skylė', ur'vas, ola'

holiday [holidei] *n* šven'tė, atos'togos

hollow [holou] *adj* tuš'čias, tuščiavidu'ris

holy [houlee] *adj* šven'tas

home [houm] *n* na'mas, tėvy'nė, prie'glauda

honest [onist] *adj* do'ras, są'žiningas

honey [hunee] *n* medus', miela'sis

honor [oner] *n* garbė' *v* gerb'ti
hoof [hoof] *n* kano'pa
hook [hūk] *n* kablys'
hoop [hoop] *n* lan'kas, ra'tas, rė'kavimas
hope [houp] *n* viltis'
horn [hōrn] *n* ra'gas
hornet [hōrnit] *n* šir'šė
horror [horer] *n* bai'mė, siau'bas, iš'gąstis
horse [hōrs] *n* arklys', žir'gas
hospitality [hospitalitee] *n* svetingu'mas,
vaišingu'mas
host [houst] *n* šeiminin'kas, minia', daugy'bė
hostess [houstis] *n* šeiminin'kė
hot [hot] *adj* karš'tas
hotel [houtel] *n* vieš'butis
hour [auer] *n* valanda'
house [hauz] *n* na'mas
how [hau] *adv* kaip', kokiu' būdu'
howl [haul] *v* staug'ti, kauk'ti
huge [hyooj] *adj* mil'žiniškas
human [hyoomen] *adj* žmogaus'
humble [humbel] *adj* nuolankus', paklusnus'
humid [hyoomid] *adj* drėg'nas
hunch [hunch] *v* kūp'rintis, lenk'ti
hundred [hundrid] *num* šim'tas
hunger [hunger] *n* ba'das *v* badau'ti

hunt [hunt] *v* medžio'ti
hurry [huree] *v* sku'binti, skubė'ti
hurt [hėrt] *v* sužeis'ti, sumuš'ti, užgau'ti
husband [huzbend] *n* vy'ras
hush [hush] *v* nutil'ti, nutil'dyti *int* ša',
tylėk'!

I

ice [īs] *n* le'das, ledai'
icicle [īsikel] *n* varvek'lis
idle [īdl] *adj* tingus', tuš'čias, nenaudin'gas
if [if] *cnj* jei'gu, jei', visuomet', kai'
ill [il] *adj* ser'gantis, nesvei'kas, blo'gas
illegitimate [ilijitemeit] *adj* netei'sėtas,
neteisin'gas
illicit [ilisit] *adj* netei'sėtas, už'draustas
image [imij] *n* at'vaizdas, paveiks'las
imagination [imajeneishen] *n* fanta'zija,
vaizduo'tė, įsivaizda'vimas
imbecile [imbiseel] *adj* silpnapro'tis, kvai'las
immediate [imeedeeit] *adj* betar'piškas,
neatidėlio'tinas, skubus'
immense [imens] *adj* didžiu'lis,
neaprė'piamas
immoral [imōrel] *adj* nepado'rus

immortal [imōrtl] *adj* nemirtin′gas, am′žinas

impart [impaart] *v* duo′ti, suteik′ti, praneš′ti, per′duoti

impatient [impeishent] *adj* nekantrus′

impeach [impeech] *v* abejo′ti, apkal′tinti

impel [impel] *v* išju′dinti, paska′tinti, pastūmė′ti

impend [impend] *v* grės′ti, pakib′ti, slink′ti, artė′ti

impetuous [impechooes] *adj* veržlus′, karš′tas, staigus′

implicate [implekeit] *v* įvel′ti, įtrauk′ti, įpai′nioti

implicit [implisit] *adj* supran′tamas, numa′nomas

important [impōrtent] *adj* svarbus′, reikšmin′gas

impossible [imposebel] *adj* nega′limas, neįvyk′domas

impost [impoust] *n* mo′kestis, duok′lė

impress [impres] *v* nuste′binti, antspauduo′ti, įteig′ti

improve [improov] *v* page′rinti, to′bulinti, gerė′ti

impudent [impyedent] *adj* begė'diškas,
aki'plėšiškas; įžūlus'
in [in] *prp* per', po'
inbred [inbred] *adj* į'gimtas, iš' prigimties'
incise [insīz] *v* įpjau'ti, išpjau'ti
incite [insīt] *v* kursty'ti, ra'ginti
inclination [inkleneishen] *n* nuo'lydis,
nuotaku'mas, palinki'mas
income [inkum] *n* pa'jamos, už'darbis
incommode [inkemoud] *v* var'ginti, trukdy'ti
increase [inkrees] *v* aug'ti, didė'ti, smarkė'ti
incredible [inkredebel] *adj* neį'tikimas
indeed [indeed] *adv* iš' tikrų'jų, nejau'gi
independent [indipendent] *adj*
nepriklau'somas, savaran'kiškas
indicate [indekeit] *v* paro'dyti, nuro'dyti,
įsaky'ti, pranašau'ti, lem'ti
indict [indīt] *v* apkal'tinti
indignation [indigneishen] *n* pasipik'tinimas
induce [indyoos] *v* paska'tinti, para'ginti,
įti'kinti
induct [indukt] *v* įkur'dinti, įtaisy'ti,
įskaity'ti
indue [indyoo] *v* apdovano'ti, suteik'ti
inept [inept] *adj* netin'kamas, ne vie'toj,
kvai'las

inference [inferens] *n* iš'vada
infect [infekt] *v* užkrės'ti
infertile [infėrtīl] *adj* bevai'sis, nederlin'gas
influence [inflooens] *n* į'taka
inherit [inherit] *v* pavel'dėti
initial [inishel] *adj* pirmi'nis, pradi'nis
injure [injer] *v* pakenk'ti, sužeis'ti, įžeis'ti
ink [ink] *n* ra'šalas
inn [in] *n* vieš'butis
inner [iner] *adj* vidi'nis, slap'tas
innocent [inesent] *adj* nekal'tas,
nežalin'gas, naivus', neišma'nėlis
inquire [inkweīer] *v* klaus'ti, teirau'tis,
tyrinė'ti
insane [insein] *adj* pami'šęs, psi'chiškai
nesvei'kas
insert [insėrt] *v* įdė'ti, išspausdin'ti
laik'raštyje
inside [insīd] *adv* viduje', į vi'dų
insist [insist] *v* primygtinai' reikalau'ti,
užsispir'ti
insolent [inselent] *adj* aki'plėšiškas, įžūlus'
instance [instens] *n* pavyzdys', reikala'vimas
instant [instent] *adj* primygti'nis,
neatidėlio'jamas
instead [insted] *adj* vie'toj, užuot'

insult [insult] *v* įžeis'ti
intend [intend] *v* ketin'ti, turė'ti galvoje'
intent [intent] *n* keti'nimas, tiks'las
interfere [interfear] *v* įsikiš'ti, trukdy'ti, susidur'ti
interrupt [interupt] *v* per'traukti
into [intū] *prp* į'
introduce [intredyoos] *v* įves'ti, supažin'dinti, pateik'ti, įtrauk'ti
intrude [introod] *v* įsiverž'ti, įsibrau'ti
invent [invent] *v* išras'ti, išgalvo'ti
invisible [invizebel] *adj* nema'tomas
involve [involv] *v* įtrauk'ti, įpai'nioti, įvel'ti
irk [ėrk] *v* nuvar'ginti, įkyrė'ti, er'zinti
iron [īren] *n* geležis', laidy'nė, lygintu'vas
irritate [iritcit] *v* er'zinti, ner'vinti
island [īlend] *n* sala'
issue [isyoo] *n* leidi'mas, leidinys', išeitis'
it [it] *prn* jis', ji', tai'
itself [itself] *prn* pats', save' patį'

J

jab [jab] *v* stum'dyti, bady'ti, įkiš'ti
jacket [jakit] *n* švar'kas, ap'valkalas
jag [jag] *n* viršū'nė, smaigalys'
jam [jam] *n* uogie'nė, *v* suspaus'ti, kimš'ti

January [janyooeree] *n* sau'sis
jar [jaar] *n* ąso'tis, stiklai'nis
jaunt [jaant] *v* pasivažinė'ti, pasivaikš'čioti
jaw [jō] *n* žandi'kaulis
jealous [jeles] *adj* pavydus', įtarus'
jest [jest] *n* juo'kas, są'mojis
jew [joo] *n* žy'das
jewel [jooel] *n* brangeny'bė, brang'akmenis
job [job] *n* dar'bas, užduotis', užsiėmi'mas, tarny'ba
jog [jog] *v* stum'dyti, stum'ti, kraty'ti
join [join] *v* sujung'ti, suriš'ti, prisidė'ti
joke [jouk] *n* juo'kas, są'mojis, pokš'tas
jolly [jolee] *adj* links'mas, gy'vas
journey [jėrnee] *n* kelio'nė, pasivažinė'jimas
joy [joi] *n* džiaugs'mas
judge [juj] *n* tesė'jas, žino'vas, *v* teis'ti, sprę's'ti
jug [jug] *n* ąso'tis
juice [joos] *n* sul'tys, sy'vai
July [joolī] *n* lie'pa
jump [jump] *v* šok'ti, šokinė'ti
June [joon] *n* birže'lis
junior [joonyer] *adj* jaunes'nis, jaunesny'sis
just [just] *adj* teisin'gas, tin'kamas, *adv* taip', kaip' tik', ką' tik'

justice [justis] *n* teisingu′mas, teisėtu′mas
justify [justefī] *v* patei′sinti, ištei′sinti,
patvir′tinti

K

keen [keen] *adj* aštrus′, ve′riantis, stiprus′,
energin′gas
keep [keep] *v* laiky′ti, sau′goti, bū′ti, toliau′
ką′ nors′ dary′ti
key [kee] *n* rak′tas, tо′nas, klavi′šas
kick [kik] *v* spir′ti, spar′dyti, atšok′ti
kid [kid] *n* ožiu′kas, vai′kas, apgau′lė
kidney [kidnee] *n* inks′tas, bū′das
kill [kil] *v* užmuš′ti, nužudy′ti, sunaikin′ti,
nuste′binti
kin [kin] *n* giminė′, šeima′
kind [kīnd] *n* rūšis′ *adj* ge′ras, malonus′,
paslaugus′
kindle [kindl] *v* uždeg′ti, padeg′ti
king [king] *n* kara′lius
kink [kink] *n* maz′gas, kil′pa
kiss [kis] *n* bučinys′, pabučia′vimas
kitchen [kichen] *n* virtu′vė
kitten [kitn] *n* kačiu′kas
knack [nak] *n* mokė′jimas, į′gūdis, į′protis

knave [neiv] *n* niek'šas, apgavi'kas, nenau'dėlis

knee [nee] *v* klaup'tis, klūpo'ti

knife [nīf] *n* pei'lis

knit [nit] *v* megz'ti, surauk'ti, jung'tis

knock [nok] *v* bels'ti, muš'ti, suduo'ti, barben'ti

knot [not] *n* maz'gas, kamuolys', sunku'mas

know [nou] *v* žino'ti, pažin'ti, sužino'ti

known [noun] *adj* ži'nomas, garsus'

L

labor [leiber] *n* da'rbas, triū'sas

lace [leis] *n* bat'raištis, nėriniai'

lack [lak] *n* trū'kumas, stoka'

lad [lad] *n* vaiki'nas

lade [leid] *v* krau'ti, pakrau'ti

ladle [leidl] *n* sam'tis, *v* semti

lady [leidee] *n* ponia', dama'

lake [leik] *n* e'žeras

lamb [lam] *n* ėriu'kas

lame [leim] *adj* rai'šas, luo'šas

land [land] *n* sausuma', že'mė, *v* išlip'ti, nusileis'ti

landscape [landskeip] *n* peiza'žas, landšaf'tas

lane [lein] *n* ta'kas, skers'gatvis, praėjimas

languid [langwid] *adj* išgle'bęs, neveiklus', nuobodus'

lank [lank] *adj* lie'sas, ištį'sęs

lapse [laps] *n* klaida', neapsižiūrė'jimas, tar'pas

lard [laard] *n* kiau'lės taukai'

large [laarj] *adj* di'delis, erdvus'

lark [laark] *n* vieversys', juokai', pokš'tas

lash [lash] *n* bota'gas, blakstie'na

lassitude [lasityood] *n* nuo'vargis, pavargi'mas

last [laast] *adj* paskuti'nis, praė'jęs, *v* tęs'tis, truk'ti

late [leit] *adj* vėly'vas, vėlus', pavėla'vęs

latter [later] *adj* nese'nas, pastara'sis

laud [lōd] *v* gir'ti, gar'binti

laugh [laaf] *n* juo'kas, *v* juok'tis

law [lō] *n* įsta'tymas, dės'nis, tei'sė

lawn [lōn] *n* pieve'lė, gazo'nas, veja'

lax [laks] *adj* silp'nas, neapi'brėžtas, palai'das

lay [lei] *v* dėti

lazy [leizee] *adj* tingus'

lead [leed] *v* ves'ti, vadovau'ti, ra'ginti

leaf [leef] *n* la'pas

leak [leek] *v* tekė'ti, prakiur'ti, prasisunk'ti
lean [leen] *v* palink'ti, atsirem'ti, atsišlie'ti
learn [lėrn] *v* mo'kytis, sužino'ti
lease [lees] *v* išnuomo'ti
least [leest] *adj* mažiau'sias
leather [lether] *n* oda', dir'žas
leave [leev] *n* leidi'mas, *v* iškeliau'ti, palik'ti, apleis'ti
leech [leech] *n* siurbėlė', dėlė', prievartau'tojas
left [left] *adj* kairy'sis, kairė'
leg [leg] *n* ko'ja
legible [lejebel] *adj* įskai'tomas, aiš'kus
leisure [lezher] *n* laisva'laikis
lemon [lemen] *n* citrina'
lend [lend] *v* sko'linti, suteik'ti, duo'ti
length [length] *n* il'gis, nuo'tolis, ilgu'mas
less [les] *adj* mažes'nis, *adv* mažiau'
lesson [lesen] *n* pamoka'
let [let] *v* leis'ti
letter [leter] *n* raidė', laiš'kas
level [level] *n* ly'gis, lyguma'
liar [līer] *n* mela'gis
lick [lik] *v* laižy'ti, muš'ti, pralenk'ti
lid [lid] *n* dang'tis, viršus', akies' vo'kas
lie [lī] *n* me'las, apgavys'tė

lie [lī] *v* gulė'ti, bū'ti
life [līf] *n* gyve'nimas
lift [lift] *v* pakel'ti, pakil'ti
light [līt] *n* šviesa', apšvieti'mas, ugnis', žiburys'
lightning [lītning] *n* žai'bas
like [līk] *adj* panašus' *v* patik'ti, mėg'ti
likely [līklėe] *adj* ga'limas, tin'kamas
liken [līken] *v* paly'ginti
lime [līm] *n* lie'pa
line [līn] *n* li'nija, riba', sie'na, brūkšnys'
linen [linen] *n* dro'bė, baltiniai'
link [link] *n* grandis', jungtis'
lion [līen] *n* liū'tas
lip [lip] *n* lū'pa, kraš'tas
liquid [likwid] *n* skys'tis
list [list] *n* są'rašas, pakraštys'
lithe [līth] *adj* lankstus'
little [litl] *adj* ma'žas, men'kas *adv* nedaug', mažai'
live [liv] *v* gyven'ti, gyvuo'ti
live [līv] *adj* gy'vas, tik'ras, realus'
liver [liver] *n* ke'penys, kepenė'lės
lizard [lizerd] *n* drie'žas
loaf [louf] *n* ke'palas, bulku'tė, dykinė'jimas
loan [loun] *n* paskola'

local [loukel] *adj* vie'tinis, papli'tęs
locate [loukeit] *v* įsikur'ti, apsigyven'ti
lock [lok] *n* gar'bana, sruo'ga, už'raktas, spyna'
lodge [loj] *n* name'lis, būde'lė, lo'žė
loft [loft] *n* palė'pė, aukš'tas, dar'žinė
log [log] *n* rąs'tas, rasti'galis
lone [loun] *adj* vie'nišas, negyve'namas, nuošalus'
long [long] *v* aistrin'gai norė'ti, steng'tis, *adj* il'gas, lė'tas
look [lūk] *v* žiūrė'ti, pažvelg'ti, sek'ti, atro'dyti
loop [loop] *n* kil'pa
lose [loos] *adj* lais'vas, platus', palai'das
lose [looz] *v* pames'ti, praras'ti
loss [los] *n* neteki'mas, praloši'mas, nuos'tolis
lot [lot] *n* bur'tas, daugy'bė, ai'bė
loud [laud] *adj* garsus', triukšmin'gas
louse [laus] *n* utėlė'
love [luv] *n* mei'lė, įsimylė'jimas, *v* norė'ti, mylė'ti, mėg'ti
low [lou] *adj* že'mas, silp'nas, niūrus'
lucid [loosid] *adj* šviesus', skaidrus', aiš'kus
luck [luk] *n* liki'mas, pasiseki'mas, lai'mė

lucre [looker] *n* pel'nas, nauda'

lug [lug] *v* tampy'ti, trauk'ti, vilk'ti

lumber [lumber] *n* šlamš'tas, staty'binis miš'kas

lump [lump] *n* ga'balas, kąs'nis, lui'tas, krūva'

lunch [lunch] *n* prieš'piečiai

lung [lung] *n* plau'tis

lure [lūr] *v* vilio'ti, gun'dyti, žavė'ti

luscious [lushes] *adj* saldus', sultin'gas

lust [lust] *n* geidulys', geis'mas

lynx [links] *n* lūšis'

M

mad [mad] *adj* pakvai'šęs, be'protis

magic [majik] *adj* ma'giškas, stebuklin'gas, bur'tų

magnificent [magnifisent] *adj* didin'gas, puošnus', nuostabus'

magpie [magpī] *n* šar'ka, plepys'

maid [meid] *n* mergai'tė, mergina', kambari'nė, tarnai'tė

main [mein] *adj* svarbiau'sias, pagrindi'nis, vyriau'sias

maintain [meintein] *v* palaiky'ti, parem'ti, tvir'tinti, teig'ti

maize [meiz] *n* kukurū′zai

major [meijer] *adj* dides′nis, vyres′nis, svarbes′nis

make [meik] *v* dary′ti, dirb′ti, gamin′ti, privers′ti

male [meil] *n* vy′ras, pa′tinas

malice [malis] *n* pyk′tis

malign [melīn] *adj* prie′šiškas, žalin′gas, blo′gas

man [man] *n* žmogus′, vy′ras

manage [manij] *v* vadovau′ti, susidoro′ti, mokė′ti, pajėg′ti

manful [manfel] *adj* vy′riškas

mankind [mankīnd] *n* žmonija′, vy′rai

mansion [manshen] *n* pas′tatas, rū′mai

manual [manyooel] *adj* ran′kinis, ran′kų

manufacture [manyefakcher] *v* gamin′ti

manuscript [manyeskript] *n* rank′raštis, origina′las

many [menee] *adv* dau′gelis, daug′

map [map] *n* žemė′lapis, pla′nas

maple [meipel] *n* kle′vas

March [maarch] *n* ko′vas

mariner [marener] *n* jū′rininkas

mark [maark] *n* žymė′, ženk′las, pažymys′

market [maarkit] *n* tur′gus, rin′ka

marriage [marij] *n* san'tuoka, vedy'bos, vestu'vės

marry [maree] *v* ves'ti, ištekė'ti, sutuok'ti

marvelous [maarveles] *adj* stebuklin'gas, nuostabus'

mash [mash] *v* sutrin'ti, sugrūs'ti

master [maaster] *n* šeiminin'kas, mo'kytojas, meist'ras

match [mach] *n* degtu'kas, pora', varžy'bos

mate [meit] *n* drau'gas, pa'tinas, vy'ras

material [meteeriel] *n* medžiaga'

maternity [metėrnitee] *n* motinys'tė

matter [mater] *n* daly'kas, klau'simas, medžiaga'

mature [metyūr] *adj* pribren'dęs, suno'kęs

may [mei] *v* galiu', man' leis'ta

May [mei] *n* gegužė'

maybe [mcibee] *adv* galbūt'

me [mee] *prn* man', mane'

meadow [medou] *n* pie'va

meal [meel] *n* val'gis, val'gymas

mean [meen] *v* turė'ti galvoje', reikš'ti, ketin'ti

meaning [meening] *n* reikšmė', prasmė'

means [meenz] *n* prie'monė, bū'das, tur'tas

measure [mezher] *v* matuo'ti, išmatuo'ti

meat [meet] *n* mėsa'
medial [meediel] *adj* viduri'nis
meek [meek] *adj* nuolankus', švelnus',
kuklus'
meet [meet] *v* susitik'ti, susirink'ti,
susipažin'ti
mellow [melou] *adj* nuno'kęs, išsir'pęs,
sultin'gas, sodrus'
melt [melt] *v* tirp'ti, ly'dyti, susigraudin'ti,
atsileis'ti
member [member] *n* narys'
menace [menis] *n* grąsi'nimas, grėsmė',
pavo'jus
mend [mend] *v* pataisy'ti, page'rinti
mental [mentl] *adj* pro'tinis, psi'chinis
mention [menshen] *v* minė'ti, užsimin'ti
mercury [mėrkyeree] *n* gyv'sidabris
mere [meer] *adj* aiš'kus, tik'ras
merge [mėrj] *v* įsiurb'ti, įtrauk'ti, susilie'ti
merit [merit] *n* nuo'pelnas
merrily [merilee] *adv* linksmai', gyvai'
mess [mes] *n* netvarka', maišatis',
nemalonu'mai
message [mesij] *n* praneši'mas, žinia',
laiš'kas

mettle [metl] *n* į'karštis, ener'gija, tempera'mentas

middle [midl] *n* vidurys'

midge [mij] *n* uo'das, ma'šlas

might [mīt] *n* galy'bė, galia'

mild [mīld] *adj* švelnus', romus', minkš'tas

milk [milk] *n* pie'nas

mince [mins] *v* kapo'ti, mal'ti, minkš'tinti

mind [mīnd] *n* pro'tas, atmintis', nuo'monė, mintis'

mine [min] *prn* ma'no

minor [mīner] *adj* mažes'nis, jaunes'nis

mint [mint] *n* mėta'

miracle [mirekel] *n* stebuk'las

mire [mīer] *n* pur'vas, liū'nas

mirror [mirer] *n* veid'rodis, *v* atspindė'ti

misery [mizeree] *n* nelai'mė, var'gas, skur'das

misfortune [misfōrchen] *n* nelai'mė, nepasiseki'mas

misguide [misgīd] *v* suklaidin'ti

miss [mis] *v* nepatai'kyti, praleis'ti, ilgė'tis

mist [mist] *n* migla', šerkš'nas

mistake [misteik] *n* klaida', suklydi'mas

mistress [mistris] *n* šeiminin'kė, mo'kytoja

mistrust [mistrust] *v* nepasitikė'ti

misunderstand [misunderstand] *adj*
neteisin'gai supras'ti

mix [miks] *v* sumaišy'ti, sujung'ti

moan [moun] *v* dejuo'ti, skųs'tis, apverk'ti

mock [mok] *v* er'zinti, pajuok'ti, ty'čiotis

moderate [modereit] *adj* nuosaikus',
viduti'nis, susival'dantis

modest [modist] *adj* kuklus'

moist [moist] *adj* drėg'nas, šla'pias

molest [melest] *v* var'ginti, kankin'ti, įkyrė'ti

Monday [mundee] *n* pirma'dienis

money [munee] *n* pinigai', tur'tai

monger [munger] *n* prekiau'tojas

monkey [munkee] *n* beždžio'nė

monster [monster] *n* pabai'sa, baidyk'lė,
išsigi'mėlis

month [munth] *n* mė'nuo

mood [mood] *n* nuo'taika

moon [moon] *n* mėnu'lis

more [mōr] *adj* dides'nis *adv* daugiau'

morning [mōrning] *n* ry'tas

moss [mos] *n* pel'kė, durpy'nė, sa'manos

most [moust] *adv* daugiau'sia

moth [moth] *n* kan'dis, druge'lis

mother [muther] *n* mo'tina

motion [moushen] *n* judė'jimas

mount [maunt] *n* kalva', kal'nas
mountain [maunten] *n* kal'nas
mourn [mōrn] *v* liūdė'ti, gedė'ti, raudo'ti
mouse [mauz] *n* pelė'
moustache [mestash] *n* ū'sai
mouth [mauth] *n* burna', anga', žio'tys
move [moov] *v* judė'ti, ju'dinti, kilno'ti
much [much] *adv* daug'
muck [muk] *n* mėš'las, pur'vas
mud [mud] *n* pur'vas, dumb'las
mushroom [mushroom] *n* gry'bas
must [must] *v* turiu', privalau'
mute [myoot] *adj* tylus',*n* nebylys'
mutton [mutn] *n* avie'na
mutual [myoochooel] *adj* abi'pusiškas,
savitar'pinis, bend'ras
my [mī] *prn* ma'no
mysterious [misteeries] *adj* paslaptin'gas,
neaiš'kus

N

nail [neil] *n* vinis', na'gas
naked [neikid] *adj* nuo'gas, pli'kas, at'viras,
aiš'kus
name [neim] *n* var'das, pavardė'
nap [nap] *v* snaus'ti

napkin [napkin] *n* servetė'lė, vys'tyklas

narrate [nareit] *v* pa'sakoti, atpa'sakoti

narrow [narou] *adj* siau'ras, ankš'tas, ribo'tas

nasty [nastee] *adj* bjaurus', šlykštus', baisus'

nation [neishen] *n* na'cija, tauta', valsty'bė, šalis'

native [neitiv] *adj* gimta'sis, į'gimtas, tėvy'ninis

naughty [nōtee] *adj* išdy'kęs, nepaklusnus', sugadin'tas

near [near] *v* arti', šalia', apie'

neat [neet] *adj* švarus', tvarkin'gas, tikslus', dailus'

necessary [nesiseree] *adj* bū'tinas, reikalin'gas, neišven'giamas

neck [nek] *n* kak'las, kakle'lis

need [need] *n* rei'kalas, stoka', bū'ti reikalin'gam, privalė'ti

needle [needl] *n* a'data

negate [neegeit] *v* neig'ti

neglect [niglekt] *v* nesirū'pinti, užleis'ti

neighbor [neiber] *n* kaimy'nas

neither [nīther] *adv* taip pat' ne', nė' vie'nas

nephew [nevyoo] *n* sūnė'nas, brola'vaikis

nest [nest] *n* liz'das, gūž'ta

never [never] *adv* niekada', nė' kar'to
new [nyoo] *adj* nau'jas, šviežias
news [nyooz] *n* žinia', ži'nios, naujie'na
next [nekst] *adv* ki'tas, se'kantis,
artimiau'sias
nice [nīs] *adj* ge'ras, malonus', dailus',
puikus'
niece [nees] *n* dukterė'čia
niggardly [nigerdlee] *adj* šykštus'
night [nīt] *n* naktis', va'karas, su'temos
nightingale [nītingeil] *n* lakštin'gala
nimble [nimbel] *adj* šaunus', vikrus', judrus'
nine [nīn] *num* devyni'
nip [nip] *v* gnai'byti, žnai'byti
no [nou] *neg* ne'
noble [noubel] *adj* kilnus'
nobody [noubedee] *n* nie'kas, menkys'ta
nod [nod] *v* link'telėti galva'
node [noud] *n* maz'gas
noise [noiz] *n* triukš'mas, nemalonus'
gar'sas
none [nun] *prn* nie'kas
nonsense [nonsens] *n* niekai', nesą'monė
noon [noon] *n* vidur'dienis, pusiau'dienis
noose [noos] *n* kil'pa
nor [nōr] *cnj* nei', taip pat'

north [nōrth] *n* šiau're

nose [nouz] *n* no'sis, nujauti'mas, uoslė'

nostril [nostre] *n* šner've

not [not] *adv* ne', nė'

note [nout] *n* pastaba', užrašai', gaida'

nothing [nuthing] *n* nie'kas, menk'niekis, nu'lis

notice [noutis] *v* pastebė'ti, *n* skelbi'mas, įspėji'mas, dėmesys'

notion [noushen] *n* suprati'mas, nuo'monė, keti'nimas

nourish [nurish] *v* maitin'ti, puo'selėti

novel [novel] *n* roma'nas, nove'lė

November [nouvember] *n* lap'kritis

now [nau] *adv* dabar', tuojau'

nowhere [nouwier] *adv* nie'kur

noxious [nokshes] *adj* kenksmin'gas, žalin'gas, nesvei'kas

nuclear [nyookleer] *adj* branduoli'nis, ato'minis

nude [nood] *adj* nuo'gas, pli'kas, negalio'jantis

nuisance [nyoosens] *n* sutriki'mas, truk'dymas

numb [num] *adj* sustin'gęs, susti'ręs, sugru'bęs

number [number] *n* skai'čius, kie'kis
nun [nun] *n* vienuo'lė
nurse [nėrs] *n* auk'lė, slau'gė
nut [nut] *n* rie'šutas

O

oak [ouk] *n* ą'žuolas
oar [ōr] *n* irk'las
oat [out] *n* a'vižos
oath [outh] *n* prie'saika
obedient [oubeedient] *adj* paklusnus',
nuolankus'
obese [oubees] *adj* nutu'kęs, apkūnus'
obey [oubei] *v* klausy'ti, nusilenk'ti, vyk'dyti
reikala'vimus
object [objikt] *n* daik'tas, tiks'las, ob'jektas
object [ebjekt] *v* prie'šintis, prieštarau'ti,
protestuo'ti
obligate [oblɛgeit] *v* įpareigo'ti
oblivious [eblivies] *adj* užmaršus',
išsiblaš'kęs
obscene [ebseen] *adj* nešvankus',
begė'diškas
obscure [ebskyūr] *adj* neaiš'kus, neryš'kus,
nepa'stebimas, įtar'tinas
observe [ebzerv] *v* stebė'ti, dary'ti pas'tabas

obsess [obses] *v* per'sekioti

obsolete [obseleet] *adj* pase'nęs, nebevarto'jamas

obstacle [obstekel] *n* kliūtis', truk'dymas

obstinate [obstenit] *adj* atkaklus', užsispy'ręs

obstruct [ebstrukt] *v* užvers'ti, užgrioz'dinti, užkimš'ti

obtain [ebtein] *v* gau'ti, laimė'ti, įgy'ti, tik'ti

obtrude [ebtrood] *v* įsiū'lyti, įpirš'ti

obtuse [ebtoos] *adj* bu'kas, nesupratin'gas, neišma'nėlis

obviate [obvieit] *v* veng'ti, ša'lintis, išvėng'ti

obvious [obvies] *adj* aiš'kus, akivaizdus'

occassion [ekeizhen] *n* proga', aplinky'bė, į'vykis

occupy [okyepī] *v* užim'ti, valdy'ti, okupuo'ti

occur [ekėr] *v* atsitik'ti, įvyk'ti, atei'ti į' gal'vą

ocean [oushen] *n* vandeny'nas, okea'nas

October [oktouber] *n* spa'lis

odd [od] *adj* nely'ginis, keis'tas, neį'prastas, lais'vas

odor [ouder] *n* kva'pas, aroma'tas, garbė'

of [ov] *prp* apie', iš'

off [of] *prp* nuo' *adj* to'limas, šaluti'nis

offense [ofens] *n* nusižengi'mas, skriauda'
offend [efend] *v* pažeis'ti, sulau'žyti, įžeis'ti
offer [ofer] *v* auko'ti, siū'lyti, teik'ti
office [ofis] *n* parega', vieta', raš'tinė, konto'ra
officer [ofiser] *n* pareigū'nas, ka'rininkas
often [ofen] *adv* dažnai', pakarto'tinai
oil [oil] *n* alie'jus, nafta'
old [ould] *adj* se'nas, įsisenė'jęs, seno'vinis
olive [oliv] *n* aly'va', alyv'medis
omen [oumen] *n* ženk'las, pranašys'tė
on [on] *prp* ant'
once [wuns] *adv* kar'tą, kadai'se
one [wun] *adj* vie'nas
oneself [wunself] *prn* save', save' patį'
onion [unyen] *n* svogū'nas
only [ounlee] *adv* tiktai', išimtinai', *cnj* bet', tik'
onto [ontoo] *prp* ant'
open [oupen] *adj* atidary'tas, at'viras, nuoširdus'
opinion [epinyen] *n* nuo'monė
opportunity [opertyoonitee] *n* proga', galimy'bė
or [ōr] *cnj* ar', ar'ba
oral [ōrel] *adj* žo'dinis, žodžiu'

orange [orinj] *n* apelsi′nas

orchard [orcherd] *n* vai′sių so′das

order [ōrder] *n* tvarka′, įsa′kymas, užsa′kymas

ordinary [ōrdneree] *adj* pa′prastas, eili′nis, įprasti′nis

ordure [ōrdyer] *n* mēš′las, at′matos, pur′vas

ore [ōr] *n* rūda′

origin [orijin] *n* šalti′nis, pradžia′, kilmė′

orphan [ōrfen] *n* našlai′tis

other [uther] *adj* ki′tas, kiti′

ought [ōt] *v* privalė′ti, turė′ti

our [auer] *prn* mū′sų

out [aut] *adv* už′, iš′orėj, iš

outcome [autkum] *n* rezulta′tas, iš′dava

outdated [autdeited] *adj* pase′nęs

outlet [autlet] *n* išėji′mas, anga′

outlook [autlūk] *n* vaiz′das, po′žiūris, perspekty′va

outrageous [autreijes] *adj* žiaurus′, įsiu′tęs, bepro′tiškas

outside [autsīd] *prp* už′ *adv* iš′ lau′ko, iš′orėje

oven [uven] *n* kros′nis

over [ouver] *prp* virš′, aukščiau′, po′, per′, apie′

overcoat [ouverkout] *n* apsiaus'tas, pal'tas, mili'nė

overcome [ouverkum] *v* nugalė'ti, įveik'ti, apim'ti

overcrowd [ouverkraud] *v* per'pildyti

overeat [ouvereet] *v* apsival'gyti, per'sivalgyti

overrun [ouverun] *v* užtvin'dyti, nioko'ti, siaub'ti

overtake [ouverteik] *v* pavy'ti, užklup'ti

owe [ou] *v* bū'ti skolin'gam, bū'ti dėkin'gam

owl [aul] *n* pelė'da

own [oun] *adj* sa'vas, nuo'savas

ox [oks] *n* jau'tis

oyster [oister] *n* aus'trė

P

pace [peis] *n* žings'nis, ei'sena

pacific [pesifik] *adj* ramus', taikin'gas

pack [pak] *n* ryšulys, pake'tas, kupri'nė, *v* sudė'ti

padlock [padlok] *n* spyna'

pain [pein] *n* skaus'mas, kentė'jimas

paint [peint] *n* dažai', *v* dažy'ti, tapy'ti

pair [pier] *n* pora', pamaina'

palace [palis] *n* rū'mai

pale [peil] *adj* išblyš'kęs, blankus'

palm [paam] *n* del'nas, pal'mė

palmful [paamfūl] *n* sau'ja

palmy [paamee] *adj* kles'tintis, žy'dintis

palsy [pōlzee] *n* paraly'žius

pamper [pamper] *v* le'pinti

pan [pan] *n* keptu'vė, prikaistu'vis

pang [pang] *n* aštrus' skaus'mas, šird'gėla

pantry [pantree] *n* san'dėlys, po'dėlis

pants [pants] *n* kel'nės, apati'nės kel'nės

paper [peiper] *n* po'pierius, laik'raštis, dokumen'tas

par [paar] *n* lygy'bė

paradise [paredīz] *n* ro'jus, dau'sos

paramount [paremaunt] *adj* svarbiau'sias, pirmaei'lis

parcel [paarsel] *n* ryšulys', pake'tas, siuntinys'

parch [paarch] *v* džiovin'ti, de'ginti, išdžiū'ti, sukep'ti

parent [pierent] *n* tė'vas, mo'tina, tėvai'

parley [paarlee] *n* dery'bos, pasitari'mas, aptari'mas

parrot [paret] *n* papū'ga

parsley [paarslee] *n* petra'žolė

part [paart] *n* dalis', or'ganas, dalyva'vimas, pu'sė

partake [paarteik] *v* dalyvau'ti, paragau'ti

participate [paartisipeit] *v* dalyvau'ti

particular [pertikyeler] *adj* ypatin'gas, savo'tiškas, skirtin'gas

party [paartee] *n* grupė', būrys', priėmi'mas, vakarė'lis, par'tija

pass [paas] *v* praei'ti, pravažiuo'ti, praleis'ti, per'duoti

passenger [pasenjer] *n* kelei'vis

passion [pashen] *n* aistra', mei'lė, prie'puolis

past [paast] *n* praeitis

pastry [peistree] *n* pyragai'tis, sausai'nis

patch [pach] *n* lo'pas, lopinys', dėmė', skiau'tė

path [paath] *n* ta'kas, ke'lias, šali'kelė

patience [peishens] *n* kantry'bė, atkaklu'mas

patter [pater] *v* barben'ti, tcšken'ti, trepsė'ti

pattern [patern] *n* pavyzdys', mo'delis, raš'tas

pauper [pōper] *n* betur'tis, el'geta

pavement [peivment] *n* grindinys', šali'gatvis

paw [pō] *n* le'tena

pawn [pōn] *n* už'statas, į'kaitas

pay [pei] *n* mo'kestis, alga', *v* mokė'ti, išmokė'ti

pea [pee] *n* žir'nis

peace [pees] *n* taika', ramy'bė

peach [peech] *n* per'sikas

peak [peek] viršū'nė, smaigalys'

pear [pier] *n* kriau'šė

peasant [pezent] *n* valstie'tis

peat [peet] *n* dur'pės

peck [pek] *v* les'ti, kapo'ti

peculiar [pikyoolyer] *adj* ypatin'gas, sa'vitas, keis'tas

peek [peek] *v* pažvelg'ti, pažiūrė'ti, žvilg'telėti

peel [peel] *v* valy'ti, lup'ti, skus'ti

peep [peep] *v* žvelg'ti, pasiro'dyti, žiūrė'ti pro' plyše'lį

peeve [peev] *n* ap'maudas

pelt [pelt] *n* kai'lis

pen [pen] *n* plunks'na, ra'šymo prie'monė

pencil [pensel] *n* pieštu'kas

penetrate [penitreit] *v* prasiskverb'ti, įei'ti, apim'ti, per'sisunkti

peony [pienee] *n* bijū'nas

people [peepl] *n* liau'dis, tauta', žmo'nės, gyven'tojai

pepper [peper] *n* pipi′ras
percent [persent] *n* pro′centas
perceptible [perseptebel] *adj* jun′tamas,
apčiuo′piamas, suvo′kiamas
perfect [pėrfikt] *adj* puikus′, to′bulas,
išbaigtas′
perform [perform] *v* atlik′ti, įvyk′dyti,
vaidin′ti
perfume [perfyoom] *n* kvepalai′, kva′pas,
aroma′tas
perhaps [perhaps] *adv* gal būt′
peril [perel] *n* pavo′jus, ri′zika
perish [perish] *v* žū′ti, mir′ti, žudy′ti,
naikin′ti
permit [permit] *v* leis′ti, prileis′ti
perplex [perpleks] *v* apstul′binti, supai′nioti,
pritrenk′ti
persecute [pėrsckyoot] *v* per′sekioti, įkyrė′ti
persist [persist] *v* užsispir′ti, atsilaiky′ti
person [pėrsen] *n* žmogus′, asmuo′,
asmeny′bė
persuade [persweid] *v* įti′kinti, įkalbė′ti
pervert [pervėrt] *v* iškraipy′ti, suvedžio′ti
pet [pet] *v* le′pinti, glamonė′ti
petrol [petrel] *n* benzi′nas, gazoli′nas
petroleum [petrouliem] *n* nafta′, ži′balas

pick [pik] *v* rink'ti, parink'ti, rūšiuo'ti
picture [pikcher] *n* paveiks'las,
paveikslė'lis, *v* piešti, įsivaizduo'ti
pie [pī] *n* pyra'gas, pyragai'tis
piece [pees] *n* ga'balas, dalis'
pierce [pears] *v* per'durti, per'smeigti,
per'verti
pig [pig] *n* kiau'lė, paršiu'kas
pigeon [pijen] *n* karve'lis, balandė'lė
pile [pīl] *n* krūva', šūs'nis *v* krau'ti, sukaup'ti
pillar [piler] *n* stul'pas, kolo'na
pillow [pilou] *n* pa'galvė, prie'galvis
pimple [pimpel] *n* spuo'gas
pin [pin] *n* segtu'kas, smeigtu'kas
pincers [pinserz] *n* rep'lės, žnyp'lės,
pince'tas
pinch [pinch] *v* įgnyb'ti, įžnyb'ti, spaus'ti, *n*
žiupsne'lis
pine [pīn] *n* pušis'
pineapple [pīnapel] *n* anana'sas
pink [pink] *n* gvazdi'kas *adj* ro'žinis,
ru'žavas
pipe [pīp] *v* vamz'dis, pyp'kė, švilpu'kas
pit [pit] *n* duobė', įdubi'mas, duobu'tė
pitcher [picher] *n* ąso'tis
pity [pitee] *n* gai'lestis, *v* gailė'ti, užjaus'ti

place [pleis] *n* vieta', vieto've, *v* de'ti, patalpin'ti

placid [plasid] *adj* le'tas, taikus'

plain [plein] *adj* aiš'kus, pa'prastas, supran'tamas, at'viras, lygus'

plait [pleit] *v* pin'ti, klos'tyti

plant [plaant] *n* au'galas, gamykla', fab'rikas, *v* sodin'ti

plate [pleit] *n* lekšte', la'pas, plokšte'le

play [plei] *n* žaidi'mas, pje'se, elgi'masis, *v* žais'ti, loš'ti, vaidin'ti

plea [plee] *n* pasitei'sinimas, dingstis', pre'tekstas

pleasant [plezent] *adj* malonus', links'mas

please [pleez] *v* patik'ti, suteik'ti malonu'mą

pleasure [plezher] *n* malonu'mas, po'megis

pledge [plej] *n* už'statas, į'kaitas

plenty [plentee] *adv* daug', gau'siai

plot [plot] *n* siuže'tas, fa'bula, są'mokslas

pluck [pluk] *v* skin'ti, peš'ti, rau'ti

plug [plug] *n* kamš'tis, kaiš'tis, uždegi'mo žva'ke

plum [plum] *n* sly'va

plump [plump] *adj* apvalus', apkūnus, pil'nas

plunge [plunj] *v* nar'dyti, pasiner'ti

plural [plūrel] *n* daugis'kaita, gausus'

pneumonia [nyūmounye] *n* plau'čių uždegi'mas

pocket [pokit] *n* kiše'nė, dėžė'

point [point] *n* taš'kas, punk'tas

poison [poizen] *n* nuodai', *v* nuo'dyti, užkrės'ti

Pole [poul] *n* len'kas, len'kė

polite [pelīt] *adj* mandagus'

poll [poul] *n* rinkė'jų są'rašas, balsa'vimas, balotira'vimasis

pond [pond] *n* basei'nas, tvenkinys', kū'dra

ponder [ponder] *v* apgalvo'ti, apsvarsty'ti, apmąsty'ti

pool [pool] *n* kla'nas, tvenkinys', basei'nas

poor [pūer] *adj* skurdus', vargin'gas, neturtin'gas

poppy [popee] *n* aguo'na

pork [pōrk] *n* kiaulie'na

porter [pōrter] *n* švei'corius, neši'kas, por'teris

possess [pezes] *v* valdy'ti, turė'ti

possibility [posebilitee] *n* galimy'bė

possibly [poseblee] *adv* kiek' ga'lima, ga'limas daik'tas, gal būt'

post [poust] *n* paš'tas, pos'tas

postman [poustmen] *n* laiškanešys'

post office [poustofis] *n* paš'tas, paš'to sky'rius

postpone [poustpoun] *v* atidė'ti

pot [pot] *n* puo'das, katiliu'kas

potato [peteitou] *n* bul'vė

pour [pōr] *v* ly'ti, lie'tis, pil'ti

poverty [povertee] *n* netur'tas, skur'das

powder [paudcr] *n* milte'liai, dul'kės, pud'ra

power [pauer] *n* jėga', galia', sugebė'jimas

praise [preiz] *v* gir'ti, gar'binti, liaup'sinti

pray [prei] *v* mels'tis, maldau'ti, prašy'ti

precaution [prikōshen] *n* įspėji'mas, atsargu'mas

precede [priseed] *v* bū'ti, įvyk'ti, vir'šyti

preceding [priseeding] *adj* ankstes'nis, ligšio'linis

precious [preshes] *adj* brangus', vertin'gas, rinkti'nis

precise [prisis] *adj* tikslus', api'brėžtas, punktualus', skrupulin'gas

predict [pridikt] *v* pranašau'ti

preface [prefis] *n* pratarmė', į'žanga

prefer [prifėr] *v* teik'ti pirmeny'bę, beve'lyti

pregnant [pregnent] *adj* nėščia'

prejudice [prejedis] *n* prie'taras, išanksti'nė nuo'monė

prepare [pripier] *v* ruoš'ti, pasiruoš'ti

presence [prezens] *n* buvi'mas, dalyva'vimas

present [prezent] *n* dabartis', dovana', *adj* e'santis, dalyvau'jantis

present [prizent] *v* atstovau'ti, bū'ti, pateik'ti, apdovano'ti

presently [prezentlee] *adv* netru'kus, tuojau' pat'

preserve [prizėrv] *v* sau'goti, konservuo'ti

press [pres] *v* spaus'ti, presuo'ti, sku'binti

pretend [pritend] *v* apsimes'ti, dė'tis, pretenduo'ti

pretty [pritee] *adj* gražus', puikus', malonus', žymus'

prevail [priveil] *v* vyrau'ti, nugalė'ti, paskleis'ti

prevent [privent] *v* sutrukdy'ti, įspė'ti, užkirs'ti ke'lią

previous [previes] *adj* ankstyves'nis, pirmes'nis, parengti'nis

price [prīs] *n* kai'na

prick [prik] *v* įdur'ti, dur'ti

pride [prīd] *n* išdidu'mas, pasididžia'vimas

priest [preest] *n* ku'nigas, šventi'kas

primal [prīmel] *adj* pirmi'nis, pagrindi'nis, pirmykš'tis

print [print] *n* ats'paudas, pėd'sakas, spauda', *v* spaus'dinti

prison [prizen] *n* kalė'jimas

private [prīvit] *adj* asme'ninis, privatus', atskir'tas, slap'tas

probable [probebel] *adj* ga'limas, spė'jamas, tikė'tinas

proceed [preseed] *v* tęs'ti, im'tis, pradė'ti

proceeds [prouseedz] *n* pa'jamos, į'plaukos

proclaim [prekleim] *v* paskelb'ti, praneš'ti, uždraus'ti

procreate [proukrieit] *v* pagimdy'ti

procure [proukyūr] *v* gau'ti, parū'pinti, tiek'ti

produce [predyoos] *v* pateik'ti, pristaty'ti, gamin'ti

proffer [profer] *n* pasiū'lymas, *v* siū'lyti

profit [profit] *n* nauda', pel'nas, pa'jamos

profound [prefaund] *adj* gilus', nuodugnus', valgus', išmintin'gas

profuse [prefyoos] *adj* gausus', dosnus', išlaidus'

prohibit [prouhibit] *v* uždraus'ti, trukdy'ti

prolong [prelong] *v* prail'ginti

prominent [promenent] *adj* žymus´, garsus´, iški´lęs

promise [promis] *n* pa´žadas

promote [premout] *v* paaukš´tinti, padė´ti, pagel´bėti

prompt [prompt] *v* paska´tinti, para´ginti, sufleruo´ti

pronounce [prenauns] *v* ištar´ti, paskelb´ti, pasisaky´ti

proof [proof] *n* įro´dymas, paro´dymas

proper [proper] *adj* tik´ras, teisin´gas, tin´kamas, į´prastas

property [propertee] *n* tur´tas, nuosavy´bė

propose [prepouz] *v* siū´lyti, pasipirš´ti, ketin´ti

propriety [reprīitee] *n* teisingu´mas, tinkamu´mas, padoru´mas

prosper [prosper] *v* klestė´ti, tarp´ti, dary´ti pa´žangą

protect [pretekt] *v* sau´goti, gin´ti, užtar´ti

protrude [proutrood] *v* išsikiš´ti

proud [praud] *adj* išdidus´, pasipū´tęs

prove [proov] *v* įro´dyti, paliu´dyti, bandy´ti

proverb [proverb] *n* patar´lė

provide [prevīd] *v* aprū´pinti, tiek´ti, im´tis prie´monių

pub [pub] *n* ali'nė, smuk'lė, vieš'butis
publish [publish] *v* leis'ti, skelb'ti
puff [puf] *n* dvelki'mas, pūs'telėjimas
pull [pūl] *v* trauk'ti, temp'ti, vilk'ti, tampy'ti
pulpy [pulpee] *adj* minkš'tas, mėsin'gas
pump [pump] *n* siurblys', pom'pa
punish [punish] *v* baus'ti
punishment [punishment] *n* bausmė'
pupil [pyoopel] *n* auk'lėtinis, mokinys',
praktikan'tas
puppet [pupit] *n* lėlė', marione'tė
puppy [pupee] *n* šuniu'kas
purchase [pėrches] *n* pirkinys', įsigiji'mas, *v*
pirk'ti, įsigy'ti
pure [pyūr] *adj* gry'nas, tik'ras, ty'ras,
pa'prastas
purpose [pėrpes] *n* tiks'las, keti'nimas
purse [pėrs] *n* pinigi'nė
pursue [persoo] *v* per'sekioti, vy'tis, tęs'ti
push [pūsh] *v* stum'ti, spaus'ti, ju'dinti į'
prie'kį
put [pūt] *v* padė'ti, staty'ti, patalpin'ti
puzzle [puzel] *n* nustebi'mas, sunku'mas,
mįslė', galvo'sūkis

Q

quaint [kweint] *adj* keis'tas, neį'prastas

quake [kweik] *v* drebė'ti, virpėti

qualm [kwōm] *n* šleikštulys

quantity [kwontitee] *n* kieky'bė

quarrel [kworel] *n* gin'čas, kivir'čas

quarry [kworee] *n* gro'bis, laimi'kis, žinių' šalti'nis

quarter [kwōrter] *n* ket'virtis, kvarta'las

quash [kwosh] *v* anuliuo'ti, slopin'ti

queen [kween] *n* karalie'nė

queer [kwear] *adj* keis'tas, ekscent'riškas, įtarti'nas

quench [kwench] *v* gesin'ti, atšal'dyti, nuslopin'ti

question [kweschen] *n* klau'simas, problema'

quick [kwik] *adj* gy'vas, grei'tas, vikrus'

quiet [kwīit] *adj* tylus', ramus'

quilt [kwilt] *n* vati'nė ant'klodė

quit [kwit] *v* palik'ti, apleis'ti, mokė'ti, atsily'ginti

quite [kwīt] *adj* visiškai', visai', užtektinai', labai'

quiz [kwiz] *v* pajuok'ti, egzaminuo'ti, apklaus'ti, *n* apklausa'

R

rabbit [rabit] *n* triu'šis, bailys'

race [reis] *n* lenkty'nės, grei'tas judė'jimas, ra'sė

rack [rak] *n* ė'džios, pakaba', lenty'na

racy [reisee] *adj* būdin'gas, originalus', smarkus', energin'gas

radish [radish] *n* ridikė'lis, ridi'kas

rag [rag] *n* skar'malas, sku'duras

ragamuffin [ragemufin] *n* dris'kius, nusku'rėlis

rage [reij] *n* pyk'tis, įnirši'mas

ragged [ragid] *adj* nuply'šęs, apdris'kęs, apleis'tas

raid [reid] *n* užpuoli'mas, ant'skrydis

rail [reil] *n* skersi'nis, turėk'las, bė'gis, geležin'kelis

rain [rein] *n* lietus'

raise [reiz] *v* pakel'ti, iškel'ti, augin'ti, paža'dinti

rally [ralee] *n* susirinki'mas, su'eiga, susivie'nijimas

ramble [rambel] *n* ekskur'sija, pasivažinė'jimas, klajo'jimas

ramp [ramp] *n* šlai'tas, *v* šėl'ti, siau'tėti

rancid [ransid] *adj* apkar'tęs, gaižus'

random [randem] *adj* atsitikti'nis
range [reinj] *n* eilė', virti'nė, kryptis',
ra'diusas
ranger [reinjer] *n* val'kata, klajū'nas
rank [rank] *n* eilė', greta', laips'nis, ran'gas
rankle [rankel] *v* pūliuo'ti, kankin'ti
ransack [ransak] *v* apieško'ti, knis'tis, plėš'ti
ransom [ransem] *v* išpirk'ti, atpirk'ti
rap [rap] *v* lengvai' suduo'ti, pabarben'ti
rape [reip] *n* ro'pė, rap'sas
rapid [rapid] *adj* grei'tas, smarkus'
rapt [rapt] *adj* sužavė'tas, pasinė'ręs,
pagrob'tas
rare [rier] *adj* re'tas, prare'tintas, puikus'
rascal [raskel] *n* suk'čius, nenau'dėlis
rash [rash] *adj* veržlus', skubo'tas,
neatsargus'
rasp [raasp] *n* trintu'vė, dil'dė, brūžik'lis
raspberry [raazberee] *n* avie'tė
rat [rat] *n* žiur'kė
rate [reit] *n* grei'tis, tem'pas, mo'kestis,
tari'fas
rather [raather] *adv* greičiau', verčiau',
mieliau'
ration [reishen] *n* por'cija, davinys'
ravage [ravij] *v* nunioko'ti, sunaikin'ti

rave [reiv] *v* kliedė´ti, dūk´ti

ravel [ravel] *v* supai´nioti, išaiš´kinti, išnarp´lioti

raven [raven] *n* var´nas, kranklys´, *v* plėš´ti, go´džiai ry´ti

ravish [ravish] *v* pagrob´ti, prievartau´ti, sužavė´ti

raw [rō] *adj* ža´lias, neišdirb´tas, neišvi´ręs

ray [rei] *n* spindulys´

raze [reiz] *v* sunaikin´ti, sugriau´ti, ištrin´ti

razor [reizer] *n* skustu´vas

reach [reech] *v* pasiek´ti, siek´ti, pasivy´ti, pristaty´ti

read [reed] *v* skaity´ti, supras´ti, mo´kytis

ready [redee] *adj* ga´tavas, pagamin´tas, pa´ruoštas

real [reel] *adj* tik´ras, realus´, nekilno´jamas

rear [rear] *v* staty´ti, iškel´ti, augin´ti, auk´lėti

reason [reezen] *n* priežastis´, pa´grindas, paaiš´kinimas

reassure [reeashūr] *v* nuramin´ti, vėl´ užtik´rinti

rebellion [ribelyen] *n* sukili´mas, pasiprie´šinimas

rebuke [ribyook] *v* priekaištau´ti, papeik´ti

receive [riseev] *v* gau'ti, priim'ti
recent [reesent] *adj* nese'nas, nau'jas,
paskuti'nis, dabarti'nis
recess [reeses] *n* atos'togos, įdubi'mas, ni'ša
recognize [rekegnīz] *v* pažin'ti, pripažin'ti
recover [rikuver] *v* atsigau'ti, pasveik'ti,
atsipei'kėti
red [red] *adj* raudo'nas, parau'dęs
reduce [ridyoos] *v* suma'žinti, prives'ti,
pavers'ti, privers'ti
reek [reek] *v* dvok'ti, rūk'ti, garuo'ti
reel [reel] *v* svirduliuo'ti, suk'tis
refer [rifėr] *v* rem'tis, kreip'tis, minė'ti, lies'ti
refrigerator [rifrijereiter] *n* šaldytu'vas
refuse [rifyooz] *v* atsisaky'ti, atmes'ti,
paneig'ti
regard [rigaard] *n* pagarba', dėmesys',
rū'pinimasis
region [reejen] *n* kraš'tas, sritis', rajo'nas
regret [rigret] *v* apgailestau'ti, atgailau'ti
reject [reejekt] *v* atmes'ti, atstum'ti,
išmes'ti, išvem'ti
relate [rileit] *v* pa'sakoti, būti susi'jusiam
relative [reletiv] *n* giminai'tis
relax [rilaks] *v* atpalaiduo'ti, pailsė'ti,
atsikvėp'ti, susilpnė'ti

release [rilees] *n* atleidi'mas,
palengvė'jimas, *v* paleis'ti
relief [rileef] *n* paguo'da, pagal'ba,
pašalpa', paleng'vinimas
relish [relish] *n* sko'nis, prie'skonis, kva'pas
rely [rilī] *v* pasitikė'ti, pasikliau'ti
remain [rimein] *v* pasilik'ti
remark [rimaark] *n* pastaba'
remedy [remidee] *n* vais'tas, prie'monė
remember [rimember] *v* atsimin'ti, atmin'ti
remind [rimīnd] *v* primin'ti
remiss [rimis] *adj* apsilei'dęs,
nerūpestin'gas, neatidus'
remit [rimit] *v* ma'žinti, mažė'ti, siųs'ti
remorse [rimōrs] *n* są'žinės grauži'mas,
gai'lestis
remote [rimout] *adj* to'limas, nuto'lęs,
men'kas, nežy'mus
remove [rimoov] *v* paša'linti, nuim'ti, nuneš'ti
render [render] *v* atsimokė'ti, teik'ti
rent [rent] *n* nuo'ma, ren'ta
repair [ripier] *v* taisy'ti, remontuo'ti
repeat [ripeet] *v* pakarto'ti
resist [rizist] *v* prie'šintis, atsispir'ti,
susilaiky'ti
respect [rispekt] *n* pagarba'

respond [rispond] *v* atsaky'ti, reaguo'ti

rest [rest] *n* liku'tis, lie'kana, likusie'ji, ramy'bė, po'ilsis

restrict [ristrikt] *v* apribo'ti

return [ritėrn] *v* sugrįž'ti, sugrąžin'ti, atsaky'ti

reveal [riveel] *n* atskleis'ti, atras'ti

revenge [rivenj] *v* ker'šyti

review [rivyoo] *n* apžvalga', žurna'las, per'žiūra, recen'zija

revise [rivīz] *v* patik'rinti, ištaisy'ti, pakeis'ti

reward [riwōrd] *n* atly'ginimas, at'pildas, bausmė'

rib [rib] *n* šon'kaulis, briauna'

ribald [ribeld] *adj* nepadorus', nešvankus', šiurkštus'

ribbon [riben] *n* juos'ta, kas'pinas

rice [rīs] *n* ry'žiai

rich [rich] *adj* turtin'gas, gausus', sodrus'

rid [rid] *v* išvaduo'ti, išgel'bėti

riddle [ridl] *n* mįslė'

ride [rīd] *v* jo'ti, važiuo'ti

ridicule [ridekyool] *v* išjuok'ti

rifle [rīfel] *n* šau'tuvas

right [rīt] *adj* dešinė', tiesus', teisin'gas

rigid [rijid] *adj* kie'tas, griež'tas
nepalen'kiamas

rind [rīnd] *n* žievė', oda', pluta'

ring [ring] *v* skambė'ti, skam'binti *n*
žie'das, apskriti'mas

rinse [rins] *v* skalau'ti, plau'ti

riot [rīet] *n* maiš'tas, siau'tėjimas, šėli'mas

ripe [rīp] *adj* subren'dęs, prino'kęs

rise [rīz] *v* kel'tis, kil'ti, iškil'ti, patekė'ti

river [river] *n* u'pė

roach [rouch] *n* tarako'nas

road [roud] *n* ke'lias, gat'vė

roar [rōr] *v* mauro'ti, rė'kauti, griaus'ti

roast [roust] *v* kep'ti

rob [rob] *v* grob'ti, plėš'ti

rock [rok] *n* uola', uolie'na, *v* sup'tis,
svyruo'ti

rod [rod] *n* meškerė', rykštė'

rogue [roug] *n* suk'čius, niek'šas,
pokš'tininkas

roll [roul] *n* są'rašas, bulku'tė, *v* suk'tis,
riedė'ti, siūbuo'ti

roof [roof] *n* sto'gas

room [room] *n* kambarys'

rooster [rooster] *n* gaidys'

root [root] *n* šaknis'

rope [roup] *n* vir'vė, ly'nas, vėrinys', py'nė
rose [rouz] *n* ro'žė
rosy [rouzee] *adj* ro'žinis, raus'vas, ru'žavas
rough [ruf] *adj* grubus', šiurkštus', nely'gus
round [raund] *adj* aps'kritas, apvalus', ištisi'nis
rouse [rauz] *v* ža'dinti, kel'ti, įkvėp'ti, suža'dinti
route [raut] *n* ke'lias, maršru'tas
rove [rouv] *v* klajo'ti, keliau'ti, basty'tis
row [rou] *n* eilė, *v* ir'tis, irkluo'ti
royal [roiel] *adj* kara'liškas, puikus'
rub [rub] *v* trin'ti, lies'ti, er'zinti
rubber [ruber] *n* guma', kaučiu'kas, trintu'kas
rubbish [rubish] *n* šlamš'tas, niekai'
ruck [ruk] *n* raukšlė, klos'tė
rude [rood] *adj* grubus', nedailus', šiurkštus'
ruin [rooin] *v* griau'ti, ardy'ti, naikin'ti
rule [rool] *n* taisyk'lė, nor'ma
rumor [roomer] *n* gan'das, pas'kalos, kal'bos
run [run] *v* bėg'ti, bėgio'ti, judė'ti, plauk'ti
rush [rush] *v* lėk'ti, dum'ti, rūk'ti, pul'ti
rust [rust] *n* rū'dys
rye [rī] *n* rugiai'

S

sack [sak] *v* plėš'ti, grob'ti, *n* mai'šas
sacrifice [sakrefīs] *v* auko'ti
sad [sad] *adj* liūd'nas, nesmagus',
nelinks'mas
safe [seif] *adj* apsau'gotas, saugus', svei'kas,
nesugadin'tas
sail [seil] *v* plaukti, keliau'ti, būriuo'ti
salad [saled] *n* salo'tos, mišrai'nė
salary [salcrcc] *n* alga, atly'ginimas
sale [seil] *n* pardavi'mas, pardavinė'jimas
saliva [selīve] *n* sei'lės
salmon [samen] *n* laši'ša
salt [sōlt] *n* druska'
salute [selool] *n* svei'kinimas, saliu'tas
same [seim] *adj* tas' pats'
sample [saampel] *n* pavyzdys', šablo'nas
sand [sand] *n* smėlys'
sandwich [sandwich] *n* sumušti'nis
sane [sein] *adj* svei'kas, svei'ko pro'to
sash [sash] *n* juos'ta, dir'žas, lan'go rė'mas
satisfy [satisfī] *v* paten'kinti, numalšin'ti,
įvyk'dyti
saturate [sachereit] *v* per'sunkti, per'siimti,
primirky'ti
Saturday [saterdei] *n* šešta'dienis

sauce [sōs] *n* pa'dažas

saucer [sōser] *n* lėkšte'lė

sausage [sōsij] *n* dešra', dešre'lė

savage [savij] *adj* lauki'nis, žiaurus', negailestin'gas

save [seiv] *v* gel'bėti, taupy'ti

savor [seiver] *n* sko'nis, aroma'tas, kva'pas

say [sei] *n* nuo'monė, žo'dis, *v* saky'ti, kalbė'ti

scald [skōld] *v* nupli'kinti, nude'ginti

scale [skeil] *n* laip'tai, mas'tas, ska'lė, gama'

scallop [skalep] *n* srai'gė, kiau'kutas

scant [skant] *adj* men'kas, nepakan'kamas, ribo'tas

scare [skier] *n* iš'gąstis, pa'nika

scent [sent] *n* kva'pas, kvepalai', uoslė'

schedule [shedyool] *n* katalo'gas, są'rašas, pla'nas, gra'fikas

school [skool] *n* mokykla'

science [sīens] *n* moks'las, mokė'jimas

scissors [sizers] *n* žirk'lės

scold [skould] *v* bar'ti

scorch [skōrch] *v* nuside'ginti, svi'linti, nudeg'ti

score [skōr] *n* į'ranta, žymė, apskaita'

scorn [skōrn] *n* panieka', pajuoka'

scoundrel [skaundrel] *n* nenau´dėlis

scrape [skreip] *v* skus´ti, gran´dyti, valy´ti, brū´žinti

scratch [skrach] *v* įbrėž´ti, įdrėks´ti

scream [skreem] *v* rėk´ti, šauk´ti, klyk´ti, spieg´ti

screen [skreen] *n* už´danga, ekra´nas

screw [skruu] *n* sraig´tas, varž´tas

scribble [skribel] *v* rašy´ti, keverzo´ti

scrub [skrub] *v* plau´ti, šveis´ti, trin´ti

sea [see] *n* jū´ra, vandeny´nas

seal [seel] *n* ants´paudas, ruo´nis

search [sėrch] *v* ieško´ti, tir´ti, sek´ti

seat [seet] *n* kėdė´, vieta´, sėdy´nė

second [sekend] *n* sekundė, mo´mentas, *adj* ant´ras, antraei´lis

secret [seekrit] *n* paslaptis´, *adj* slap´tas

secure [sikyūr] *adj* saugus´, ramus´, tik´ras, tvir´tas

sedate [sideit] *adj* ramus´, šaltakrau´jis, rim´tas, solidus´

seduce [sidyoos] *v* vilio´ti, gun´dyti, suvedžio´ti

see [see] *v* maty´ti, žiūrė´ti, stebė´ti

seed [seed] *n* sėk´la, grū´das

seek [seek] *v* ieško´ti, steng´tis

seem [seem] *v* ro'dytis, atro'dyti

seize [seez] *v* pagrieb'ti, pačiup'ti

select [silekt] *v* parink'ti, atrink'ti, išrink'ti

self [self] *prn* pats, aš', ma'no asmeny'bė

selfish [selfish] *adj* savanau'dis, egois'tiškas

sell [sel] *v* parduo'ti, prekiau'ti

send [send] *v* siųs'ti, pasiųs'ti, mes'ti, per'duoti

sense [sens] *n* jaus'mas, juti'mas

sensible [sensebel] *adj* protin'gas, supran'tantis

sensitive [sensitiv] *adj* jautrus', juslus', įžeidus'

sentence [sentens] *n* nuo'sprendis, sakinys'

separate [sepereit] *v* atskir'ti, rūšiuo'ti, išsklaidy'ti

September [september] *n* rugsė'jis

sequel [seekwel] *n* padarinys', iš'dava, pasekmė'

sequence [seekwens] *n* eilės' tvarka', nuoseklu'mas

serious [seeries] *adj* rim'tas, svarbus'

serpent [sėrpent] *n* gyva'tė, žaltys', išdavi'kas

servant [sėrvent] *n* tar'nas, tarnai'tė

serve [sėrv] *v* tarnau'ti, paduo'ti, aptarnau'ti, elg'tis

service [sėrvis] *n* tarny'ba, paslauga', patarna'vimas

set [set] *v* staty'ti, dė'ti, talpin'ti, leis'tis, sodin'ti

settle [setl] *v* įsikur'ti, susitvarky'ti, apsigyven'ti, nutar'ti

seven [seven] *num* septyni'

several [sevrel] *prn* ke'letas, keli'

severe [sivear] *adj* grierž'tas, žiaurus', smarkus'

sew [sou] *v* siū'ti

sex [seks] *n* lytis'

shabby [shabee] *adj* nudėvė'tas, nusku'ręs, nudris'kęs

shade [sheid] *n* šešė'lis, paunks'nė

shadow [shadou] *n* šešė'lis, tamsa', šmėk'la, atspindys'

shake [sheik] *v* kraty'ti, sukrės'ti, drcbė'ti

shallow [shalou] *adj* seklus', negilus', paviršuti'niškas, lėkš'tas

shame [sheim] *n* gė'da, nešlovė'

shank [shank] *n* blauzda', ko'ja

shape [sheip] *n* pavi'dalas, for'ma, iš'vaizda

share [shier] *v* dalin'ti, padaly'ti

sharp [shaarp] *adj* aštrus', smailus', staigus', protin'gas

shave [sheiv] *v* skus'ti, drož'ti, prasmuk'ti

she [shee] *prn* ji'

sheep [sheep] *n* avis', a'vinas, tyle'nis

sheet [sheet] *n* paklo'dė, lakš'tas, juos'ta

shelf [shelf] *n* lenty'na, pako'pa, iškišulys'

shell [shell] *n* kiau'tas, lukš'tas

shelter [shelter] *n* prie'globstis, prie'glauda, pasto'gė, būs'tas

shift [shift] *v* keis'ti, per'kelti, gudrau'ti, išsisukinė'ti

shine [shīn] *v* švies'ti, švytė'ti, blizgė'ti, poliruo'ti

ship [ship] *n* lai'vas

shirt [shėrt] *n* marškiniai'

shiver [shiver] *v* krūp'čioti, drebė'ti, suduž'ti, subyrė'ti

shock [shok] *n* smū'gis, sukrėti'mas, šo'kas

shoe [shoo] *n* ba'tas, avaly'nė, pasaga'

shoot [shoot] *v* šau'ti, pralėk'ti, pradum'ti, sprog'ti

shop [shop] *n* krau'tuvė, parduotu'vė

shore [shōr] *n* kran'tas, rams'tis, atrama'

short [shōrt] *adj* trum'pas, že'mo ū'gio

shoulder [shoulder] *n* pety's

shout [shaut] *v* šauk'ti, rėk'ti

show [shou] *v* ro'dyti, demonstruo'ti

shower [shauer] *n* liūtis', du'šas

shriek [shreek] *v* rėk'ti, klyk'ti, spieg'ti

shrink [shrink] *v* susitrauk'ti, sumažė'ti, vengti

shut [shut] *v* uždary'ti, uždeng'ti

shy [shī] *adj* drovus', bailus'

sick [sik] *adj* nesvei'kas, nuvar'gęs, atsibo'dęs

side [sīd] *n* pu'sė, šo'nas

sight [sīt] *n* regė'jimas, žvilgs'nis

sign [sīn] *n* ženk'las, žymė', iš'kaba

signature [signecher] *n* pa'rašas

significant [signifekent] *adj* reikšmin'gas, svarbus'

silence [sīlens] *n* tylė'jimas, tyla'

silk [silk] *n* šil'kas

silly [silee] *adj* kvai'las, silpnapro'tis, absur'diškas

silver [silver] *n* sidab'ras

similar [simeler] *adj* panašus'

simple [simpel] *adj* pap'rastas, nesudėtin'gas

sin [sin] *n* nuodėmė'

since [sins] *prp* nuo', nuo to' lai'ko kai'

sincere [sinsear] *adj* nuoširdus', tik'ras

sing [sing] *v* dainuo'ti, giedo'ti

single [singel] *adj* vienin'telis, vie'nas, vie'nišas, neve'dęs

sink [sink] *n* kriauk'lė, *v* skęs'ti, grimz'ti, apsem'ti

sip [sip] *n* gurkš'nis

sister [sister] *n* sesuo'

sit [sit] sėdė'ti, posėdžiau'ti, perė'ti

six [siks] *num* šeši'

size [sīz] *n* dy'dis, apimtis', kalib'ras, klijai'

skate [skeit] *v* čiuož'ti

skew [skyoo] *adj* žvai'ras, krei'vas, įžambus'

ski [skee] *n* sli'dės, *v* slidinė'ti

skill [skil] *n* sumanu'mas, įgudi'mas

skin [skin] *n* oda', kai'lis, žieve'lė

skirt [skėrt] *n* sijo'nas, skver'nas

sky [skī] *n* dangus', padan'gė

slack [slak] *adj* lė'tas, silp'nas, išgle'bęs

slander [slander] *v* šmeiž'ti, liežuvau'ti, apkalbė'ti

slang [slang] *n* žargo'nas

sledge [slej] *n* ro'gės, rogu'tės

sleek [sleek] *adj* švelnus', glotnus'

sleep [sleep] *n* mie'gas, *v* miego'ti, užmig'ti

sleeve [sleev] *n* ranko'vė

slice [slīs] *n* riekė', dalis'

slide [slīd] *v* slys'ti, slidinė'ti, slink'ti

slightly [slītlee] *adv* lengvai

slim [slim] *adj* plo'nas, grakštus', lai'bas, men'kas

sling [sling] *v* svies'ti, mes'ti, blokš'ti

slip [slip] *v* slys'ti, paslys'ti, suklys'ti

slow [slou] *adj* lė'tas, ramus'

sluggard [slugerd] *n* tinginys'

sly [slī] *adj* gudrus', suk'tas, klastin'gas

small [smōl] *adj* ma'žas, men'kas, smulkus'

smart [smaart] *adj* stiprus', smarkus', vikrus', protin'gas

smash [smash] *v* lauž'ti, lūž'ti, suduž'ti, sutriuš'kinti

smell [smel] *n* kva'pas, uoslė', *v* kvepė'ti, uos'tyti

smile [smīl] *n* šypsena', *v* šypso'tis

smoke [smouk] *n* dū'mai, *v* rūk'ti, rūky'ti

smooth [smooth] *adj* ly'gus, ply'nas, sklandus'

smother [smuther] *v* uždu'sinti, troškin'ti, dus'ti

smoulder [smoulder] *v* smilk'ti, rusen'ti, deg'ti

snack [snak] *n* už'kanda

snail [sneil] *n* srai'gė

snake [sneik] *n* gyva'tė

sneeze [sneez] *v* čiau'dėti

snore [snōr] *v* knark'ti

snout [snaut] *n* snu'kis

snow [snou] *n* snie'gas

so [sou] *adv* taip', tai'gi, tuo' būdu', vadi'nasi, tiek'

soak [souk] *v* įmerk'ti, išmirky'ti, įsiger'ti, prisisunk'ti

soap [soup] *n* mui'las

sob [sob] *v* raudo'ti, kūk'čioti

society [sesīitee] *n* visuo'menė

sock [sok] *n* kojinai'tė, pus'kojinė

soft [soft] *adj* minkš'tas, švelnus', malonus', tylus'

soil [soil] *n* že'mė, dirva', dirvo'žemis, *v* pur'vinti, tep'ti

soldier [souljer] *n* karei'vis, karys', kariš'kis

solemn [solem] *adj* iškilmin'gas, didin'gas, rim'tas

solid [solid] *adj* kie'tas, tvir'tas, vien'tisas

solution [selooshen] *n* tir'palas, skiedinys', sprendi'mas

solve [solv] *v* spręs'ti

somber [somber] *adj* tamsus', niūrus', liūd'nas

some [sum] *adj* kažkoks', tam' tik'ras,
kuris', ke'letas, keli', trupu'tis, šiek' tiek'
somebody [sumbodec] *prn* kažkas', kas nors'
somehow [sumhau] *adv* kaip nors', kažkaip'
something [sumthing] *n* kažkas', kas nors'
son [sun] *n* sūnus'
song [song] *n* daina, daina'vimas, giesmė
son-in-law [sun in lō] *n* žen'tas
soon [soon] *adv* greit', netru'kus, anksti'
sore [sōr] *adj* jautrus', ser'gantis,
skausmin'gas
sorrel [sorel] *n* rūgšty'nės
sorrow [sorou] *n* liūdesys', šird'gėla, var'gas
sorry [soree] *adj* liūd'nas, nelaimin'gas,
apgailestau'jąs
soul [soul] *n* siela', dvasia', vėlė'
sound [saund] *n* gar'sas, skambė'jimas, *v*
skambė'ti, aidė'ti, *adj* svei'kas, stiprus'
soup [soop] *n* sriuba'
sour [sauer] *adj* rūgštus', surū'gęs, gaižus',
irzlus'
souse [saus] *v* marinuo'ti, sū'dyti
south [sauth] *n* pie'tūs, pietų' kraš'tas
sow [sou] *v* sė'ti, apsė'ti
space [speis] *n* vieta', erdvė', nuo'tolis

spare [spier] *v* taupy'ti, sau'goti, *adj* atsargi'nis, atlie'kamas

sparkle [spaarkel] *v* žėrė'ti, žibė'ti, kibirkščiuo'ti

sparrow [sparou] *n* žvirb'lis

speak [speek] *v* kalbė'ti, šnekė'ti, saky'ti, tar'ti

spectacle [spektekel] *n* akiniai', reginys', spektak'lis

spectator [spekteiter] *n* žiūro'vas, stebė'tojas

speed [speed] *n* grei'tis, tem'pas, *v* skubė'ti

spend [spend] *v* išleis'ti, eikvo'ti, leis'ti lai'ką

spice [spīs] *n* prie'skonis, prie'maiša

spider [spīder] *n* voras

spill [spil] *v* išpil'ti, palie'ti, išbarsty'ti

spinster [spinster] *n* sen'mergė

spirit [spirit] *n* dvasia', siela', šmėk'la, nuo'taika, spi'ritas

spit [spit] *n* sei'lės, *v* spjau'dyti

splash [splash] *v* aptašky'ti, pliušken'ti, pliump'telėti

split [split] *v* skil'ti, skal'dyti, *n* plyšys', skylė'

spoil [spoil] *v* gadin'ti, le'pinti, plėš'ti, grob'ti

spoon [spoon] *n* šaukš'tas

spot [spot] *n* dėmė', šlake'lis, vieta'

spread [spred] *v* sklis'ti, skleis'ti, plis'ti,
paties'ti

spring [spring] *n* pava'saris, *v* šok'ti, užšok'ti

square [skwier] *n* kvadra'tas, stačiakam'pis,
aikšte'lė, skve'ras

squash [skwosh] *v* suspaus'ti, sutraiš'kyti,
grūs'tis

squirrel [skwėrel] *n* voverė

staff [staaf] *n* tarnau'tojai, persona'las

stage [steij] *n* sce'na, pakyla', teat'ras

stair[stier] *n* laipte'lis

stammer [stamer] *v* mik'čioti

stamp [stamp] *v* tryp'ti, užklijuo'ti, *n*
ant'spaudas, paš'to ženk'las

stand [stand] *v* stovė'ti, atsisto'ti, pakęs'ti

star [staar] *n* žvaigždė'

stare [stier] *v* atidžiai' žiūrė'ti, spokso'ti

start [staart] *v* krūp'telėti, pradė'ti, išvyk'ti,
im'tis

starve [staarv] *v* badau'ti, marin'ti badu'

state [steit] *n* bū'sena, padėtis', valstija'

station [steishen] *n* vieta', punk'tas, stotis'

stay [stei] *v* sulaiky'ti, pasilik'ti, apsisto'ti,
dels'ti

steady [stedee] *adj* pastovus', tvir'tas, patvarus', vieno'das

steal [steel] *v* vog'ti, sė'linti

steam [steem] *n* garai', *v* garuo'ti, ga'rinti

steel [steel] *n* plie'nas

step [step] *v* ženg'ti, ei'ti, *n* žings'nis, laip'tas

stew [styoo] *v* troškin'ti, prakaituo'ti, šus'ti

stick [stik] *n* lazda', ran'kena, *v* dur'ti, priklijuo'ti, prilip'ti

still [stil] *adj* tylus', ramus', *adv* dar', iki šiol', tačiau'

stingy [stinjee] *adj* šykštus'

stocking [stoking] *n* ko'jinė

stomach [stumek] *n* pil'vas, skil'vis

stone [stoun] *n* akmuo

stool [stool] *n* suoliu'kas, taboure'tė

stop [stop] *v* susto'ti, nutrauk'ti, baig'ti

store [stōr] *n* atsarga, gausu'mas, san'dėlis, parduotu'vė

storm [stōrm] *n* audra', štor'mas

story [stōree] *n* pa'saka, apy'saka, padavi'mas

stout [staut] *adj* stiprus', tvir'tas, stambus', apkūnus'

straight [streit] *adv* tie'siai, tiesiog', nedel'siant, tuojau', *adj* tiesus'

strain [strein] *v* įtemp'ti, steng'tis, per'vargti

strange [streij] *adj* keis'tas, nej'prastas, sve'timas

strangle [strangel] *v* du'sinti, smaug'ti

straw [strō] *n* šiau'das

strawberry [strōberee] *n* braš'kė, žem'uogė

stream [streem] *n* srovė', u'pė, upe'lis, tekė'jimas

street [street] *n* gat've

strength [strength] *n* jėga', tvirtu'mas, atsparu'mas

stress [stres] *v* spaus'ti, pabrėž'ti, kirčiuo'ti

stretch [strech] *v* temp'ti, ties'ti, įtemp'ti

strict [strikt] *adj* tikslus', grież'tas, reiklus'

strike [strīk] *v* muš'ti, suduo'ti, kal'ti, ding'telėti

string [string] *n* vir'vė, virve'lė, styga'

strong [strong] *adj* stiprus', tvir'tas, garsus'

struggle [strugel] *v* kovo'ti, grum'tis

study [studee] *v* mo'kytis, tir'ti, studijuo'ti

stupid [styoopid] *adj* kvai'las, bukapro'tis

subject [subjikt] *n* pavaldinys', tema', daly'kas, veiksnys'

submit [sebmit] *v* paklus'ti, pasiduo'ti, nusileis'ti

subscribe [sebskrīb] *v* pasirašy'ti,
užsisaky'ti, prenumeruo'ti

suburb [subėrb] *n* prie'miestis

success [sekses] *n* pasiseki'mas, sėkmė'

such [such] *prn* toks'

suck [suk] *v* čiulp'ti, žįs'ti

suddenly [sudenlee] *adv* stai'giai, netikė'tai

suffer [sufer] *v* kęs'ti, kentė'ti, pakęs'ti

sugar [shūger] *n* cuk'rus

suggest [sejest] *v* pasiū'lyti, patar'ti, įteig'ti,
užsimin'ti

suicide [sooisīd] *n* savižudy'bė

suit [soot] *n* kostiu'mas, *v* pritai'kyti, tik'ti

sullen [sulen] *adj* niūrus', pik'tas,
apsiniau'kęs

summer [sumer] *n* va'sara

summit [sumit] *n* viršū'nė

sun [sun] *n* sau'lė

Sunday [sundei] *n* sekma'dienis

sunflower [sunflauer] *n* saulė'grąža

superior [sūpeerier] *adj* geres'nis,
pranašes'nis, vyres'nis

supply [seplī] *v* aprū'pinti, tiek'ti,
paten'kinti

support [sepōrt] *v* palaiky'ti, parem'ti,
išlaiky'ti

suppose [sepouz] *v* galvo'ti, many'ti, prileis'ti

sure [shūr] *adj* tik'ras, įsiti'kinęs

surface [sėrfis] *n* pavir'šius, iš'orė

surgeon [sėrjen] *n* chirur'gas

surname [sėrneim] *n* pavardė', pravardė'

surprise [serprīz] *n* nustebi'mas, netikėtu'mas, staigmena'

surrender [serender] *v* pasiduo'ti, atsisaky'ti

surround [seraund] *v* apsup'ti, apspis'ti

survive [servīv] *v* per'gyventi, lik'ti gyvam', išlaiky'ti

suspect [sespekt] *v* įtar'ti, nepasitikė'ti

suspend [sespend] *v* pakabin'ti, nutrauk'ti, atidė'ti

suspicion [sespishen] *n* įtari'mas

swallow [swolou] *n* kregž'dė, *v* ry'ti, prary'ti

swan [swon] *n* gul'bė

swear [swier] *v* prisiek'ti, prižadė'ti

sweat [swet] *n* pra'kaitas, *v* prakaituo'ti

sweep [sweep] *v* šluo'ti, valy'ti, dum'ti

sweet [sweet] *adj* saldus', kvapus', *n* saldai'nis

swell [swel] *v* tin'ti, brink'ti, kil'ti

swift [swift] *adj* grei'tas, sraunus', ūmus'

swim [swim] *v* plauk'ti, plau'kioti

swine [swīn] *n* kiau′lė

swing [swing] *v* siūbuo′ti, sup′tis, svyruo′ti, suk′tis

switch [swich] *v* įjung′ti, išjung′ti švie′są, plak′ti

swoon [swoon] *v* apalp′ti

syringe [serinj] *n* švirkš′tas

T

table [teibel] *n* sta′las

tail [teil] *n* uodega′, eilė′

tailor [teiler] *n* siuvė′jas

take [teik] *v* im′ti, paim′ti, nugalė′ti, užim′ti

tale [teil] *n* pa′saka, pa′sakojimas, pas′kalos

talk [tōk] *n* pasikalbė′jimas, po′kalbis, *v* kalbėti

tall [tōl] *adj* aukš′tas, di′delio ū′gio

tame [teim] *v* prijaukin′ti, numalšin′ti, nuramin′ti

tangle [tangel] *v* susipai′nioti, sunarp′lioti

tap [tap] *n* čiau′pas, kamš′tis, rūšis′

tape [teip] *n* kas′pinas, juoste′lė, raiš′tis

tape recorder [teip rikōrder] *n* magnetofo′nas

target [taargit] *n* taikinys′

tart [taart] *n* pyra'gas, tor'tas, *adj* aitrus', rūgštus'

task [taask] *n* užduotis', pamoka', pareiga', dar'bas

taste [teist] *n* sko'nis, raga'vimas, *v* ragau'ti

tax [taks] *n* mo'kestis, našta', įtempi'mas

tea [tee] *n* arbata'

teach [teech] *v* mo'kyti, dės'tyti, pripra'tinti

team [teem] *n* koman'da, būrys', brigada'

tear [tier] *v* plėš'ti, plė'šyti, nusidėvė'ti, *n* a'šara

tease [teez] *v* er'zinti, py'kinti

tedious [teedies] *adj* nuobodus', var'ginantis

teenager [teeneijer] *n* paauglys'

tell [tel] *v* pa'sakoti, kalbė'ti, saky'ti, įsaky'ti

temper [temper] *n* kantry'bė, bū'das, charak'teris, nuo'taika

tempest [tempist] *n* audra', vėt'ra

temple [tempel] *n* šventykla', švento'vė

tempt [tempt] *v* gun'dyti, vilio'ti, bandy'ti, kėsin'tis

ten [ten] *num* de'šimt

tenant [tenent] *v* nuomo'ti

tender [tender] *adj* švelnus', jautrus', silp'nas, meilus'

tense [tens] *adj* į'temptas, standus'

tent [tent] *n* palapi'nė, tampo'nas

term [tėrm] *n* tam tik'ras lai'kas, ter'minas, semes'tras

terrible [terebel] *adj* siaubin'gas, baisus', smarkus'

terror [terer] *n* siau'bas, tero'ras

terse [tėrs] *adj* trum'pas, su'glaustas, raiškus'

test [test] *v* bandy'ti, tik'rinti, *n* ban'dymas

than [than] *cnj* negu', kaip'

thank [thank] *v* dėko'ti

that [that] *prn* anas', *adv* taip', *cnj* kad', kai'

their [thier] *cnj* jų', sa'vo

them [them] *prn* juos', jas', jiems', joms'

then [then] *adv* tada', po to', paskui'

there [thier] *adv* ten', čia', šioje' vie'toje

they [thei] *prn* jie'

thick [thik] *adj* sto'ras, drū'tas, stambus', tirš'tas, tankus'

thief [theef] *n* vagis'

thigh [thī] *n* šlaunis'

thin [thin] *adj* plo'nas, lie'sas, skys'tas, re'tas

thing [thing] *n* daik'tas, daly'kas, fak'tas, rei'kalas

think [think] *v* galvo'ti, many'ti

thirteen [thėrteen] *num* try'lika

thirty [thėrtee] *num* tris'dešimt

thorough [thurou] *adj* pil'nas, nuodugnus'

though [thou] *adv* tačiau', vis' dėl to, bet',
cnj nors', nepai'sant

thought [thōt] *n* mintis', mąs'tymas

thousand [thauzend] *num* tūks'tantis

thread [thred] *n* siū'las

threat [thret] *v* grąsin'ti

three [three] *num* trys'

thrill [thril] *n* šiurpulys', virpesys',
jau'dinimasis

throat [throut] *n* gerklė

through [throo] *prp* per', pro', dėka', dėl'.
adv kiaurai', visiškai'

throw [throu] *v* mes'ti, svies'ti, mė'tyti

thumb [thum] *n* nykštys'

thunder [thunder] *n* griaus'mas, griausti'nis,
perkū'nas

Thursday [thėrzdei] *n* ketvirta'dienis

ticket [tikit] *n* bi'lietas, etike'tė, skelbi'mas

tidy [tīdee] *adj* tvarkin'gas, švarus'

tie [tī] *v* riš'ti, per'rišti, vars'tyti

tighten [tītn] *v* sutrauk'ti, suspaus'ti

till [til] *prp* i'ki, li'gi, *cnj* kol'

timber [timber] *n* rąs'tas, sija'

time [tīm] *n* lai′kas, laiko′tarpis, kar′tas, ter′minas

timid [timid] *adj* drovus′, baugus′, nedrąsus′

tiny [tīnee] *adj* ma′žas, smulkus′

tire [tīer] *v* var′ginti, pavarg′ti, nusibos′ti

tissue [tishoo] *n* au′deklas, audinys′

title [tītl] *n* var′das, pavadi′nimas, ant′raštė

to [tū] *prp* į′, pas′, prie′, i′ki

today [tėdei] *adv* šiandien′

toe [tou] *n* ko′jos pirš′tas

together [tūgether] *adv* kartu′, drauge′, tuo′ pačiu′ laiku′

toil [toil] *v* dirb′ti, triūs′ti

tomato [temaatou] *n* pomido′ras

tomb [tomb] *n* ka′pas, ant′kapis

tomorrow [temorou] *adv* rytoj′, *n* ryt′diena

tongue [tung] *n* liežu′vis, kalba′

tonight [tenīt] *adv* šią′nakt, šį va′karą

too [too] *adv* taip pat′, per daug′

tool [tool] *n* į′rankis, stak′lės

tooth [tooth] *n* dan′tis

top [top] *n* viršū′nė, viršus′

torch [tōrch] *n* žibintu′vas, žibin′tas, žiburys′

tortoise [tėrtes] *n* vėžlys

torture [tōrcher] *n* kančia, kanki′nimas

total [toutl] *adj* pil′nas, vi′siškas, vi′sas

touch [tuch] *v* lies'ti, lytė'ti

tough [tuf] *adj* kie'tas, ištvermin'gas, tvir'tas

tour [tūr] *n* kelio'nė, turnė, *v* keliau'ti

towards [tōrdz] *prp* link', į', apie'

towel [tauel] *n* rankš'luostis

tower [tauer] *n* bokš'tas, tvirto'vė

town [taun] *n* mies'tas, mieste'lis

toy [toi] *n* žais'las

trace [treis] *n* pėd'sakas, bruo'žas, take'lis

track [trak] *n* vėžė', ta'kas, bė'giai

trade [treid] *n* a'matas, profe'sija, preky'ba

traffic [trafik] *n* judė'jimas, eis'mas, trans'portas

train [trein] *v* mo'kyti, treniruo'ti, *n* traukinys'

traitor [treiter] *n* išdavi'kas

transfer [transfėr] *v* per'kelti, per'duoti, per'leisti

translate [transleit] *v* išvers'ti

trash [trash] *n* at'matos, šlamš'tas, šiukš'lės

travel [travel] *v* keliau'ti, vaikš'čioti, ei'ti

treasure [trezher] *n* tur'tai, brangeny'bės

treat [treet] *v* elg'tis, gy'dyti, vaišin'ti, traktuo'ti

tree [tree] *n* me'dis

tremble [trembl] *v* drebė'ti

trick [trik] *n* gudry′bė, apgau′lė, pokš′tas

trifle [[trīfel] *n* niekai′, maž′možis, arbat′pinigiai

trim [trim] *v* tvarky′ti, dai′linti, kirp′ti, taisy′ti

trip [trip] *n* ekskur′sija, kelio′nė, iš′vyka

trouble [trubel] *n* rū′pestis, var′gas, bėda′, *v* nerimau′ti, rū′pintis, kamuo′ti

trousers [trauzers] *n* kel′nės

true [troo] *adj* tik′ras, teisin′gas, iš′tikimas

trunk [trunk] *n* liemuo′, kamie′nas

trust [trust] *v* paves′ti, patikė′ti, tikė′tis

truth [trooth] *n* tiesa′, teisy′bė, teisingu′mas

try [trī] *v* bandy′ti, mėgin′ti, steng′tis

Tuesday [tyoosdee] *n* antra′dienis

turn [tėrn] *v* suk′ti, pasuk′ti, kreip′ti, tap′ti, pavirs′ti

turnip [tėrnip] *n* ro′pė

tutor [tyooter] *v* globo′ti, auk′lėti, mo′kyti

twelve [twelv] *num* dvy′lika

twenty [twentee] *num* dvi′dešimt

twice [twīs] *adv* du′kart

twin [twin] *n* dvyniai′, dvynu′kai

twist [twist] *v* suk′tis, vy′ti, vingiuo′tis, iškraipy′ti

two [too] *num* du

U

ugly [uglee] *adj* negražus′, bjaurus′, šlykštus′
umbrella [umbrele] *n* skė′tis, liet′sargis
unable [uneibel] *adj* nega′lintis, nemo′kantis
unbearable [unbierebel] *adj* nepa′kenčiamas
uncle [unkel] *n* dė′dė
uncommon [unkomen] *adj* nepa′prastas, nuostabus′
unconscious [unkonshes] *adj* be są′monės, nesą′moningas
under [under] *prp* po′, žemiau′, apačioje′
undergo [undergou] *v* patek′ti, papul′ti, kentė′ti, patir′ti
underground [undergraund] *adv* po žeme′, slaptai′, po′grindyje
understand [understand] *v* supras′ti, žino′ti
undo [undoo] *v* atriš′ti, ardy′ti, žlugdy′ti, gadin′ti
uneven [uneeven] *adj* nely′gus, nely′ginis
unfortunate [unfōrchenit] *adj* nelaimin′gas, nesėkmin′gas
unhappy [unhapee] *adj* nelaimin′gas
unify [yoonefī̄] *v* suvie′nyti
union [yoonyen] *n* są′junga, vieny′bė, susivie′nijimas
unit [yoonit] *n* vie′netas, elemen′tas

unite [yoonīt] *v* suvie'nyti, sujung'ti

unprejudiced [unprejedist] *adj* beša'liškas, objektyvus'

unreal [unreel] *adj* netik'ras, nerealus', pramany'tas

until [until] *prp* i'ki, *cnj* kol'

up [up] *adv* į vir'šų, aukštyn'

upper [uper] *adj* viršuti'nis, aukščiau'sias

upset [upset] *v* apvers'ti, nuliū'dinti, prislėg'ti, sujau'dinti

up-to-date [up tū deit] *adj* šiuolaiki'nis, naujau'sias, modernus'

urge [ėrj] *v* ra'ginti, vary'ti, įtikinė'ti, reikalau'ti

us [us] *prn* mums', mus', mumis'

use [yooz] *n* nauda', varto'jimas, *v* varto'ti, naudo'ti

used [yoozd] *adj* įpra'tęs, į'prastas

useful [yoosfel] *adj* naudin'gas

usual [yoozhooel] *adj* pa'prastas, į'prastas

utensil [yootensel] *n* in'dai, rakan'dai, į'rankis

utility [yootilitee] *n* nauda', naudingu'mas

utter [uter] *v* tar'ti, prabil'ti, surėk'ti

utterly [uterlee] *adv* labai', be ga'lo, visiškai'

V

vagabond [vagebond] *n* val'kata, bastū'nas, neti'kėlis

vague [veig] *adj* neaiš'kus, miglo'tas

vain [vein] *adj* tuš'čias, bergž'džias, išdidus'

valise [velees] *n* sakvoja'žas, kupri'nė

valley [valee] *n* slė'nys

value [valyoo] *v* ver'tinti, įkaino'ti

vanish [vanish] *v* ding'ti, pranyk'ti

vanity [vanitee] *n* tušty'bė, tuštu'mas, niekingu'mas

vanquish [vankwish] *v* nugalė'ti, laimė'ti, numalšin'ti

vapid [vapid] *adj* neskanus', be sko'nio, blankus'

various [vieries] *adj* skirtin'gas, įvairus'

vary [vieree] *v* keis'tis, skir'tis, įvai'rinti, nesutap'ti

vast [vaast] *adj* platus, didžiu'lis

vaunt [vaant] *v* gir'tis

vegetable [vejitebel] *n* daržo'vė

vehicle [veekel] *n* veži'mas, prie'monė, į'rankis

vend [vend] *v* pardavinė'ti, prekiau'ti

venerate [venereit] *v* gerb'ti

venture [vencher] *v* rizikuo'ti, išdrįs'ti

verdict [verdikt] *n* sprendi´mas, nuo´monė
verge [vėrj] *n* kraš´tas, *v* nusileis´ti, nulip´ti
verse [vėrs] *n* eilė´raštis, poe´zija
very [veree] *adj* tik´ras, tas pats´, *adv* labai´
vex [veks] *v* er´zinti, py´kinti
vice [vīs] *n* yda´, trū´kumas
vice versa [vīse vėrse] *adv* atvirkščiai´, prie´šingai
victim [viktim] *n* auka´, *v* per´sekioti, apgaudinė´ti
victory [vikteree] *n* per´galė
view [vyoo] *n* vaiz´das, po´žiūris, nuo´monė
village [vilij] *n* kai´mas
villain [vilen] *n* niek´šas
vinegar [vineger] *n* ac´tas
violate [vīeleit] *v* prievartau´ti, įsiverž´ti, suterš´ti, išnie´kinti
violet [vīelit] *n* žibuok´lė, žibu´tė, viole´tinė spalva´
viper [vīper] *n* gyva´tė
virgin [vėrjin] *n* mergai´tė, merge´lė
virtue [vėrchoo] *n* dory´bė, vertingu´mas, jėga´, skaisty´bė
vision [vizhen] *n* regė´jimas, svajo´nė, įžvalgu´mas, numa´tymas
vital [vītl] *adj* gyvy´binis, esmi´nis, svarbus´

vitiate [vishieit] *v* gadin'ti, dary'ti negalio'jantį

vivid [vivid] *adj* gy'vas, ryškus'

vivify [vivefī] *v* atgaivin'ti, pagy'vinti

vocabulary [voukabyeleree] *n* žody'nas, žo'džių atsarga'

vogue [voug] *n* mada', populiaru'mas

voice [vois] *n* bal'sas

volume [volyoom] *n* to'mas, knyga', tū'ris, apimtis'

volunteer [volenteer] *n* savanau'dis

vomit [vomit] *v* vem'ti, išvers'ti, išstum'ti

vote [vout] *v* balsuo'ti, pripažin'ti

voyage [voij] *n* kelio'nė

W

wade [weid] *v* bris'ti, brai'džioti

wage [weij] *n* alga', dar'bo už'mokestis

wager [weijer] *v* la'žintis, rizikuo'ti

wail [weil] *v* dejuo'ti, raudo'ti, apverk'ti

waist [weist] *n* juosmuo', ta'lija

wait [weit] *v* lauk'ti, aptarnau'ti

wake [weik] *v* pabus'ti, ža'dinti, sukel'ti

walk [wōk] *n* ėji'mas, *v* ei'ti, vaikš'čioti

wall [wōl] *n* sie'na, siene'lė

wallet [wōlit] *n* pinigi'nė

wander [wonder] *v* klajo'ti, keliau'ti, basty'tis

wane [wein] *v* mažė'ti, dil'ti

want [wont] *v* norė'ti, reikė'ti, stoko'ti, reikalau'ti

war [wōr] *n* ka'ras

ward [wōrd] *v* sau'goti, gin'ti, ser'gėti

warily [wierelee] *adv* atsargiai'

warm [wōrm] *adj* šil'tas, karš'tas

warn [wōrn] *v* įspė'ti, per'spėti

warrant [worent] *v* įgalio'ti, garantuo'ti, užtik'rinti

wash [wosh] *v* plau'ti, skalb'ti, praus'ti, mazgo'ti

wasp [wosp] *n* vapsva'

waste [weist] *v* švaisty'ti, eikvo'ti, vel'tui leis'ti

watch [woch] *n* laik'rodis, sargy'ba, *v* sek'ti, stebė'ti, žiūrė'ti

water [wōter] *n* vanduo'

wave [weiv] *n* banga', *v* banguo'ti, mojuo'ti

way [wei] *n* ke'lias, nuo'tolis, sritis', atžvilgis

we [wee] *prn* mes'

weak [week] *adj* silp'nas, neryžtin'gas

wealth [welth] *n* tur'tai, lo'bis, gausu'mas

weapon [wepen] *n* gink'las

wear [wier] *v* nešio'ti, dėvė'ti, išse'kinti, nuvar'ginti

weather [wether] *n* o'ras

weave [weev] *v* aus'ti, pin'ti

wed [wed] *v* susituok'ti

wedding [weding] *n* vedy'bos, sutuoktu'vės

Wednesday [wenzdee] *n* trečia'dienis

weed [weed] *n* pikt'žolė

week [week] *n* savai'tė

weep [weep] *v* verk'ti

weigh [wei] *v* sver'ti, paly'ginti

weight [weit] *n* svo'ris, svars'tis, sunku'mas, našta'

welcome [welkem] *int* sveiki'!, *v* svei'kinti

welfare [welfier] *n* gero'vė, aprū'pinimas

well [wel] *n* šulinys', *adv* gerai', gero'kai, labai'

west [west] *n* vakarai'

wet [wet] *adj* šla'pias, *v* šla'pinti, mirky'ti

whale [weil] *n* bangi'nis

wharf [wōrf] *n* prie'plauka

what [wut] *prn* kas', koks', kokia', kokie'

whatever [wutever] *adj* bet kuris', kuris', kas bebū'tų

wheat [weet] *n* kviečiai'

wheedle [weedl] *v* prisige'rinti, įsiteik'ti

wheel [weel] *n* ra'tas, vai'ras, *v* riedė'ti, suk'tis

when [when] *adv*, *cnj* kada', kai'

whence [whens] *adv* iš kur', kaip', kokiu'būdu'

whenever [whenever] *adv* kada' tik', kai' tik'

where [wier] *adv* kur', kame'

which [wich] *prn* kuris'

while [wīl] *n* lai'kas, valandė'lė, *cnj*, *adv* tuo' metu', kai'

whim [wim] *n* už'gaida, į'noris, į'geidis

whirl [wėrl] *v* suk'tis, skrie'ti

whisk [wisk] *v* mosuo'ti, nudul'kinti, nuvaly'ti, plak'ti

whisky [wiskee] *n* degti'nė, vis'ki

whisper [wisper] *v* šnabždė'ti

whistle [wisel] *v* švilp'ti

white [wīt] *adj* bal'tas, skaistus'

who [hoo] *prn* kas', kuris'

whole [houl] *adj* vi'sas, iš'tisas, nenukentė'jęs, svei'kas

wholly [houlee] *adv* visiškai'

whom [hoom] *prn* ką', kam'

whose [hooz] *prn* kieno', ko'

why [wī] *adv* kodėl', kaip'

wicked [wikid] *adj* nege'ras, pik'tas, nedo'ras

wide [wīd] *adj* erdvus', platus'

widow [widou] *n* našlė'

wife [wīf] *n* žmona'

wild [wīld] *adj* lauki'nis, smarkus', pasiu'tęs, pašė'lęs

will [wil] *n* valia', no'ras

willow [wilou] *n* gluos'nis, kark'las

win [win] *v* išloš'ti, laimė'ti, užkariau'ti, nugalė'ti

wince [wins] *v* krūp'telėti, atšok'ti, susigūž'ti

wind [wīnd] *v* raity'tis, rangy'tis, pūs'ti

window [windou] *n* lan'gas

wine [wīn] *n* vy'nas

wing [wing] *n* spar'nas, *v* skraidy'ti

wink [wink] *v* mirk'čioti, mirgė'ti

winter [winter] *n* žiema'

wipe [wīp] *v* šluos'tyti, valy'ti

wire [wīer] *n* viela', lai'das

wisdom [wizdem] *n* išmintis'

wise [wīz] *adj* išmintin'gas

wish [wish] *n* no'ras, pageida'vimas, linkė'jimas

wit [wit] *n* pro'tas, sa'mojis

witch [wich] *n* ra'gana, bur'tininkė

with [with] *prp* su´, kartu´ su´, iš´, nuo´

withdraw [withdrō] *v* atsiim´ti, atšauk´ti,
atsitrauk´ti, nuei´ti

wither [wither] *v* vysti, džiū´ti, džiovin´ti

withhold [withhould] *v* sulaiky´ti,
sustabdy´ti, neduo´ti, neleis´ti

within [within] *prp* viduje´, ribose´

without [withaut] *prp* be´

withstand [withstand] *v* prie´šintis, spir´tis,
išlaiky´ti

wizard [wizerd] *n* bur´tininkas, kerė´tojas

woe [wou] *n* nelai´mė, siel´vartas

wolf [wūlf] *n* vil´kas

woman [wūmen] *n* moteris´

wonder [wunder] *n* nustebi´mas, stebuk´las,
v stebė´tis, norė´ti žino´ti

wood [wūd] *n* miš´kas, mal´kos, me´dis

wool [wūl] *n* vil´na

word [wėrd] *n* žo´dis, įsa´kymas, praneši´mas

work [wėrk] *n* dar´bas, veiki´mas, veikla´

world [wėrld] *n* pasau´lis, visuo´menė

worm [wėrm] *n* kirmėlė´, sraig´tas

worry [wuree] *v* nerimau´ti, rū´pintis,
var´ginti

worse [wėrs] *adj* bloges´nis, *adv* blogiau´

worst [wėrst] *adj* blogiau´sias, *adv* blogiau´sia

worth [werth] *n* vertė', *adj* ver'tas, nusipel'nęs
wound [woond] *n* žaizda', *v* sužeis'ti
wrap [rap] *v* apvynio'ti, apsup'ti
wrestle [resel] *n* kova', imty'nės,
grumty'nės, *v* kovo'ti
wretch [rech] *n* niek'šas, varg'šas, nelai'mėlis
wring [ring] *v* gręž'ti, spaus'ti, išsiverž'ti,
išplėš'ti
wrinkle [rinkel] *n* raukšlė, *v* surauk'ti,
suraukšlė'ti
wrist [rist] *n* rie'šas
write [rīte] *v* rašy'ti
wrong [rong] *adj* neteisin'gas, neteisus',
klaidin'gas
wry [rī] *adj* krei'vas, iš'kreiptas

X

x-ray [eksrei] *n* Rent'geno spinduliai
xylograph [ksilegraaf] *n* graviū'ra me'dyje

Y

yard [yaard] *n* kie'mas
yarn [yaarn] *n* ver'palas, siū'lai, gi'jos
yawn [yōn] *v* žio'vauti, žiojė'ti, vėpso'ti
year [yier] *n* me'tai

yearn [yėrn] *v* kankin'tis, ilgė'tis, trokš'ti

yeast [yeest] *n* mie'lės, rau'galas

yell [yel] *v* šauk'ti, rėk'ti

yellow [yelou] *adj* gelto'nas

yes [yes] *prt* taip', tai'gi

yesterday [yesterdee] *n* vakarykš'tė diena', *adv* va'kar

yet [yet] *adv* dar, vis' dar, jau', *cnj* bet'gi, tačiau', vis'dėlto

yield [yeeld] *v* gamin'ti, duo'ti der'lių, nusileis'ti, pasiduo'ti

yolk [youlk] *n* kiauši'nio trynys'

you [yoo] *prn* jūs', tu', jums', tau', jus', tave'

young [yung] *adj* jau'nas, nepaty'ręs

your [yōr] *prn* jū'sų, ta'vo

yourself [yōrself] *prn* save', pa'tys save'

youth [yooth] *n* jaunuo'lis, jaunys'tė, jauni'mas

Z

zany [zeinee] *n* juokdarys', kvailys', *adj* kvai'las

zealous [zeles] *adj* uolus', stropus', karš'tas

zero [zeerou] *n* nu'lis, nie'ko

zest [zest] *n* pries'konis

zip [zip] *v* prazvimb'ti, grei'tai lėk'ti